After *the* PYRAMIDS

To my wife

By the same author:

Egyptian Rock-cut Tombs
The Canopic Equipment of the Kings of Egypt
Monarchs of the Nile
With Salima Ikram:
The Royal Mummies in the Egyptian Museum
The Mummy in Ancient Egypt

After *the* PYRAMIDS

The Valley of the Kings and Beyond

Aidan Dodson

THE RUBICON PRESS

The Rubicon Press
57 Cornwall Gardens
London SW7 4BE

British Libraary Cataloguing-in-Publication Data

A catalogue record for this book is available from the British Library

ISBN 0-948695-51-X (hbk)
ISBN 0-948695-52-8 (pbk)

Printed and bound in Great Britain by Biddles Ltd. of Guildford
and King's Lynn

Contents

List of Illustrations

Acknowledgments

This book has been a long time in gestation, and I am most grateful to my publishers, Anthea Page and Juanita Homan, for accepting it for publication, a decade-and-a-half after I first put pen to paper (and latterly, fingers to word-processor keys!).

Except where otherwise noted, all illustrations are by the author; for their help in producing the exceptions, my gratitude goes to Juanita, George B. Johnson, Salima Ikram, Jacke Phillips, Bob Partridge and Donald B. Redford. For provision of information and access to their current work, or collections under their care, I must thank Hartwig Altenmüller, Edwin C. Brock, Tim Kendall, Jaromír Málek, Karl-Heinz Priese, Daniel Polz, Maartin Raven, Nick Reeves, Catharine Roehrig, John Romer, Donald P. Ryan, Otto Schaden, John H. Taylor Nicholas Warner and Jean Yoyotte. I am particularly indebted to the staff of the Qurna Inspectorate of the Supreme Council for Antiquities, in particular Ibrahim Soliman, Inspector-General, and Saber Abd el-Ghany and Yasser Youssef Ahmed, Inspectors, for all their help with access to a number of important 'closed' monuments in their care.

As always I have to give additional thanks to two particular dear friends: to Salima, for accommodation in Cairo and running errands to the Cairo Museum, and to Julie Hudson for her painstaking reading of the manuscript, and excising errors and unfortunate turns of phrase. To other friends and colleagues who have helped, but I have omitted to mention: my apologies!

Preface

This book was conceived back in the very early 1980s; first as a youthful enthusiast, then as an undergraduate, and finally as a post-graduate student, I had had frequent recourse to I.E.S. Edwards' seminal *Pyramids of Egypt*, for fifty years the basic source-book for those interested in Egyptian pyramids and their surrounding buildings. However, those seeking a similarly-comprehensive book on later royal tombs and mortuary temples have long lacked such a volume. A number of excellent books exist on the Valley of the Kings and its tombs, but none tie in the subsequent royal necropoleis in the Nile Delta, nor the equally-important mortuary temples that ritually form an integral part of the royal funerary complex. Accordingly, this volume attempts to treat as a connected whole the funerary monuments of all kings from the beginning of the Thirteenth Dynasty, down to the Ptolemaic Period.

Any Egyptian tomb ideally comprised two elements, the subterranean burial place and a 'public' chapel, in which the spirit could receive offerings and commune with the living. In the case of kings, during the New Kingdom (c. 1550-1064 BC), the former comprised superbly decorated galleries in the famous Valley of the Kings, while the latter were represented by a series of massive temples, on the opposite side of the cliffs, in which the pharaohs hoped to sleep-out eternity.

The chronological narrative will thus look at both elements of the eternal homes of the kings in question. The little-known last representatives of the pyramidal genre will first be looked at, then the New Kingdom monuments, and finally the rather different tombs constructed by the kings of the Third Intermediate, Late and Ptolemaic Periods in the Nile Delta. Unlike earlier tombs, these were sunk in the courtyards of national cult-temples in the rulers' capital cities.

The architecture and decoration of the monuments will be covered in detail, together with a summary of their most important contents. As far as possible, the results of the latest research have been incorporated, but such is the volume of work at present being undertaken that it is impossible to keep track of every strand. Between the completion of work in the tomb of Tutankhamun in 1932 and the late 1970s, almost nothing was done amongst the royal tombs at Thebes. Since then, however, beginning with

John Romer's clearance of the tomb of Ramesses XI in 1979, the smaller tombs of the Valley of the Kings have been worked by Don Ryan; the tombs of Amenmesse and Bay excavated by Otto Schaden and Hartwig Altenmüller, respectively; sarcophagi reassembled by Edwin Brock; and the tomb of the sons of Ramesses II reopened by Kent Weeks. These are but a few examples of the various areas of work which have already brought to light important data to change our understanding of a number of elements of the history of royal tomb design. Another area of excavation is Dira Abu'l-Naga, where Daniel Polz may yet reveal the long-lost Seventeenth Dynasty royal necropolis.

Side-by-side with this work has been the publication of a number of key books on the Valley of the Kings, particularly by Erik Hornung and Nicholas Reeves, plus the growing series publishing the tomb of Tutankhamun. As this book went to press, there appeared the long awaited *Atlas of the Valley of the Kings*, providing at last a comprehensive series of maps and plans of the area. Away from Thebes, the remains of a Twenty-ninth Dynasty king's tomb have been revealed at Mendes by Donald Redford, with work at Tanis by Phillipe Brissaud adding to the knowledge of the royal necropolis there. The full glory of the latter site was more fully revealed to the wider audience by exhibitions in France and Scotland.

This but briefly touches on some of the more significant pieces of work over the past few years dealing with the royal tombs of the New Kingdom and later. Many individual monuments have important things to say about the history of the times, major events being reflected in variations and erasures within their decorative schemes, not to mention the information provided by the royal mummies themselves. This book aims to provide a convenient synthesis of what is currently known of the royal burial places and chapels, in the Valley of the Kings and beyond.

University of Bristol   Aidan Dodson

Introduction

The land of Egypt comprises two distinct elements: firstly, there is the narrow fertile strip that extends for a few kilometres either side of the channel of the Nile, the waterway that has always defined the country. It is here that the vast majority of the population live, and where the agricultural produce on which the nation depends is grown. Secondly, occupying by far the largest proportion of the territory of the modern Arab Republic of Egypt, there is the desert, empty of habitation, with the exception of a few distant oases.

The division between the two elements, respectively known in ancient times as the 'Black' (the colour of the wet, fertile soil) and 'Red' lands is strikingly marked, it being possible to stand with one foot in a lush field and the other in the arid desert. The same division marked the boundary between the lands of the living and the dead, cemeteries being largely restricted to the desert edge and the rocky cliffs that rise up not far beyond.

A fundamental belief in the life after death led to a high priority being placed upon the construction of funerary monuments, which would normally be built during a person's own lifetime. The earliest known Egyptian tombs are no more than holes in the low desert. In them, the body of the deceased was laid on its side, knees drawn up in the embryonic position. Accompanied by a few pots, implements and perhaps a stone palette, the body was covered over with sand. When uncovered today, such corpses are often very well preserved, the hot sand having turned them into natural mummies, the probable origin of the Egyptian belief that the soul could only survive if the mortal body did as well.

As the next stage in development, a lining was added to the pit, which was roofed over, a cross-wall sometimes dividing it into two chambers. One such tomb, at Hierakonpolis, would appear to be the earliest royal sepulchre known, to judge from the presence of unique paintings on the main chamber's walls. These include depictions of boats, men and animals, and are the first examples of such mural art in Egypt.

With the unification of Egypt, c. 3050 BC, tomb architecture developed apace, the underground chambers growing in number and gaining brick-built, rectangular superstructures - dubbed 'mastabas', owing to their resemblance to Arab benches. At the same time, the first steps were taken towards the artificial preservation of the corpse, since the construction of chambers had separated the body from the preservative action of the sand. To this end, the corpse was swathed in linen bandages, coated in plaster, and the external features modelled. Since this did nothing to prevent decomposition of the flesh, the process was later supplemented by the artificial desiccation of the body with a substance known as natron, a naturally occurring mixture of salts. While this aspect of mummification remained constant for the remainder of Ancient Egyptian history, the practice of modelling the physical features ended around the end of the Old Kingdom.

Egyptian history is nowadays divided into a number of Kingdoms and Periods, and further into thirty-one dynasties (see pp. 171 ff.). The latter are derived from the work of the Egyptian priest Manetho, who compiled a history of his country in the early days of the Greek domination. While a number of his divisions are questionable, the system is so convenient that it is unlikely to be replaced.

Royal tombs, constructed at Umm el-Qaab, part of the Abydos necropolis in Upper Egypt, initially took the form of brick chambers built in pits in the desert surface, surmounted by two stelae. Minimal superstructure actually stood above the body, huge panelled enclosures of brick being built some two kilometres away, and it was there that the cult

Fig. 1. The Shunet el-Zebib, the great brick enclosure which formed the monumental element of the tomb of the Second Dynasty Horus and Seth Khasekhemwy at Abydos. It and earlier examples at the site provide the prototypes for all later royal mortuary temples.

2

Fig. 2. The first pyramid: the Step Pyramid of Djoser, second king of the Third Dynasty, at Saqqara.

of the deceased king was celebrated. However, the Second Dynasty saw the construction of far more elaborate sepulchres at Saqqara, in the north. They comprised labyrinths of subterranean passages, above which were erected superstructures of very considerable size. Later Second Dynasty kings, however, moved back to Abydos, where the last of the brick enclosures was built by the Horus Khasekhemwy (fig. 1). At the centre of this lay a brick massif, perhaps symbolic of the primeval mound upon which the creator god was held by some to have first manifested himself.

This seems to have served as the starting point for the astounding tomb which the architect, Imhotep, built for his master, King Djoser, the founder (?) of the Third Dynasty. This monument is the Step Pyramid of Saqqara, the first pyramid and among the first stone buildings ever erected (fig. 2). In this monument the original massif had been extended into a stepped structure that seems to have represented a first 'stairway to heaven'. Although his immediate successors were powerless to complete similar monuments, seventy years later King Seneferu, founder of the Fourth Dynasty, was able to build two great pyramids at Dahshur, a third at Meidum, and erect a fourth, ritual, example at Seila. Furthermore, his son, Kheops, built the Great Pyramid of Giza: nearly four and a half thousand years old, this monument remains the most massive free-standing stone structure ever raised by man (fig. 3). At the same site, Kheops' son, Khephren, was able to build a pyramid little smaller than his father's, but after him a steady decline in size and quality set in, the later pyramids of the Old

Fig. 3. The largest of all pyramids, Kheop's Great Pyramid at Giza;
mastaba tombs of the nobility are in the foreground.

Kingdom being now little more than heaps of rubble. These monuments were all straight-sided 'true pyramids', in which the idea of the stairway to the next world had been superseded by one whereby an image of the sun's descending rays were visualised as a ramp towards the realm of the gods.

Fig. 4. The degeneration of the Old Kingdom pyramid.
The badly-denuded pyramid of Sahure (early Fifth Dynasty) at Abusir.

4

All these monuments formed part of a mortuary complex, initially including a whole series of dummy buildings for the use of the dead king's spirit, but later just a mortuary temple was erected against the pyramid's eastern face, in which offerings were made to the spirit, linked to a valley building on the edge of the cultivated land by a causeway. These buildings and structures were normally decorated with reliefs and statuary of the highest quality, but little has survived to the present day, save tantalizing scraps of offering, hunting and other scenes, plus a few statues, for example those of Khephren and Mykerinos from Giza.

The king's family and followers were often buried near him, particularly in the Fourth Dynasty, when Kheops laid out street after street of stone mastabas to create a very real 'city of the dead' around his pyramid (fig. 3). At other times, nobles' tombs tended to be scattered between the cemeteries of the capital, Memphis, and the provinces, with only a limited cluster around the king's tomb. These tombs became increasingly elaborate with time, the single-room chapel of the Third/Fourth Dynasty developing into a labyrinth of courts and offering chambers of which the most complex is to be found in the tomb of the Vizier Meruruka at Saqqara (c. 2350 BC). The scenes carved on their walls are a rich source of information on life in Old Kingdom Egypt, as well as often being remarkable works of art. Likewise great works of art are a number of the statues produced, perhaps the finest being the diorite-gneiss statue of Khephren from his valley building. Now in the Cairo Museum, it seems to capture the very essence of the god-king, serenely confident as he faces eternity. A similar quality is detectable in the sorely-mutilated face of another portrait of Khephren, the Great Sphinx, carved from a huge knoll of rock as the guardian of the Giza necropolis.

The half-millennium of the Old Kingdom was clearly a time of great prosperity, but after the end of the ninety-four(?) year reign of Pepi II (c. 2196 BC) came a period of rapid decline and eventual disintegration. The power of local governors, or nomarchs, increased considerably, while the country split up into two kingdoms, one in the north, centred on Herakleopolis and another in the south, centred on the small town of Thebes. It was not until c. 2030 BC that Egypt was once again united, as the result of a civil war from which King Montjuhotpe II of Thebes emerged victorious. His reign marks the beginning of his country's second great era of prosperity, the Middle Kingdom, which comprises the end of the Eleventh, the Twelfth and Thirteenth Dynasties.

I Pyramid Twilight

The latter part of the eighteenth century BC saw Egypt apparently at the height of her powers. The Twelfth Dynasty, founded by Ammenemes I shortly after 2000 BC, had provided a series of long-lived and effective monarchs, the latest of whom was Ammenemes III. They were considerable builders, both of temples and their own funerary monuments. Yet little more than a decade separates the great building works of Ammenemes III from King Sobkhotpe I, a ruler so obscure that he has long been confounded with a later monarch of his, Thirteenth, dynasty.

With the exception of Sesostris II, buried at Lahun in the Fayoum, the Twelfth Dynasty kings from Ammenemes II to Ammenemes III were buried at Dahshur (fig. 5), some thirty kilometres south of modern Cairo. Although badly ruined, the pyramids of Sesostris III and Ammenemes III are still visible land-marks, lying along the edge of the cultivation. They are some considerable distance from the huge stone pyramids of the Fourth Dynasty pharaoh Seneferu which dominate the site from their locations further out into the desert. Sesostris III's seems to derive its overall layout from the Third Dynasty Step Pyramid, the walls of whose enclosure are depicted around the lower part of the sarcophagus of the king, and a number of subsequent individuals.

The southernmost of these Twelfth Dynasty monuments of Dahshur is that of Ammenemes III, the so-called 'Black Pyramid'. Excavations by Dieter Arnold in the 1980s, following on from Jacques de Morgan's more

Fig. 5. The royal necropolis of the late Middle Kingdom: Dahshur. Pyramids and tombs of kings of the Thirteenth Dynasty lay along the whole area, from the left of the pyramid of Sesostris III to beyond that of Ammenemes III. The tomb of King Hor actually lay at the bottom of an old shaft alongside the latter pyramid.

6

Fig. 6. The last of the great pyramids: the second brick monument of Ammenemes III at Hawara.

summary investigations in 1894-5, revealed a number of new galleries and, most significantly, that the monument had suffered from subsidence and structural failure. Although queenly burials still took place there, the damage to the substructure led to the pyramid's abandonment as the king's prospective burial place, and its replacement by a new pyramid at Hawara in the Fayoum (fig. 6).

This great monument was to be the last major pyramid to be completed in Egypt. Many of the Twelfth Dynasty pyramids had special architectural features to guard against robbers, but in this case a new approach was tried: the actual burial chamber was carved from a single immense block of quartzite, the hardest stone worked by ancient man. Into this open box was laid the king's separately-carved sarcophagus and canopic chest, the room being then roofed over by a series of three wide quartzite beams. One was raised on a pair of quartzite props, resting in chambers filled with sand. When the sand was allowed to escape from them into adjacent passages, the props descended, lowering the ceiling block and sealing the chamber.

Ammenemes III was succeeded by Ammenemes IV, but although he was the author of a number of monuments, nothing certain is known of his burial place; likewise obscure is the last resting place of his successor, Sobkneferu, one of those rare women to have held the throne of Egypt. With her, the Twelfth Dynasty was over, and the Thirteenth begun. Unlike the well-documented Twelfth, the new dynasty is obscure in the extreme. For the names and succession of many of its kings, we are beholden unto the Turin Canon of Kings, a sadly-wrecked document that once apparently listed every king of Egypt from the days of the gods to Ramesses II. Certain points in time are illuminated by contemporary documents, but the whole period is replete with problems.

For the period beginning with the death of Ammenemes III, down to the dissolution of the Thirteenth Dynasty in the wake of a take-over by a group of Palestinian rulers known as the Hyksos, some eight pyramids and a shaft-tomb can be identified with fair certainty as tombs of pharaohs. This is either on the basis of their excavated architecture and contents, or their position where they still await archaeological attention. Of the excavated pyramids, only two are 'named'; thus, they have to provide the chronological pegs around which the remainder must be hung, a task in which the design of their substructures and, particularly, sarcophagi are the key pieces of evidence.

One of the unexcavated monuments may also have given us the name of its owner. Near the ruined pyramid of Ammenemes II is an area of limestone rubble, some 40 metres square, unfortunately recently badly damaged by the construction of a pipeline. The rubble probably represents the remains of a casing; since the causeway appeared also to survive, it would seem that the monument had progressed some considerable way towards completion. A fragment of relief from it naming a King Ammenemes, unless a stray from Ammenemes II's complex, might indicate ownership by Ammenemes IV.

The superstructures of the excavated Thirteenth Dynasty pyramids are generally more or less totally destroyed, as a result of quarrying, or simply lack of completion: few rulers of the dynasty are known to have ruled for more than a handful of years. The substructures, however, feature massive quartzite portcullises and elaborate arrangements of galleries and chambers, which tend to multiply with time. The example of the carved burial chamber in the Hawara pyramid is developed further, by sculpting the sarcophagus, canopic chest and lower part of the chamber out of a single block of stone.

The earliest 'named' pyramid of the Thirteenth Dynasty seems to be that of Ameny-Qemau, at South Dahshur, around one and a half kilometres south of the pyramid of Ammenemes III (fig. 7). It was discovered in 1957 by an expedition led Charles A. Muses; publication was finally carried out by the Italian architects, Vito Maragioglio and Celeste Rinaldi, in 1968. The pyramid was originally c. 50 m square, while its substructure, now very considerably damaged, embodied what is typologically the earliest example of a combined sarcophagus/canopic chest. This formed the floor of the burial chamber, and was sealed by a lid which was slid on top from the antechamber-area, lying directly north of the sarcophagus. The lid was locked into place by a sideways-sliding portcullis-slab; owing to its being in contact with the chamber walls on

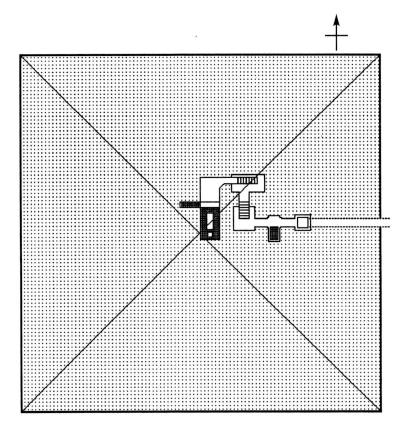

Fig. 7. Plan of the pyramid of Ameny-Qemau, at South Dahshur,
typical of early Thirteenth Dynasty pyramids.

three sides, and the portcullis on the other, the inevitable tomb robbers had
to resort to smashing the north end of the lid to gain access to the coffin,
and then pushing the remains northwards, to rifle the canopic cavity. After
all the trouble to which they had been put as a result of the pyramid's
elaborate architectural design, the robbers were thorough: all that
remained of the king and his equipment were his canopic jars, reduced to
fragments, which provide us with one of their owner's names.

A kilometre further south lies the Northern Pyramid of Mazghuna.
Not one block of the superstructure has survived, but the arrangement of
the substructure resembles that of Ameny-Qemau, in expanded form.
Both pyramids share the feature of huge blocks which were set to slide
laterally and block roof-trapdoors that gave access from one gallery to the
next. First found at Hawara, such blocks were unbreakable, since the
hardness of the stone required pounding, which cannot be carried out from
beneath. At Mazghuna, however, they were never tested, since open

9

portcullises and an unclosed sarcophagus indicate that the pyramid never received the body of 'its lord'. Its excavator, Ernest Mackay, provisionally ascribed the pyramid to one of the last two rulers of the Twelfth Dynasty, Ammenemes IV or Sobkneferu, on account of its similarities to the Hawara pyramid, but this was before the excavation of other Thirteenth Dynasty monuments that prove its correct date. The Northern Pyramid's close resemblance to Ameny-Qemau's, and its position next-south, makes it rather more probable that its chronological position is a reign or two later than that of Ameny.

A further pyramid lies at Mazghuna; rather more of its 55 metre-square superstructure is preserved, while the form of its substructure closely links it with that of Khendjer, built at the opposite end of the Middle Kingdom necropolis, some way south of a site where a number of Old Kingdom monarchs had built their tombs. As in the cases of Mazghuna-North and Ameny-Qemau, this pair of pyramids' substructures feature quartzite portcullises and sarcophagi, but the latter are more advanced. The coffer has been considerably deepened, leaving a void above the coffin- and canopic-cavities, thus making it rather more like the Hawara chamber, while a straight-forward lid was abandoned in favour of two much more massive blocks, once again reminiscent of Ammenemes III's prototype. One was intended as a fixture, cut away below to give additional head-room for the burial party, but the other was supported by a pair of quartzite props, equipped to sand hydraulics, after the manner of Hawara.

Fig. 8. The cap-stone of the pyramid of Khendjer, at southern South Saqqara.

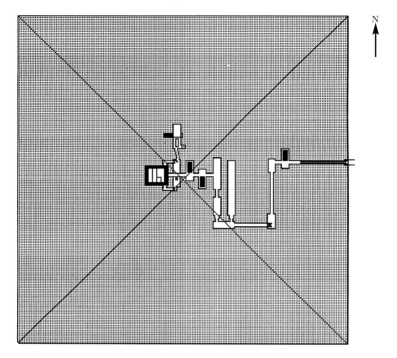

Fig. 9. Plan of the Thirteenth Dynasty Unfinished Pyramid at southern South Saqqara, the possessor of the most elaborate substructure ever built into a pyramid.

No trace of the king's name was found at Mazghuna-South; only a fragment of calcite kohl pot and a piece of steatite inlay remained from the burial. In the pyramid of Khendjer, the owner's name was only recovered by the fortunate discovery of the monument's inscribed pyramidion, now in the Cairo Museum (fig. 8). With a base-measurement of 51.8 metres, Khendjer's pyramid was rather smaller than the Mazghuna monument; however, since its sarcophagus-cum-burial chamber is both the deeper and the larger, indications are that it was built at a slightly later date, with both pyramids posterior to Ameny-Qemau's and the other Mazghuna example.

Khendjer's pyramid is the only one of the Thirteenth Dynasty group known to have had a small adjacent pyramid. This lay north of the site of the mortuary temple and had two burial chambers, with quartzite sarcophagi, which had never been used. It almost certainly belonged to Khendjer's wives, its features and position being inconsistent with its being a 'subsidiary', 'ritual' or 'ka' pyramid, an element in any case last seen with any degree of certainty in the pyramid complex of Sesostris I at Lisht.

The fifth excavated pyramid lies just south of Khendjer's, and was apparently never finished. Its substructure is one of the most elaborate of any Egyptian sepulchral monument (fig. 9), while, at 91 metres square, it is

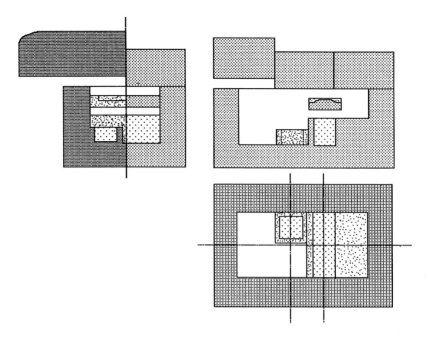

Fig. 10. The quartzite burial chamber of the Unfinished Pyramid; the sarcophagus and canopic chest were carved as one with the chamber.

by far the largest pyramid of the dynasty. One of its most remarkable features is its possession of two burial chambers, the principal of which was carved out of a block of quartzite, with a conventional-looking sarcophagus and canopic chest within, but carved as one with the chamber (fig. 10). Closure of the chamber was to be by the same means as in the pyramids of Khendjer, Hawara and Mazghuna-South, but the tomb was never used; as in the Northern Mazghuna pyramid, this probably represents the outcome of some coup or palace intrigue which lost a king his throne and/or his life. To judge from the number and brevity of the dynasty's reigns, such was probably not uncommon.

The other burial chamber lay to the west and had an arrangement of sarcophagus/lid/portcullis similar to Ameny-Qemau's, but reversed, with a separate canopic chest. The chamber has been described as a queen's, but no similar installation is known. Given the elaboration of the substructure, clearly inspired by the desire for security, the most attractive solution is that the room was a decoy, to draw plunderers away from the real burial. The elaboration and scale of the monument would suggest that it is the latest of the known pyramids, but of its owner, no indication was forthcoming from its excavation.

The remaining unexcavated probable Thirteenth Dynasty pyramids are Ameny-Qemau's neighbours at South Dahshur and were first noticed by Dieter Arnold and Rainer Stadelmann. Their position argues most strongly for their being part of the Middle Kingdom necropolis, and, within that, for their attribution to kings subsequent to Ammenemes III. Nothing else is thus far known of them, save their positions, having been missed even by such a keen observer as Carl Richard Lepsius, the German Egyptologist who had mapped almost every pyramid-ruin in the late 1840s.

Apart from the pyramids, one other king's tomb of the dynasty is known, a tomb of a type which one suspects was a common one for the many ephemeral kings of the Thirteenth Dynasty: King Auibre Hor was laid to rest in the easternmost of a row of shaft-tombs cut between the inner and outer temenos-walls of the Dahshur pyramid of Ammenemes III. Originally excavated for a member of Ammenemes's court, it had been enlarged by the construction of an emplacement for the sarcophagus and canopic chest, plus an antechamber-area, at a lower level than the tomb's original chamber. These additions were gable-roofed. With the rims of the coffer and chest level with the antechamber floor, from which the sarcophagus lid was slid into place, the arrangements conformed (with the exception of a locking portcullis) to earlier-Thirteenth Dynasty practice, as exhibited in the pyramid of Ameny-Qemau.

The great interest of the tomb derives from the fact that it had suffered relatively lightly at the hands of the tomb-robbers, thus providing us with our only sizable body of information as to what accompanied a Middle Kingdom monarch to the grave. The antechamber contained, principally, a celebrated statue of the king's *ka*, or guardian spirit, in its naos, two calcite stelae, one with an offering formula, a case for staves and a number of pottery and (dummy) wooden vessels. Inside his sarcophagus, the king's rifled body lay within a badly-decayed rectangular coffin, decorated with an eye-panel and inscribed gold strips.

The coffin (and accompanying canopic chest) were very simple confections, with a flat lids. These contrast with the quite elaborately decorated boxes, with curved and end-boarded lids, that are ubiquitous in the later Middle Kingdom - and are found on the coffin of the Princess Nubheteptikhered, buried in the tomb next to Hor's, and perhaps his daughter. The distinctly archaic appearance of Hor's *ensemble* is perhaps unexpected. Among sarcophagi, those of kings were at the forefront of development; in particular, the introduction of the panelled lower part under Sesostris III comes to mind, something much imitated in the immediately following years. Likewise, the royal tombs of the Middle Kingdom show dramatic innovations in their design. However, interestingly enough, a similar situation exists concerning the royal coffins of the New Kingdom and early Third Intermediate Period, when an otherwise-obsolete coffin design was retained solely for kingly burials. It may be, therefore, that a conscious decision to place the divine body in a 'primeval' container is involved, not wishing to entrust this sacred duty to a 'new fangled' piece of magical apparatus.

Although stripped of much of his finery, Hor retained some of his equipment: his once-gilded mask, and the remains of two falcon collars and a dagger. The mummy itself had been reduced to a damaged skeleton: the king's skull today lies in the Cairo Museum, its facial skeleton missing, and sawn through the temples - the work of the anatomist Daniel Fouquet in 1894. Alongside him lay a stave, two long sceptres, an inlaid flail, two small calcite vases and a wooden mallet, the latter perhaps left by robbers. The wooden inner canopic chest, which closely matched the coffin, and still contained four human-headed canopic jars, was found with its two seals intact, these reading 'Nimaetre', the erstwhile prenomen of Ammenemes III. This led some early scholars to identify Hor as a defunct co-regent of the latter. While his placement in the Thirteenth Dynasty is not now generally questioned, the sealings do, however, require explanation.

One might be that Hor's probable successor, (Kay-)Ammenemes VII, used Nimaetre as his prenomen at the beginning of his reign, only to change it to Sedjefakare later; such changes were not unknown in the sweep of Egyptian history. An alternative, and perhaps more probable, explanation is that it is the amuletic use of the prenomen of the last great king of the Middle Kingdom: it appears to have occurred as a divine name in what seems to be a variant prenomen of Hor's third successor, Khendjer, Nikhanimaetre, who is more usually Userkare. Such uses of revered predecessors' names are not uncommon, particularly at times of national weakness: certain royal prenomina retained their potency for millennia.

Attempting to historically fix the owners of the pyramids noted so far is difficult, but certain possibilities and probabilities may be delineated. Of the two kings firmly associated with pyramids, Ameny-Qemau does not appear in any lists - or elsewhere. However, the ninth king of the Dynasty, Sehetepibre Sihornedjhiryotef, appears to have been the son of Ameny-Qemau, which might suggest his approximate position. Khendjer, on the other hand, appears securely placed as the sixteenth king, two places after Hor. Since the two Mazghuna pyramids are to be placed typologically between those of Ameny-Qemau and Khendjer, they might be attributable to two of the longer-reigning intervening kings. Jéquier suggested that the Unfinished Pyramid might have belonged to Khendjer's successor, but the great leap forward in architecture represented by it might suggest ownership by one of a slightly later group of kings.

Allocation of unexcavated pyramids must rest largely upon their position and guesswork; a basic premise is that within any group of monuments there is a North-South trend, with time. On this basis, the two unexcavated South Dahshur pyramids would be earlier than Ameny-Qemau's; a possibility is that one is the pyramid of Ammenemes IV (if not the owner of Ammenemes II's neighbour), or Sobkneferu, since its position relative to the pyramid of Ammenemes III is very similar to that of the latter to that of Ammenemes II, and Ammenemes II to Sesostris III. In any case, the South Dahshur group should probably be placed within the twenty-five years following the death of Ammenemes III. Ephemeral monarchs would have been buried after the manner of Hor, who seems to have held the throne for a mere seven months.

In the foregoing there has, perhaps, been an underlying assumption that the tombs of all Thirteenth Dynasty kings are to be looked for in that part of the Memphite necropolis that served as the burial ground for the Residence of *Itj-tawy*, the capital city founded near Lisht by Ammenemes I early in the Twelfth Dynasty. That some were buried elsewhere is quite possible, and some monuments from rather further north may represent evidence for this. From near Faqus came a large fragment of the granite pyramidion of the pyramid of Merneferre Ay, the twenty-seventh king of the dynasty, while from near Tell el-Dab'a, at Ezbet Rushdi el-Kebira, came a basalt pyramidion, originally fitted with a metal covering. These might suggest a royal cemetery associated with what was soon to be the capital of a new set of rulers - Avaris. On the othe hand, it is probably far more likely that these pieces, along with such Middle Kingdom sculpture found re-inscribed in the same area, may represent plunder brought back by the Palestinian rulers who would soon emerge from the area to take over much of the rest of Egypt. In addition, at Athribis, at the apex of the Delta, were the remains of a destroyed brick pyramid which, by its material, might appear to be Middle Kingdom/Second Intermediate Period in date, although it may have been very much later in date, particularly in view of its location, within a Ptolemaic city.

Thus, it would appear that for its first forty or more years, the kings of the Thirteenth Dynasty had their tombs in the necropolis used by their Twelfth Dynasty predecessors, the greater in pyramids, the lesser in shaft-tombs; later, they may have been buried further afield, as their kingdom broke down.

This decline was caused by a group known as the Hyksos. For generations, people of Palestinian origin had settled in the eastern Delta, perhaps finding an echo in the Biblical stories of Abraham and Joseph. Their centre was at Avaris, and at some point around 1650 BC, the whole of Lower (northern) Egypt, came under the rule of one of their number. Whether this was the result of military action, or merely a political coup, for the next

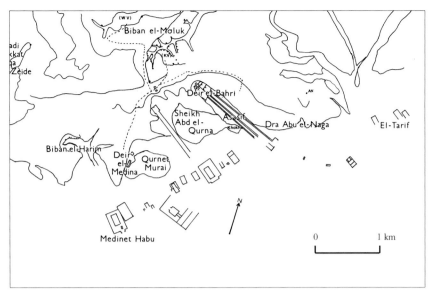

Fig. 11. Sketch-map of Western Thebes.

century these 'Hyksos' kings reigned as pharaohs at Avaris; the full extent of their power is still the subject of debate, but there is evidence that their nominal power stretched a long way into the south, possibly embracing even Thebes for a relatively short period. Nothing is as yet known of these kings' tombs, although the ongoing excavations of Manfred Bietak at Tell el-Dab'a (Avaris) may yet reveal something. Of the tombs of their Egyptian predecessors in the old cemeteries at Memphis, it seems likely that a number were plundered by the Hyksos - witness the pyramidion of King Ay.

While the Palestinians ruled in the north, down in the south, from Thebes, ruled the rump of the old royal line, now referred to as the Sixteenth/Seventeenth Dynasty. At this city they initiated the royal cemetery at Dira Abu'l-Naga, in which were erected the last kings' pyramids to be built in Egypt (fig. 11, 12). Thebes had been the place of origin of the Middle Kingdom kings of the Eleventh and Twelfth Dynasties, and had been the place of burial of its earliest rulers, until Ammenemes I had abandoned it in favour of Lisht, in the north.

Some of our best information on the pyramids of the Seventeenth Dynasty kings is provided by Papyrus Abbott, which records an investigation into alleged robberies amongst certain royal tombs at Western Thebes during the reign of Ramesses IX. Included in them were a series of small royal pyramids on the hillside of Dira Abu'l-Naga. Unfortunately, none have yet been properly excavated or recorded; one was cleared by Auguste Mariette in 1860, but his excavation records are lost. Others had their substructures opened by local plunderers and their contents

16

Fig. 12. Dira Abu'l-Naga, the royal cemetery of the Seventeenth Dynasty, showing the approximate location of the pyramid of Inyotef VI.

dispersed. No real records survive of any of these 'explorations', and more recent searches for identifiable traces of the Seventeenth Dynasty royal necropolis have proved thus-far inconclusive.

Of the pyramids themselves, our only solid piece of information is provided by the cap-stone of King Sekhemre-wepmaet Inyotef (V). Now in the British Museum (fig. 13), its angle shows the brick pyramid to have

Fig. 13. The cap-stone of the pyramid of Inyotef V, bearing the king's name. Compared with that of Khendjer, fig. 8, above, it shows that the structure had a much steeper angle than the earlier, far larger, royal pyramids.

Fig. 14. The coffin of Inyotef VI, from Dira Abu'l-Naga.

been tall and slender, much like the later private pyramids, now restored on the hillside of Deir el-Medina. It would appear that a chapel was built into the brick pyramid core and/or the rock-face below it. It is possible that a twelve metre-square pyramid described and sketched by Robert Hay in the first half of the nineteenth century may have been one such monument, but it is also possible that what he saw was one of the pyramids that top a number of Ramesside tombs in the area. A pair of obelisks stood outside the chapel of Nubkheperre Inyotef (VI); unluckily, both were lost in the Nile en route to Cairo in the last century. A late tomb of the group may now have been rediscovered by a German-US expedition (see below, p. 28).

The burial chamber was apparently reached by a shaft in the bed-rock; in one case, that of Inyotef VI, the chamber contained a rock-cut sarcophagus, holding his coffin, now in the British Museum (fig. 14). In the tomb of Inyotef V, the entrance to the substructure seems to have been a brick-lined pit, about twenty feet deep, half way up the hill, from which a corridor led to a chamber in which two coffins lay, 'covered with cloth and dirt thrown over them'. Both coffins are now in the Louvre Museum, one being that of Inyotef V himself; the other was a private coffin, hurriedly adapted to hold the body of King Sekhemre-heruhirmaet Inyotef (VII). The latter seems to have been the next-but-one king, buried after the briefest of reigns in a recent predecessor's tomb.

The coffins from these tombs are of a distinctive form. At the beginning of the Seventeenth Dynasty, coffins followed the Thirteenth Dynasty rectangular type, largely black-varnished, with painted decorative elements. Most of them were of a straightforward box form, with an arched lid and end pieces, a shape reflected also in contemporary canopic chests. An interesting exception, however, was the coffin of Queen Montjuhotpe, the wife of King Djehuty, one of the very earliest kings of the new dynasty. It had a flared rim and sloped lid, thus taking the form of the primitive shrine, the naos.

By the time of Inyotef V, however, a new, mummiform, design had come into use, depicting the deceased as a human-headed bird, whose feathered wings enfold the whole body. From this feathering derives the modern name for such cases - *rishi*, the Arabic for 'feathered'. The coffin inscriptions of Inyotef V are interesting in that they state that it was a gift from his brother, another King Inyotef who, on the basis of the spelling of the nomen, is clearly the sixth king of the name.

Besides the coffins, a number of royal canopic chests have also come to light, those of Djehuty, Inyotef V and Sobkemsaf II (fig. 15) being found by local plunderers. Also known is the heart scarab of, probably, the last named king. Now in the British Museum, there is some confusion over its

Fig. 15. The canopic chest of Sobkemsaf II, from his lost tomb on Dira Abu'l-Naga.

exact provenance, since the first information was that it came from the mummy of Inyotef VI, in spite of clearly naming a King Sobkemsaf. A set of arrows was allegedly found with the mummy of Inyotef VI.

The latter wore a silver diadem, now in Leiden; curiously enough, a very similar item has recently appeared on the antiquities market, almost certainly from another Seventeenth Dynasty royal burial. However, nothing deriving from outside a coffin or canopic chest seems to be known, perhaps implying that the kings of the Seventeenth Dynasty went without the kind of ancillary funerary equipment that was found with Hor. This may be confirmed by the confession of the robbers responsible for the pillaging of the tomb of Sobkemsaf I during the reign of Ramesses IX (Papyrus Leopold II-Amhurst), which seems to mention only material removed from the mummies and coffins:

> We found the pyramid of King Sekhemre-Shedtawi Sobkemsaf (I), this being unlike the pyramids and tombs of the nobles that we were used to rob. We took our copper tools and forced a way into the pyramid of this king through

its innermost part. We found the substructure, and we took our lighted candles in our hands and went down. Then we broke through the blocking that we found at the entrance to his crypt, and found this god lying at the back of his burial place. And we found the burial-place of Queen Nubkhaes, his wife, situated beside him, it being protected and guarded by plaster and enclosed by a stone blocking. This we also broke through, and found her resting there in the same way.

We opened their sarcophagi and their coffins in which they were, and found the noble mummy of this king equipped with a *khepesh*-sword; many amulets and jewels were upon his neck, and his headpiece of gold was upon him. The noble mummy of the king was completely bedecked with gold, and his coffins were adorned with gold and silver inside and out and inlaid with all kinds of precious stones...

On the other hand, when enumerating the amount of gold taken by each robber in the share-out of the loot, there is an oblique reference to this not including booty from 'the furniture', so one cannot be absolutely certain on this point.

On the basis of the Abbott Papyrus itinerary, the Dira Abu'l-Naga necropolis remained in use down to at least the time of Kamose, the last king of the dynasty. The papyrus implies that the tomb was the southernmost of the cemetery, and at around the likely spot, the Metropolitan Museum of Art expedition, under H.E. Winlock, discovered a small pyramid that he believed could be that of the king. It lay in an area known as the Birabi at the bottom of the causeways leading up to Deir el-Bahari, where lie the Eleventh Dynasty temple of Montjuhotpe II and the Eighteenth Dynasty monuments of Hatshepsut and Tuthmosis III. Here it formed the focus of a cemetery datable to the very beginning of the Eighteenth Dynasty.

Next north seem to have been the pyramids of Kamose's predecessors, the two Taas, the second of whom (Seqenenre) is known as the apparent initiator of the struggle against the Hyksos, in which he died from severe head-wounds inflicted by Asiatic battle-axes.

While the Inyotefs and Sobkemsafs seem to have been left in their tombs, to be robbed in ancient (Sobkemsaf I) or modern (Inyotef V-VII, Sobkemsaf II) times, the mummies of Taa II and Kamose received more attention from the later necropolis commissioners. This was perhaps prompted by their being close kin of the first kings of the great Eighteenth Dynasty - the father and brother(?) of Amosis, the dynastic founder. Thus, like most of the kings of the New Kingdom, their bodies were removed from their vulnerable sepulchres and reinterred elsewhere during the

Twenty-first Dynasty, in a series of caches.

Taa's coffin was accordingly relieved of most of its gilding (and perhaps an inner case as well) and was placed in a great cache which was established south of Deir el-Bahari (TT 320), where it was found in the 1870s. Kamose, on the other hand, had been originally buried in a makeshift coffin (on which his name had even been written without a cartouche!); this was simply reburied in the rubble below the northern end of Dira Abu'l-Naga, not far from site of the pyramid of Inyotef VI. Here, it was found by Mariette in 1857. Regrettably, the mummy disintegrated on exposure to the air, but the coffin is now on display in Cairo. In the same area was placed at least one other coffin removed from its tomb by the necropolis authorities, the famous case of Queen Ahhotpe, wife of Taa II, also now in Cairo, together with the jewellery found on her mummy. The giant outer coffin that seems once to have been associated with it was found, however, in the TT 320 cache.

The war of liberation from the Hyksos, begun by Taa II and Kamose, was continued and brought to a successful conclusion by Amosis, the founder of the New Kingdom. With him, Egypt was reunited and its period of greatest glory arrived.

II   A New Beginning

Amosis, first king of both the Eighteenth Dynasty and the New Kingdom, reigned for some twenty-five years, a quarter-century which saw the transformation of the kingdom from the rather impoverished rump of Hyksos days into a prosperous, united nation on the verge of an Imperial future. His tomb remains something of an enigma: one might have expected him to seek burial amongst his immediate forefathers, on the slopes of Dira Abu'l-Naga, but no certain trace has been found of him there. A tomb in a wadi behind the Theban cliffs has been suggested as his (KV 32), but on tenuous typological grounds. There is, however, a tomb that bears his name, but is unlikely to ever have been used to contain his mummy. This lies at the holy city of Abydos, sacred city to the mortuary god, Osiris, and is part of one of the more intriguing groups of funerary monuments.

The site lies somewhat to the south of the well-known temples of Sethos I and Ramesses II, and comprises three axes, only two of which seem to have been finished (fig. 16). The most northerly was the work of

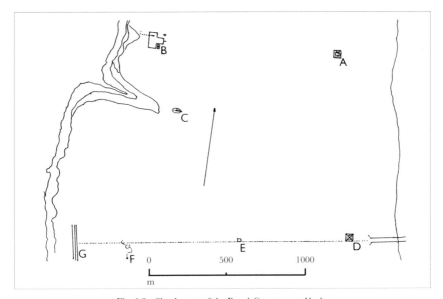

Fig. 16. Sketch-map of the Royal Cemetery at Abydos.

the Twelfth Dynasty king, Sesostris III, and comprised a chapel at the desert edge, due west of which was a complex at the base of the cliff. This included a temple and a tomb, the latter a series of passageways and rooms, one of which contained a sarcophagus and canopic chest.

This remarkable tomb would seem to have been only a cenotaph, since Sesostris had a pyramid at Dahshur, in which he was almost certainly buried, although some recent suggestions have revived the idea that the king was actually interred at Abydos. There are plenty of private parallels to such a cenotaph, large numbers of worthies building small chapels, or erecting stelae, to assure their posthumous participation in the cult of Osiris, King of the Dead. Accordingly, one should probably take a similar view of the complex that Amosis built a few hundred metres south of Sesostris III's.

It was even more elaborate than the Twelfth Dynasty structure, including a pyramid near the cultivation, the last such monument to be built for a pharaoh until the Twenty-fifth Dynasty (figs. 16D, 17). At the opposite end of its axis was a temple, rising in terraces against the cliff face (fig. 16G). This form of building is relatively uncommon in Egyptian architecture, the best known examples being two temples built at Deir el-Bahari, those of the Eleventh Dynasty Montjuhotpe II and the Eighteenth Dynasty Hatshepsut. However, as discussed later, it is fully in keeping with the mythic functions of the temple, and was utilised to a greater or lesser extent by a number of monarchs of the New Kingdom for their mortuary chapels.

Fig. 17. The ruined Pyramid of Amosis at Abydos, viewed from the cultivation.

24

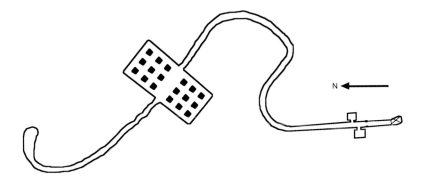

Fig. 18. Plan of the cenotaph-tomb of Amosis at Abydos.

In the expanse of desert between the pyramid and temple, Amosis constructed two monuments. The first was a brick chapel dedicated to the king's grandmother, Tetisherit (fig. 16E), containing a fine stela, now in the Cairo museum. The second was a subterranean tomb of unusual form (fig. 16F). Mostly cut only a few metres below the surface, a pit entrance gives access to a twisting passageway that eventually opens into a great hall, its roof formerly held up by eighteen columns (fig. 18). However these supports gave way many years ago, and it was the clue supplied by the hollow in the ground created by the room's collapse that led to the tomb's discovery by Charles Currelly in 1903/4. Below the hall, a further passage, seemingly unfinished, leads deeper into the matrix.

Little was found by the excavators, apart from a few bricks, stamped with Amosis' prenomen, and a number of fragments of gold leaf, all found in the debris of the pillared hall. An interesting point is that the pyramid's core contained rubble from the construction of the tomb; in a similar way, the spoil from Sesostris III's 'tomb' had been concealed within dummy mastabas constructed nearby.

From either here, or his lost resting place at Thebes, came a magnificent shabti figure, now in the British Museum. Such images make their first appearance in the Middle Kingdom, and until the middle of the Eighteenth Dynasty only one normally appeared in a burial. However, from around the time of Amenophis II, there was something of an explosion in their numbers, quantities increasing over time, until a burial of the Third Intermediate Period could contain upward of four hundred figures.

The other surviving item from Amosis' burial is his mummy and coffin. As will be related in detail later, his was amongst the royal bodies removed from their tombs in the Third Intermediate Period and gathered

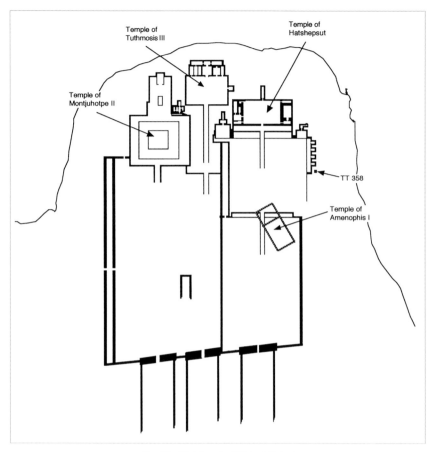

Fig. 19. Sketch-map of Deir el-Bahari

together in a number of communal hiding places. The mummy is
somewhat battered, but quite well preserved, displaying the interesting
feature that its brain had been removed through the *foramen magnum*, rather
than via the more usual nasal route. The mummy still lay in its original
coffin, remarkably well preserved, in spite of having lost its gilding in
antiquity. Made to closely fit the embalmed body, it had been decorated
with the *rishi* pattern of the previous dynasty, which was to remain in use
on royal coffins until at least the time of Psusennes I, over five hundred
years later.

The Theban funerary arrangements of Amosis' son and successor,
Amenophis I, are somewhat better known, if still obscure. In after years,
the king, together with his mother, Ahmes-Nefertiri, were worshipped as
the patron deities of the Theban necropolis, and a number of chapels are
recorded as being used for his cult in the later New Kingdom. One of
them, apparently built for the king's Sed-Festival, and finally dedicated to

26

Amenophis and Ahmes-Nefertiri jointly, lay in front of Dira Abu'l-Naga, the burial place of their Seventeenth Dynasty ancestors. However, the original mortuary chapel possibly lay at Deir el-Bahari, where a rectangular building was erected, its bricks stamped with the cartouches of the king and queen-mother (fig. 19). Janusz Karkowski believes that the structure was rather a workshop associated with restoration work in the nearby temple of Montjuhotpe II, but the point remains distinctly moot.

Nothing today can be seen of this building, it having been demolished by Hatshepsut when it stood in the way of the final extension of her own temple at the site. However, its general plan was traced during the American excavations there, showing it to be a relatively modest structure of rectangular plan. A number of items of statuary that possibly once stood in the building have been recovered in the Deir el-Bahari area, most particularly limestone statues that may have been reinstalled in the temple of Montjuhotpe II by Hatshepsut, and granite remains from the Ramesside temple further down the Asasif (cf. pp. 127-8, below).

The importance of the area to Amenophis I is further indicated by the presence there, northwest of the chapel, of the tomb of his wife, Meryetamun (TT 358). When first opened, this sepulchre was dated to the time of Amenophis II, but work by the Polish expedition at the site has now confirmed that the tomb predates the construction of Hatshepsut's temple. It is entered via a pit, two corridors leading to a deep shaft, blocking further access. Such shafts are a typical feature of New Kingdom royal tombs; it would appear that they had two functions. One was the basic practical aim of foiling the entry of thieves, something supported by the ancient Egyptian name for the room containing the shaft, *ta weskhet iseq*, 'the Hall of Hindering'. There may also have been a more esoteric function, that of facilitating the spirit's access to the subterranean regions of the netherworld.

Beyond the shaft lay an antechamber and, beyond, the unfinished burial chamber. When entered in 1929, it still contained the queen's body, enclosed in two coffins, the inner of normal size, and of the same basic design as that of the corresponding piece of the earlier queen Ahhotpe. The outer case also followed Ahhotpe's in being giant, 3.135 m long, with debris indicting that it had once been enclosed in an even more gigantic coffin. The coffins and mummy had attracted the attentions of tomb robbers, but had been restored in the Twenty-first Dynasty, the larger of the surviving two being one of the finest coffins ever recovered from an Egyptian tomb.

Meryetamun's mother-in-law, Ahmes-Nefertiri, was buried in a tomb of rather similar design, constructed near the summit of the Dira Abu'l-Naga foothills, and was also the possessor of a coffin of giant stature. The tomb has been the subject of much discussion, being frequently posited as the last resting place of Amenophis I himself, either as his original sepulchre, or after modification of the queen's tomb to accept a double burial.

No tomb has revealed unequivocal evidence of its occupation by the king; however, the Abbott Papyrus, already referred to in connexion with the tombs of the Seventeenth Dynasty, gives the following description of its location:

> The tomb of King Amenophis I is 120 cubits [c. 61 metres] below the structure/ridge related to it, called (that of) The High Path, which is north of the House-of-Amenophis-of-the Garden.

Unfortunately, no-one has succeeded in identifying the 'House-of-Amenophis-of-the Garden' with any degree of certainty. The most likely candidates would seem to be either the aforementioned temple in front of Dira Abu'l-Naga, or a chapel dedicated to the king at the workmen's village of Deir el-Medina, where lived those charged with the construction of the royal tombs.

Depending on the view one takes of these cult places, two areas have been generally admitted as candidates for containing the sepulchre of Amenophis I. One is the cliffs of Dira Abu'l-Naga, rising behind the aforementioned temple. The tomb mentioned above as being that of Ahmes-Nefertiri was identified by Howard Carter as that of the king, an equation resurrected more recently by Nicholas Reeves, who notes that its entrance lies little more than 120 cubits from a cairn on the hill side. In favour of this attribution is that the tomb seems to have been modified to take two burials, and the plentiful fragments found within naming the king.

In 1993, however, Daniel Polz found on the hillside itself a huge tomb (K93.11), comprising a double forecourt, with an entrance passage leading to a four-pillared hall. A large, ten-metre shaft opens in the centre of this hall, giving access to a spacious gallery leading to a small chamber, in front of which is an anthropoid rock-cutting, reminiscent of the 'rock-cut sarcophagus' reported in the tomb of Inyotef VI (see above, p. 19). On the basis of the sheer scale and design of the sepulchre, its excavator takes the view that a royal ownership is highly probable. Still more suggestive is the fact that large brick and sandstone structures were built over the front of the tomb from the late Eighteenth Dynasty until the late Ramesside Period, in particular by the High Priest Ramessesnakhte, who served under Ramesses IV to IX; during that very period, Amenophis I was supreme as patron deity of the Theban necropolis. All this makes Amenophis I's ownership not improbable, although some of his predecessors, particularly Amosis, are also clear candidates.

On the other hand, another school of thought, holding the 'House' to lie at Deir el-Medina, has identified the tomb with one some way to the south, now numbered KV 39. It lies a requisite distance below the pathway leading up into the hills from Deir el-Medina and, on the basis of early descriptions, appeared to be of a plan consistent with an early Eighteenth Dynasty date. However, clearance begun in 1989 by John Rose has shown a distinctly unusual plan, seemingly resulting from the extension of a 'core' 'corridor-and-chamber' tomb. A long gallery extends at right angles to the original axis, with another leading back underneath the entrance-stairway. The remains of a number of Eighteenth Dynasty burials have been found in the debris-choked tomb, with fragmentary objects bearing the names of more than one Eighteenth Dynasty king. In view of this, KV 39's candidacy for being Amenophis I's burial place must now be regarded as distinctly questionable. It may in fact be the joint tomb of a number of members of the royal family of the mid Eighteenth Dynasty.

Since the dawn of history, the body had rarely been far separated from the place where its mortuary priests placed offerings for the benefit of its spirit. If the 1993 Dira Abu'l-Naga tomb is indeed that of Amenophis I, his will have conformed to that pattern, although with an additional, perhaps principal, mortuary chapel at Deir el-Bahari. If either of the other tombs are his, however, the body and offering place will be seen as being separated by a considerable distance. This should be seen as a fairly momentous event, and the considerations leading to it must accordingly have been pressing, particularly in view of the conservatism exhibited by the Egyptians in matters pertaining to fundamental funerary matters.

The most likely must be the matter of security. The development of pyramid architecture throughout most of the Middle Kingdom had clearly been driven by the need to augment the protection afforded the body - witness the quartzite chambers and 'hydraulic' closures employed in the Thirteenth Dynasty pyramids at Saqqara, Dahshur and Mazghuna. The next step would have to be to remove the royal body completely from any superposing monument that would give away its location. Amenophis I may have been the first king known to have done this; if not, however, the step was certainly taken by his successor: Tuthmosis I.

III   The Valley

Tuthmosis I was not a son of Amenophis I, who seems to have been childless; it has recently been suggested that the new king was a son of Ahmose-Sipairi, a brother of Amosis. Tuthmosis would thus have succeeded as the late king's nearest living relative.

Whether or not Amenophis I had taken the step, Tuthmosis I certainly separated his places of burial and offerings, in which he was followed by all other rulers of the New Kingdom. Funerary chapels of increasing magnificence henceforth lined the plain that lies between the West Theban cultivation and cliffs. The royal mummies, however, lay almost without exception in a wadi behind the wall of cliffs (fig. 20, 21). Apart from any other merits, its choice may have been influenced by the presence above it of El-Qurn, the sacred mountain home of the goddess, Mertesger, 'the Lover of Silence', and the most magnificent of all natural pyramids (fig. 22). This wadi is called in Arabic the Biban el-Moluk, or 'Doors of the Kings': to the Western layman it is perhaps better known as the Valley of the Kings. KV 39, a putative candidate for tomb of

Fig. 20. The southern end of the Biban el-Moluk.

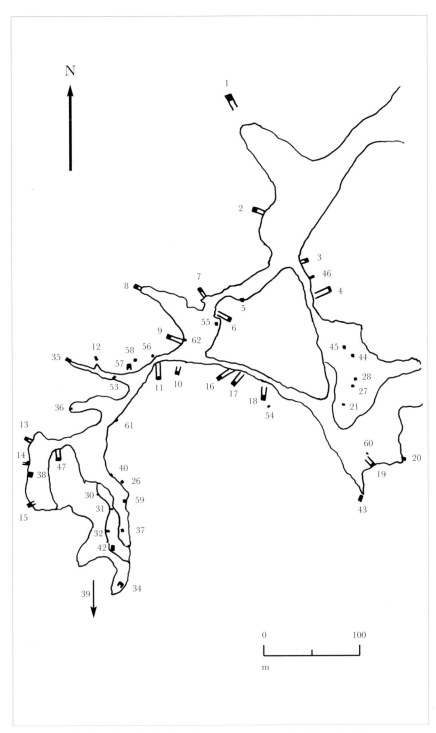

N

Fig. 21. Map of the King's Valley, the eastern branch of the Biban el-Moluk.

31

Fig. 22. El-Qurn, the pyramidal peak that overlooks the Biban el-Moluk, sacred to the goddess Mertesger: 'She Who Loves Silence'.

Amenophis I, is numbered in its series (KV = Kings' Valley), but is not really in the valley-proper.

The construction of Tuthmosis I's tomb is recorded in the celebrated biographical inscription of his high official, Ineni:

> I supervised the excavation of the tomb of His Majesty, alone, without anyone else overseeing (lit.: 'no-one seeing, no-one hearing').... I was vigilant in seeking that which is excellent. I made fields of clay, in order to plaster their tombs in the necropolis; it was a work such as the ancestors had done which I was obliged to do there.

This passage has often been quoted to show that the tombs were constructed in true secrecy, with the more imaginative writers conjuring up images of workers held incommunicado for years on end, and slaughtered once the burial had taken place. Of course, this view owes far more to Hollywood than to ancient Egypt.

In the first place, the phrase 'no-one seeing, no-one hearing' is far better interpreted as the normal boast of the Egyptian official that he had had sole responsibility for a task, without a senior 'looking and listening'. Secondly, it is abundantly clear that the workmen employed in tomb construction were by no means an expendable rabble of slaves, rather skilled artisans who could not be lightly disposed of.

These workers were accommodated in the already mentioned village

Fig. 23. Deir el-Medina,
the workmen's village of the Theban royal necropolis.

of Deir el-Medina (fig. 23), from which a path led over the cliffs into the
Valley; at the top lay a secondary settlement in which the workers spent the
night when 'on call' in the Valley. Although most of our evidence on the
workings of the community comes from the second half of the New
Kingdom, the earliest dated material from the site comes from the time of
Tuthmosis I, in whose reign the bricks of the wall surrounding the
settlement were made.

Although little is known of the history of the Deir el-Medina
community during the Eighteenth Dynasty, large quantities of
documentation are available from the succeeding Ramesside Period,
allowing much of the organization of the workmen and their activities to
be reconstructed, for this period at least. Work in the royal necropolis was
largely hereditary, with families traceable for generation after generation.
The basic work gang was divided into 'Left' and 'Right' 'sides', each under
its own foreman, with a single 'Scribe of the Tomb' in overall charge of
administration.

The procedure leading down to the completion of a royal tomb seem
to have been standardised, beginning with the selection of a site by a royal
commission, and then continuing with the drawing up of basic plans and
the cutting of the sepulchre itself. As will be seen, during most of the
Eighteenth Dynasty, decoration was essentially carried out only after the
burial, with the exception of certain border patterning. However, later on
decoration was carried out essentially as soon as a wall-area had been freed

from the rock matrix. It is possible that the apparent formalisation of the Deir el-Medina organization around the beginning of the Nineteenth Dynasty was a result of the need to have a set of experienced artists permanently available, rather than for a fairly short period near the completion of all work.

The basic procedure for any decorative work was for the overall scheme to be laid out, by a scribe, in red ink, presumably working from a draft set out on papyrus or on an ostracon. This fairly rough basis was then worked up by an 'outline draughtsman', who would use black ink to produce the definitive form of the wall surface, with fully-detailed hieroglyphs and vignettes. If the tomb was to be decorated in relief, sculptors would then carve the wall in accordance with the drawings; in any case, the final phase would be a visit by the painters, who would finish the whole scheme in polychrome. The decoration of a tomb (or any other Egyptian monument, for that matter) was thus an effort involving a series of separate individuals. Many tombs are unfinished, and allow us to see the work 'in progress', and so study the techniques employed (figs. 24, 67).

The workmen were buried in a necropolis adjoining their village. The tombs are superbly decorated, not surprisingly, given that in many cases

Fig. 24. Detail of unfinished work in the tomb of Tuthmosis IV, showing guidelines.

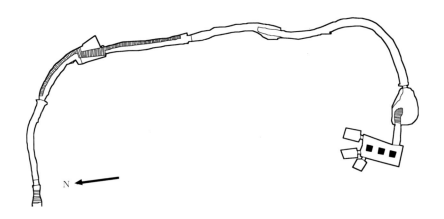

Fig. 25. Plan of the tomb of Tuthmosis I and Hatshepsut, KV20.

their owners and the artists decorating Pharaoh's tomb were one and the same. A number have been found intact, and their contents likewise display the mark of royal artists.

While Tuthmosis I is the first certain occupant of the Valley, there remains some doubt as to which tomb first had the honour of enshrining his mummy. In 1898, Victor Loret opened a tomb (KV 38) containing a canopic chest and sarcophagus bearing the king's name, but these items were shown in the 1930s to have been made for a reburial of the king by his grandson, Tuthmosis III. Another sarcophagus, adapted for Tuthmosis I by his daughter, Hatshepsut, was found a few years later, when Howard Carter cleared the burial chambers of KV 20, an immensely long tomb in the eastern part of the Valley (figs. 25, 110).

This sepulchre also contained a sarcophagus and canopic chest naming the female pharaoh, Hatshepsut. Accordingly, for many years KV20 was regarded as hers, which she planned to share with her father, whom she removed thither from KV 38. However, in 1974, John Romer published a convincing argument that only the inner pillared burial chamber was the work of Hatshepsut, the remaining parts of the tomb being Tuthmosis I's original sepulchre. According to this theory, KV 38 was the work of Tuthmosis III, who was certainly the author of the sarcophagus found within.

On this view, the body of Tuthmosis I will have been first interred in the large chamber which lies at the end of the series of passages and stairways that lead over 200 metres down from the surface of the Valley, its floor over 90 metres vertically below ground level. This great depth, the roughness of the cutting, and curiously bowed plan can be explained by the builders' vain search for good rock. Like much of the Theban necropolis, the Valley of the Kings is composed of layers of good quality limestone,

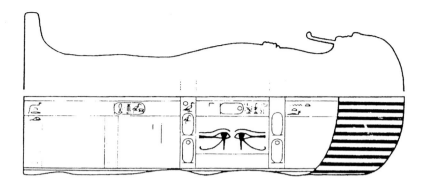

Fig. 26. A restoration of the original form of the outer coffin of Tuthmosis I, later usurped by Pinudjem I of the Twenty-first Dynasty.

interposed with layers of poorer stone, and a crumbly shale. It was into the latter that most of KV 20 is cut; clearly, the workmen hoped that they would eventually hit a layer of good stone, into which the burial chamber could be cut. This proved impossible, and thus it is likely that some lining was planned for this apartment, although nothing has been positively identified *in situ*.

It is most likely that no stone sarcophagus was employed at Tuthmosis I's original interment, a wooden one being used instead to contain his nest of coffins. The outermost coffin was later usurped by Pinudjem I of the Twenty-first Dynasty (fig. 26). This item is interesting in that, like the coffin of Amosis,

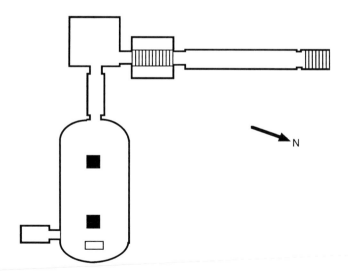

Fig. 27. Plan of the probable tomb of Tuthmosis II, KV 42.

Fig. 28. The burial chamber of KV42.

this coffin bears the tripartite heavy wig normally seen on private coffins, rather than the royal *nemes* affected by kingly coffins of earlier and later times. However, Tuthmosis' mummy was only to remain undisturbed for a few years.

He was succeeded by his son, a second Tuthmosis, who was married to his half-sister, Hatshepsut. Like those of his predecessors, the identification of this king's tomb has been the subject of debate. However, it appears most likely that it was an uninscribed tomb found by Carter in 1900, and now numbered KV 42 (fig. 27, 28). Although somewhat more regularly laid out than the tomb of the next king, Tuthmosis III, the workmanship is similar, and should not be used to argue for the necessary priority of one or the other sepulchre. Like the tombs of Ahmes-Nefertiri and Meryetamun, it has the characteristic right-angled bend that is a feature of royal tombs down to the time of Amenophis III. The antechamber has a low rock 'bench' along its right-hand side, perhaps intended to support items of funerary equipment, or alternatively an indication of the tomb's unfinished state. Its most distinctive feature, however, is its burial chamber, of an oval form that is clearly intended to replicate the cartouche, the enclosure within which are written the principal names of the kings of Egypt.

This room had had its walls plastered and a *khekher* frieze painted around its upper part. Interestingly, the upper quarter of the tinted plaster below the frieze is of a much lighter hue than the lower portion. It is possible that this reflects an intended division between the top two registers in any completed scheme. On the basis of parallels in succeeding royal tombs, this will have comprised the Book of Amduat ('What is in the Underworld'), applied by pen as if upon papyrus. However, no other decoration had been applied, and the quartzite sarcophagus lay unfinished and apparently unused at one end of the chamber (fig. 28). This great box would appear to be the earliest of all extant New Kingdom royal sarcophagi, of a simple design directly following that of the wooden box it replaced. Quartzite was the hardest stone worked by ancient man, this monument being the precursor of a series of sarcophagi in the material, the last being that used for the interment of Tutankhamun, six generations later. The non-use of the sarcophagus for the king's burial is most curious. The tomb was taken over in his son's reign for the use of Queen Meryetre, though again seemingly not used, perhaps in that case as the result of dissention in the royal family that accompanied Tuthmosis IV's apparent usurpation of the throne. It is unknown where Tuthmosis II was actually interred; what is certain is that his mummy was amongst those reburied by the necropolis officials of the Twenty-first Dynasty, with the implication that it had found rest somewhere in the area of the Valley.

A mortuary chapel of the king lies in the southern part of the Theban necropolis, west of Deir el-Medina, later to become the area of Medinet Habu; the location of that of Tuthmosis I is uncertain, perhaps near that of Amenophis I at Deir el-Bahari and later over-built. A (replacement?) chapel may have been built for him by Tuthmosis III, which was named 'Akheperkare (Tuthmosis I)-United-with-Life'. Tuthmosis II's sanctuary was a building of fairly simple design, it appears to have undergone reconstruction under Tuthmosis III, who was responsible for most of the fragmentary carved scenes that survive from the building. Amongst the

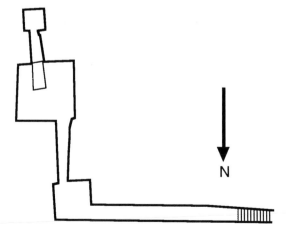

Fig. 29. Plan of the tomb of the Regent Hatshepsut.

other discoveries, made by a French team working under Bernard Bruyère in the 1920s, were the fragments of a colossus of Tuthmosis II, and a number of stelae, attesting to his posthumous cult.

Tuthmosis II left behind a young son, Tuthmosis III, for whom the dowager Hatshepsut acted as regent for some seven years. During her regency, the queen came close to completing a tomb in the remote Wadi Siqqat Taqa el-Zeide, in the southern part of the necropolis. It lies in a fairly dramatic location, the entrance being at the base of a cleft in the rock, some 70 metres above the bed of the wadi. Of a fairly simple right-angled plan (fig. 29) it contained a small quartzite sarcophagus, lacking only its final polish - in all matters a reduced version of that of Hatshepsut's late husband.

History is not without examples of dowagers acting as regents for infant kings; however, Hatshepsut did not stop there, being crowned Tuthmosis III's co-regent around the latter's seventh regnal year. She maintained this largely unprecedented position for nearly fifteen years, during which she was responsible for one of the finest of all Egyptian funerary monuments.

It was built in the great bay of Deir el-Bahari, already occupied by the Eleventh Dynasty temple of Montjuhotpe II, the probable mortuary chapel of Amenophis I, and quite possibly that of Hatshepsut's father, Tuthmosis I (figs. 18, 30). KV 20 is just on the other side of the cliff from Deir el-Bahari, which may have encouraged its appropriation. As the first

Fig. 30. The temples of Deir el-Bahari, with that of Montjuhotpe II at the left, Tuthmosis III in the centre, and Hatshepsut on the right.

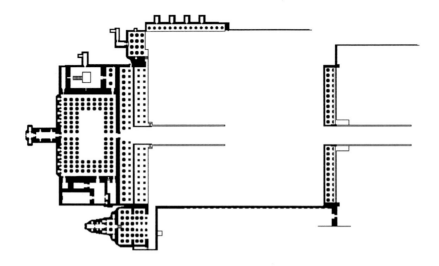

Fig. 31. Plan of the mortuary temple of Hatshepsut.

full-scale New Kingdom royal mortuary temple, it is of the greatest
interest, and provides a prototype for all succeeding examples, although
the resemblance is obscured at a superficial level by its construction in deep
terraces (fig. 31). In this, Hatshepsut's temple followed its Eleventh Dynasty
neighbour, and that of Amosis at Abydos. For its elegance and unity with
its surroundings, the building has long been recognized as a gem of
Egyptian architecture.

It is now being increasingly realised that the meaning of the New
Kingdom mortuary temple was much more complex than appears at first
sight. Indeed, even the very term 'mortuary temple' is not wholly
appropriate; other suggestions are 'memorial temple', or the Egyptian
term 'Mansion of Millions of Years'. Nevertheless, for the purposes of this
book, the old term will be maintained, with the intention of distinguishing
the cult element of the royal mortuary establishment from the tomb
chambers themselves.

The complex began in the plain, near the edge of the cultivation,
where Howard Carter and Lord Carnarvon excavated the remains of the
valley building, recalling similar structures associated with the great
pyramid complexes of the Old and Middle Kingdoms. This unfinished
construction had two levels: a lower court, and an upper terrace fronted by
a colonnade of square pillars. Battered walls bracketed the building, which
presumably linked with those that defined the causeway, lined with
sphinxes. This led for over a kilometre up to a gate in the main temple's
temenos wall. Beyond this, a path flanked with seven pairs of sphinxes led

up to the first ramp. Here lay a pair of T-shaped pools, filled with papyrus plants and accompanied by two trees, each planted in a pit cut in the desert gravel and filled with soil.

On each side of the ramp is now a colonnade, the right hand one lying directly over the site of the building of Amenophis I. It seems that these colonnades were constructed after other parts of the temple, and it is possible that it may originally have been intended to leave the chapel be, a decision later rescinded. Either end of the facade comprised by this pair of colonnades was adorned by a statue of the queen in the guise of Osiris. The southern colonnade is decorated with reliefs depicting the transport of a pair of obelisks from the granite quarries at Aswan to the great temple of Karnak. Its northern counterpart is, however, badly mutilated, although enough traces survive to show that its reliefs depicted Hatshepsut fowling, fishing, and offering to the gods.

The ramp leads up to the second court, once dominated by six sphinxes marking the way to a further ramp. The latter's balustrades are in the form of cobras, their heads protected by falcons with outstretched wings. The image of the protective falcon was by no means new, being found a millennium earlier on the famous diorite statue of Khephren, a more recently discovered figure of Neferefre from Abusir, and some mummy-masks of the Second Intermediate Period. As was the case with the first ramp, on either side lie colonnades. At their southern end lies a chapel dedicated to the goddess Hathor, a patron of the Theban necropolis. Its columns carry the distinctive Hathoric capitals, a woman's head merged with that of a cow, the goddess' sacred creature. On the walls, Hatshepsut and Tuthmosis III make offerings although, as is the case throughout the temple, the images of the queen were cut away some two decades after the date of her presumed death. Most extant reliefs depict Hatshepsut in the guise of a man - an indication of the irregularity of a woman holding the kingly office. However, two statues found in the temple area show her as a woman, and it has been suggested that they once stood in this chapel, dedicated as it was to the most feminine of goddesses.

Directly next door lies the famous Punt Colonnade, containing representations of a trading expedition sent to the land of Punt, probably located on the Red Sea coast of modern Somalia. North of the ramp is the Birth Colonnade. Here is told the tale of how Amun-Re, King of the Gods, took the form of Tuthmosis I in order to impregnate Hatshepsut's mother, Ahmes, thus making the queen regnant the physical daughter of the god. This idea of the supernatural paternity of the pharaoh is an ancient concept in Egyptian kingship, but explicit depictions have only survived in a few places. The prominence given to it by Hatshepsut is perhaps another manifestation of her need to seek the maximum justification for her assumption of power.

Fig. 32. The upper terrace of the mortuary temple of Hatshepsut; behind is the Eleventh Dynasty temple of King Montjuhotpe II.

The northern extremity of the colonnades is occupied by a chapel of Anubis, the canine-headed god of embalming and guardian of the necropolis . The right hand wall of the court, running parallel with the cliff, is occupied by a further colonnade, equipped with four niches. This structure is unfinished, and lies directly over the old tomb of Queen Meryetamun. The niches' intended dedications remain obscure.

The ramp that leads up from the second court gives access to the inner part of the temple, fronted once more by a pair of colonnades (fig. 32).

Fig. 33. Rear wall of the central sanctuary of the mortuary temple of Hatshepsut, with Tuthmosis III offering to Amun above the doorway; the other side of the tympanum showed the co-ruler, Hatshepsut, in a similar pose.

An osiride figure of the queen stood at the front of each pillar, with small kneeling figures in the intercolumnar spaces. Between the colonnades is a decorated trilithon gate, leading into the peristyle court. According to the latest reconstruction, the north, south and west sides of the court had three rows of columns, the eastern only two.

Directly across the court from the gateway is the main sanctuary of the temple, dedicated to Amun-Djeser-djeseru, the special form of the Theban god who resided in the temple, named anciently 'Holy-of-Holies' (Egyptian: *Djeser-djeseru*). The spacious anteroom originally had an osiride statue in each corner, the left and right wall having interesting scenes involving Hatshepsut's family, including her father, mother, husband and two daughters, Neferure and Neferubity (fig. 33). Beyond lies the holy-of-holies itself, decorated with offering scenes. This, with its subsidiary rooms, was originally the end of the temple, but over a thousand years after its construction, a cult room was added in honour of two deified mortals, Imhotep, architect of the Step Pyramid of Saqqara, and Amunhotpe-son-of-Hapu, the celebrated official of Amenophis III. Its decoration, executed under Ptolemy VIII Euergetes II, contrasts very badly with the exquisite Eighteenth Dynasty work elsewhere in the temple.

Either side of the entrance to the sanctuary complex, to which a columned porch was added in Ptolemaic times, extending along the back wall of the peristyle, are eighteen niches, ten shallow ones to contain osiride statues, the others small rooms originally closed by doors. Their decoration comprises the normal offering scenes, with the exception of a small scene that appears behind each door. Here, we find the kneeling figure of Senenmut, Hatshepsut's most intimate official, who has been frequently credited with the design of Deir el-Bahari. The presence of the image of an official in such positions is almost without parallel, and has been seen either as an indication of his position in the queen's favour, or as an act of monumental presumption. This man's burial chamber (TT 353) also lay within the precincts of the temple, below, and just inside the temenos wall. His mortuary chapel lies some distance away, on the summit of the Sheikh Abd el-Qurna hill (TT 71).

A doorway in the south wall of the peristyle leads into a vestibule giving access to two chapels, the smaller having been provided for Tuthmosis I. Whether or not this was intended as a replacement for a putative earlier chapel, this provision of a sanctuary dedicated to the king's late father would become standard in all royal mortuary temples. Next door is the considerably larger sanctuary of Hatshepsut herself. The two chapels' decoration is generally similar, featuring offering bringers, scenes of butchers, and schematic offering lists, with a large hardstone stela at the western end. That of Hatshepsut is lost.

To the north of the peristyle, a columned vestibule gives access to the altar court. In the centre stands a raised platform, approached by steps from the west, upon which offerings were made to the sun-god, Re, in his manifestation of Harmakhis – Horus-in-the-Horizon. This kind of offering place was always open to the sky, thus emphasising the difference between the cult of the sun and that of all other Egyptian gods, who were adored in dark, mysterious recesses. Leading off this court is a small room, dedicated to Anubis, but heavily featuring Hatshepsut's parents.

Essentially the prototype for all subsequent royal mortuary examples, the Deir el-Bahari temple had four specific cult-foci, the central one dedicated to Amun – or rather a special form of the Theban god, unique to the specific locale. The kings' specific divine essence was relegated to a secondary position, their own cult chambers lying away to the left of the principal god's. However, since by death they had also become fused with Amun, this was ameliorated by their thus sharing in his central placement and honour. The third cultic element was that of the sun. The altar court that is found to the north of the Amun sanctuary in all Theban mortuary temples may be seen as the last philosophical link with the royal tomb of the Old and Middle Kingdoms, whose central element, the pyramid, had

Fig. 34. The ruined burial chamber of Hatshepsut in KV 20. Much of the ceiling has collapsed; the rough walls were originally covered with an inscribed limestone lining.

been the supreme manifestation of the sun-god's status in the royal funerary complex. The fourth and final element was the veneration of the king's father; the scale of the provision for him seems to be the most variable in extant temples, and was doubtless influenced by personal considerations.

Some twenty years after her disappearance from the scene, the images of Hatshepsut at Deir el-Bahari were removed from the temple by Tuthmosis III: reliefs were erased, statues smashed and dumped. This phenomenon, which is to be seen at nearly all her monuments has been much discussed, but unanimity of explanation is far off.

As queen-regnant, Hatshepsut clearly intended to be buried in KV 20 in the Valley of the Kings. This is the tomb that seems have to have been made by her father, Tuthmosis I; to it she added a further chamber, equipped with store rooms and three columns. Its proportions incorporate a module used in the Deir el-Bahari temple but, significantly, not in the outer parts of the tomb. In view of the extremely poor rock from which the tomb was cut, any attempt to simply plaster the walls to receive decoration, as had been done in the tomb of Tuthmosis II, was impossible (fig. 34). Therefore, limestone lining slabs were installed, upon which were delineated in black and red a cursive version of the *Amduat*, the earliest of a series of texts that describe and illustrate the sun-god's passage through the hours of the night. The version from KV 20 is but fragmentary (fig. 35), but the intact decoration of the tomb of Tuthmosis III shows that its execution will have resembled a great papyrus, unrolled against the walls of the burial chamber.

KV 42 had certainly been intended to receive a similar decorative scheme, but only the preparation of the ground, and upper border had occurred (see above pp. 37-8). The evidence of later tombs with this kind

45

Fig. 35. Lining-blocks from the burial chamber of KV 20, bearing part of the Book of Amduat in cursive hieroglyphs.

of scheme indicates that the application of the sacred texts was carried out after the deposition of the royal mummy and its accompanying equipment, as part of the magical activation of the tomb. Thus, the presence of decoration on the lining blocks of the sepulchral chamber of Hatshepsut makes it certain that she was actually buried there, contrary to some scholars' assertions, in part influenced by the old idea that the aforementioned destruction of Hatshepsut's monuments directly followed her disappearance from the throne.

In the chamber, the queen was interred in a fine quartzite sarcophagus. For her tomb as Regent in the Wadi Siqqat Taqa el-Zeide, she had prepared a rectangular sarcophagus that directly imitated wooden

Fig. 36. The sarcophagus made for Hatshepsut and later modified for her reburial of Tuthmosis I.

examples, as had the earlier example of Tuthmosis II. When she first took the throne, she had had made another of the same form, but more elaborately decorated. However, later in the reign, yet another sarcophagus was made for her: this time it differed in having the plan of a cartouche, i.e. exhibiting a square-cut foot, but a rounded head. This form was to be almost universal for kingly sarcophagi for the rest of the New Kingdom. Most unusually, the sarcophagus head faced south, the reverse of normal practice. However, the canopic chest lay in the traditional orientation of east of the south end of the coffer, even though this meant that it lay opposite the head of the mummy.

The 'left-over' sarcophagus was partly reinscribed for Tuthmosis I (fig. 36); it was also installed in the burial chamber, with the intention that father and daughter should lie together. This sarcophagus also exhibited the strange reversal of orientation. At some point, Tuthmosis I's body was removed for reburial by Tuthmosis III; the fate of that of Hatshepsut remains obscure. The only trace is a few pieces of one of her wooden funerary items, perhaps a coffin, which were found along with other discarded fragments of royal funerary equipment in the shaft of the tomb of Ramesses XI, which suggests that her interment remained in place until the dismantling of the royal burials around the end of the New Kingdom (see p. 134 ff, below).

The corpse of Tuthmosis I, on the other hand, was provided by his grandson with a new quartzite sarcophagus, matching canopic chest, and, in all probability, new tomb. From its dimensions, it can be seen that the sarcophagus was specifically made to contain the king's rather large outer coffin. The tomb itself, KV 38, is a relatively small, roughly cut sepulchre on the opposite side of the Valley from KV 20. Nevertheless, it possesses a cartouche-form burial hall, once decorated with the typical pen-drawn Amduat and *khekher*-frieze (fig. 37). The tomb has been largely ruined by flooding. During the Twenty-first dynasty, one of the king's coffins was usurped by the priest-king, Pinudjem I, but nothing is known of the final

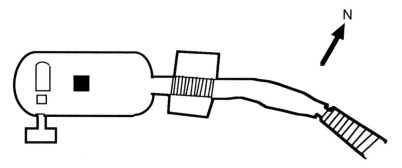

Fig. 37. Plan of the second tomb of Tuthmosis I, KV 38.

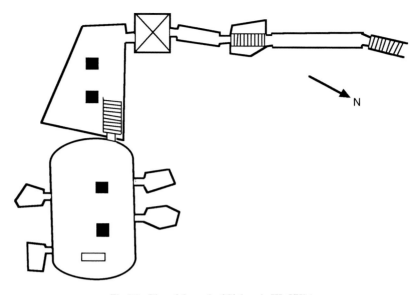

Fig. 38. Plan of the tomb of Tuthmosis III, KV34.

fate of his mummy. An early Eighteenth Dynasty mummy that happened to lie in this coffin at the time of its discovery has often been presented as his, but on arm position alone, this cannot be so. Starting with Amenophis I, kings were buried with their arms crossed at the breast: 'Tuthmosis I' has his extended.

As has already been noticed, Tuthmosis III came to the throne as a youngster; he spent the first twenty years of his reign under the tutelage of Hatshepsut, first as regent and then co-ruler. However, soon after the beginning of the third decade of his nominal rule, he achieved sole authority, and embarked upon a long career of overseas conquest and domestic development. He followed Hatshepsut's lead as a patron of art and architecture, building extensively throughout Egypt, in particular at Thebes.

His tomb in the Valley of the Kings is one of the finest of its kind. Numbered KV 34, it is not far from the probable tomb of Tuthmosis II, but lies high above the valley floor in a 'chimney' in the rock. This kind of situation is found at a number of tombs of the general period, including that of Hatshepsut as regent, and one attributed to Tuthmosis III's half-sister, Neferure. KV 34 was found by Victor Loret in 1898, and follows the general 'bent' plan of KV 42, but with various additions, and a surprising lack of right-angles (fig. 38).

From the entrance, two sets of steps and two corridors, all somewhat roughly cut into the rock, lead down to a chamber whose floor was cut away after the funeral to form a shaft some 19 metres deep. Although such a 'well' had been included in the tombs of Ahmes-Nefertiri and

Meryetamun, it is the first of its kind to be found in a king's sepulchre. The walls of the room are whitewashed and topped with a *khekher*-frieze. The preparation of the wall below this suggests that further decoration was contemplated, but never carried out. The ceiling is adorned with five-pointed yellow stars, on a deep blue background. The motif of the starred ceiling is very ancient, being found alongside the Pyramid Texts in the pyramids of the Fifth and Sixth Dynasties. The latter texts, the first to be found in royal tombs, and the ancestors of all such later compositions, comprise a wide variety of spells relating to the king's afterlife. They develop into the Coffin Texts of the First Intermediate Period and later, and their themes continue into the wide variety of funerary 'books' of the New Kingdom, of which the Amduat and the famous 'Book of the Dead' are but two.

A once-sealed doorway, painted over to match the rest of the wall, leads into the antechamber, its roof supported by a pair of pillars. The shape of the room is rather odd, each wall being of a different length. This can probably be explained as being the result of hurried completion. These walls are adorned with long lists of the denizens of the Underworld, many of them not found outside the restricted world of the royal tombs. In keeping with the fashion of the period, they are drawn in pen on a golden-yellow background, in the imitation of a papyrus roll. Certain figures so delineated are bizarre in the extreme, some with animal heads, but some with the complete form of an invertebrate atop their shoulders, or even an inanimate object where the head should be. When confronted with these strange images, it is important that we grasp what they meant to their Egyptian creators. Theologians did not actually believe that the gods and other divine entities actually looked as they were depicted on temple and tomb walls: Hathor did not 'really' have a cow's horns; Anubis did not 'really' have the head of a jackal. Rather, the reliefs, paintings and statues were seen as convenient shorthand manifestations of making concrete that which could never be concrete.

In the floor of the chamber, a sunken stairway leads down into the burial chamber. This will have been filled in level with the floor after the burial, but was opened by the ancient plunderers. These intruders had devastated the tomb's contents, whose remains were found strewn over the floors of the chambers. The burial hall is of the oval form probably introduced by Tuthmosis II, and bears the earliest intact version of the 'papyrus-written' Amduat, seen in fragmentary form in Hatshepsut's sepulchral chamber. On five faces of the two pillars is to be found an abbreviated version of another of the funerary 'books', the so-called 'Litany of Re'. The sixth face, however, has a unique scene, showing Tuthmosis with three wives and a daughter, and suckled by his mother,

Fig. 39. Representations drawn on a pillar in the burial chamber of KV 34. In the upper register, Tuthmosis III and his mother, Iset, stand in a barque; below, the king is followed by his spouse, Meryetre, his late wives, Sitiah and Nebtu, and his daughter, Neferetre.

Iset, in the guise of a tree (fig. 39). The stick figures and cursive hieroglyphs are of the same style as those in the antechamber, and were like them applied during the funerary ceremonies, perhaps as part of the 'activation' of the magical mechanism that was the tomb.

Apart from its mythological texts, the chamber shares with the other rooms of the tomb a *khekher* frieze and a starred ceiling. From it lead four small annexes, all roughly cut and undecorated. Running clockwise from the entrance to the chamber, the first room was found empty, having been swept out in the Late Period, when the next-door chamber was used to bury two nameless mummies certainly of post-New Kingdom date. Those opposite, however, still contained remains of the king's grave goods. The room opposite the foot of the sarcophagus held the remains of a large bovid and pottery containers for provisions, while the final compartment held an ape and nine broken funerary statues. Many other items lay about the main chambers, but, surprisingly, no shabti-figure of the king has ever come to light. This may be explained by the fact that, until the middle of the Eighteenth Dynasty, only single shabtis were provided in a burial; this would only change in the next reign.

Tuthmosis III's sarcophagus is a further development of those of Hatshepsut. The sky-goddess Nut features on both faces of the lid, as well as on the bottom of the coffer, her arms thus being spread protectively above and below the dead king. On the head and foot of the coffer are depicted respectively the kneeling figures of Nephthys and Isis, the sisters of Osiris, and particularly associated with the protection of the dead. They are perched on the hieroglyphic signs for 'gold', and flanked by texts. Panels on the sides show the male mortuary deities Hapy, Anubis-Khentysehnetjer and Qebehsenuef (left) and Imseti, Anubis-Imywet and Duamutef (right); one panel on the right side bears a long hieroglyphic text, that on the opposite side a panelled design and a pair of wadjet-eyes. The latter were intended to allow the dead to see out, and go back to the Middle Kingdom, when the mummy lay on its left side, rather than supine, as was New Kingdom practice. With typical Egyptian conservatism, the eyes retained their position long after the burial posture had been changed, and were often retained even when eyes had been added to the lid.

The sarcophagus of Tuthmosis III is generally regarded as the finest of its kind, both in terms of design and execution. This verdict appears to have been shared in ancient times, for nearly a thousand years after Tuthmosis' death, an almost exact copy was made for one Hapymen. The Saite and early Late Periods were ones of considerable antiquarianism, including the direct copying of many ancient works of art. Today, this example of the trait stands in the British Museum, having been found used as a ritual bath in Cairo's Ibn Tulun mosque.

The copying may have coincided with the introduction of the two mummies into the first annex, although the dating of these bodies is problematic. Hapymen's commission may explain one of the mysteries of the tomb, the absence of the canopic chest, presumably identical to that provided by Tuthmosis for his grandfather's reburial. Perhaps the king's actual canopic chest was removed to accompany the new sarcophagus to Hapymen's unknown tomb.

The king's mummy was found in TT 320, the larger of the two great caches made for royal corpses removed from their original tombs in the Third Intermediate Period. It lay within what had once been his outer coffin: made of Lebanese cedar, and just over two metres long, it had closely fitted the sarcophagus. It is now in very poor condition, the entire

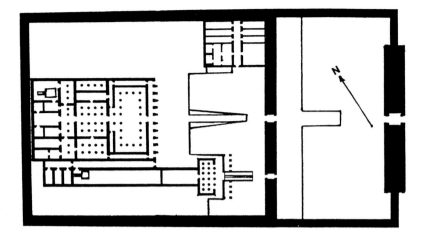

Fig. 40. Plan of the mortuary temple of Tuthmosis III.

surface having been lost when its thick coating of inscribed plaster, topped with gold foil, was hacked away. Even so, it may be seen that the king was depicted wearing the nemes headdress. In this, it reverts to Seventeenth Dynasty practice, the coffins of Amosis and Tuthmosis I having affected the heavy 'tripartite' wig instead.

Tuthmosis III constructed his mortuary temple at the edge of the cultivation, some way to the south of the valley building of Hatshepsut. Built on rising ground, it resembles that of the queen in being arranged on three levels (fig. 40), but is in a far worse state of preservation. Of its structure of limestone, sandstone and mud-brick, most is destroyed, although various broken pieces of relief and statuary have been recovered from the site. Entrance to the complex was by way of a large brick pylon. The first court gave access, via a ramp, to a terrace at a higher level, paved with limestone slabs. This was divided in two by a wall, pierced by two doorways and a series of statue niches. From the rear section, a brick ramp led up to another court, partly rock cut, partly the result of filling and grading, supported by a brick retaining wall. In this court stood the main temple, fronted by a portico of osiride figures. Behind this lay the peristyle court, in turn giving access to the hypostyle hall, and finally the three sanctuaries. As at Deir el-Bahari, the northernmost was open to the air, and contained an altar dedicated to Re; the central was that of Amun (in this case 'of Henketankh', the ancient name of the temple), roofed with images of the goddesses of the day and night. The southern chapel belonged to the king himself, and once contained a magnificent false door now at Medinet Habu, whence it seems to have been moved in Roman times.

An interesting feature of the temple is the complex built on the south side of the main temple, with its own ramp and portico leading up from the middle terrace. This was dedicated to Hathor, and corresponds to the same goddess' cult place in Hatshepsut's temple. Tuthmosis III appears to have been particularly interested in worship of the cow-goddess, since he was also responsible for the construction of a second Hathor-chapel at Deir el-Bahari, in the northern part of the old temple of Montjuhotpe II. This structure contained a very fine statue of Hathor in bovine form, placed there by the next king, Amenophis II. It, together with the sanctuary itself, adorned with reliefs of Tuthmosis III, is now in the Cairo Museum.

Tuthmosis' principal wife for much of his reign, Meryetre, left foundation deposits outside KV 42, the unused tomb of Tuthmosis II, seemingly indicating her intended appropriation of the sepulchre, although in the event she may have been buried elsewhere. At least some of the king's family were buried in the southern part of the necropolis. His possible first wife, Neferure, the elder daughter of Hatshepsut, seems to have had a grave in the Wadi Qubbanet el-Qirud, not far from Hatshepsut's intended resting place as regent, while three Syrian minor wives were interred together in a tomb in the same wadi, about 150 metres to the west. Flooding had severely damaged its contents, but modern looters recovered considerable quantities of grave-goods, including jewellery, now in the Metropolitan Museum of Art, New York. Both these tombs follow the style of the day, in being cut at the bottom of clefts in the rock, thus making their presence very difficult to detect. At least one son was buried in the area that later became the Valley of the Queens, whence came a fragmentary canopic jar.

After an outstanding reign of fifty-four years, Tuthmosis III was succeeded by his son, Amenophis II, who had already served as his co-regent for some two years. For his tomb (KV 35), the new king chose a spot at the base of the western cliffs of the Kings' Valley. Its plan (fig. 41) follows the general arrangement of KV 34, but is more regular and, most importantly, abandons the cartouche-form burial hall, in favour of one of rectangular plan, approached via an additional corridor.

This room is the only one of the tomb to be decorated. The walls carry the Amduat in the same cursive style as found previously, with the exception that the ground colour is somewhat lighter. The pillars, however, now six in number, show the king receiving the sign of life (*ankh*) from various deities, and the doorways of the four annexes have polychrome borders. The floor was first intended, as in earlier tombs, to be on one level. However, at a relatively late stage in the construction of the tomb, its south end was lowered by around 1.5 metres, thus forming a kind of crypt. In this was placed the king's sarcophagus, similar to that of his predecessor,

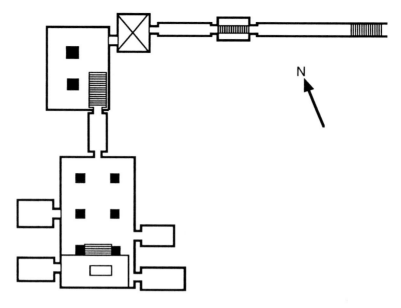

Fig. 41. Plan of the tomb of Amenophis II, KV 35.

but somewhat larger and less elegant. The construction of the crypt may be explained by the desire to surround the sarcophagus with one or more wooden shrines. Four or more are known to have been employed during the late Eighteenth and Twentieth Dynasties, and the sunken floor was the easiest way of gaining the requisite vertical clearance.

Although comprehensively robbed in antiquity, large quantities of funerary equipment survived when the tomb was opened, shortly after KV 34. Much of the material was of the kind already seen in the earlier tomb, but a number of Amenophis II's shabtis were found, along with fragments of his canopic chest. This differed completely from those of Hatshepsut and Tuthmosis I, which had been made from the same material as their sarcophagi. It had been carved from a block of translucent calcite (Egyptian alabaster), and on each corner bore the raised figure of each of the protective goddesses, Isis, Nephthys, Nut and Selqet. Inside, canopic jars were carved as one with the box, each stopped with a small head of the king. This basic design was retained for royal canopics down to the middle of the Nineteenth Dynasty.

In addition to these objects, the tomb still retained an almost unique one: the mummy of its owner. Almost all other royal mummies had been removed from their original sepulchres in the Third Intermediate Period, but King Amenophis still rested in his own sarcophagus, albeit enclosed in a later substitute coffin. This was because KV 35 had been selected as a cache for displaced royal persons, nine of whom lay in one of the annexes to the burial chamber. Three other mummies lay in another of these small chambers, a middle-aged woman, a male youth, and a young woman. Unlike the nine other bodies, they lacked containers, and most probably represent members of Amenophis II's family, who predeceased him and were buried in his tomb. The youth is most likely to have been prince Webensenu, whose presence in the sepulchre is attested by the recovery of his canopic jars and shabti figures. The identity of the women is less certain, particularly that of the elder, since Amenophis II's mother, Meryetre, seems to have out-lived him, as did his only known wife, Tia. This is the mummy identified some years ago as Amenophis III's wife, Tiye, on the basis of the comparison of hair samples from the tomb of Tutankhamun. However, it has now been demonstrated that the grounds for such an identification are not secure, and the archaeological evidence seems better fitted to attributing the corpse to the first occupation of KV 35, perhaps to an otherwise unattested wife (and/or sister?) of Amenophis II. A final mummy, perhaps removed by robbers from one of the above-mentioned groups, and found upon a model boat in the antechamber, plus a pair of skulls from the shaft, complete the list of human remains found in Amenophis II's tomb.

The funerary temple of Amenophis II was built just south of that of Tuthmosis III. Unfortunately, it was almost entirely destroyed in antiquity, part having been used for a Twenty-second Dynasty cemetery. Flinders Petrie, who explored the site in 1896, was only able to recover a small part of its plan, comprising the portico and peristyle court of the main temple. Both seem to have undergone some rebuilding under Tuthmosis IV and Amenophis III; on the basis of sculptured fragments it is possible that the latter appropriated the building for his eldest daughter, Sitamun.

To the temple's original author belonged a series of foundation deposits, a grey granite osiride statue, and perhaps another in calcite. The granite figure was one of a pair that had guarded the doorway leading from the peristyle to the now-vanished hypostyle hall. The foundation deposits contained principally calcite vases and model tools. Such deposits, often augmented, were made at the inauguration of all major buildings; amongst the most comprehensive were those delineating Hatshepsut's Deir el-Bahari project. Comparing the visible portion of Amenophis II's temple with the corresponding part of Tuthmosis III's, an additional row of columns is added around the inside of the peristyle, as well as to the rear of the fronting colonnade. The corridor that had surrounded the court is deleted. The temple of Amenophis' successor, Tuthmosis IV, continues this trend, the sides and rear of the peristyle now having three rows of columns (fig. 42).

The main body of this temple otherwise follows the plan of Tuthmosis III's quite closely, although, significantly, it lacks the latter's Hathor complex. Part of Tuthmosis IV's first pylon, built of sun-dried brick,

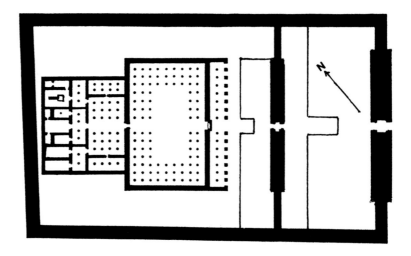

Fig. 42. Plan of the mortuary temple of Tuthmosis IV.

still remains standing to some height: its thickness is around 8.6 metres (fig. 43). Behind it, the temple rose on two terraces, but little more than a grey granite doorsill and some paving remains in situ. Some fragmentary statues and reliefs, of limestone and sandstone respectively, were found in the ruins, together with pieces that suggest the reuse of older material in the building's construction. Along with bricks from the temenos wall were found pieces of faience stelae, some of which seem to have had gilded elements.

Tuthmosis IV constructed his tomb in the Valley of the Kings not far

Fig. 43. The ruins of the mortuary temple of Thutmosis IV.

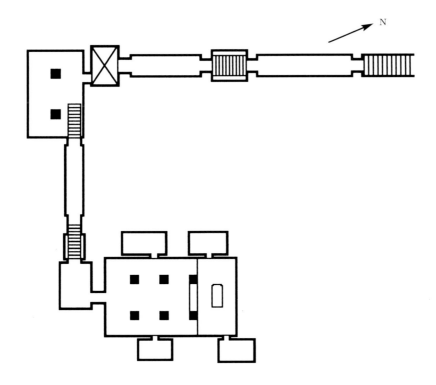

Fig. 44. Plan of the tomb of Tuthmosis IV, KV 43.

from the last resting place of Hatshepsut (KV 20: see fig. 109), and thus on the opposite side of the wadi from his father. It is instructive to note that Amenophis II had also selected a site a considerable distance from the tomb of his predecessor, as had Tuthmosis II. This practice continues down to the end of the dynasty, but not beyond. It is a reflection of the change that later takes place, from the tomb being simply a concealed burial place, to becoming a monument in its own right. This culminated in late Ramesside tombs that were incapable of concealment.

The tomb (KV 43) was discovered by Howard Carter in 1902/3, and represents a further development of that of Amenophis II, most notably adding a third flight of stairs and antechamber before the burial chamber, which is turned through a further ninety degrees (fig. 44). The latter's walls are bare, not even having received their basic ground colour. This is surprising, even given the king's relatively short reign of around a decade. However, the antechamber and well-room did receive their decoration. In contrast to the outline-only work in earlier tombs, the figures are fully coloured in, and represent the king before various deities (fig. 45). They begin a trend which culminates in the adoption of painted relief for the

Fig. 45. The end wall of the antechamber of the tomb of Tuthmosis IV, showing him, left to right, before Hathor, Anubis, Hathor, Osisris, and Hathor again.

decoration of royal tombs in the Valley in the final years of the Eighteenth Dynasty.

The pillared room that in the previous two tombs has been termed the 'antechamber' will henceforth be termed the 'mid-length pillared hall' (MLPH), since further chamber(s) now interpose between it and the sepulchral chamber. In KV 43, its walls, and those of the burial chamber, are bare limestone, the surfaces still exhibiting the bands left by the quarrymen's removal of successive layers of stone. The great sarcophagus that still stands in the midst of the burial chamber's sunken crypt is, however, completely carved and painted (fig. 46). It is twice the height and width of that of Tuthmosis III, with a somewhat differently arranged decorative scheme. When found, its lid lay upturned on the floor, evidently moved by the necropolis authorities, since it had been carefully supported on piles of stone and a wooden cow's head.

The tomb had clearly been robbed on more than one occasion. The first had been within a century of the burial, the restoration of the tomb being recorded in a hieratic graffito on the south wall of the antechamber (fig. 65):

Year 8 ..., under the Person of King ... Horemheb. His person commanded that the fan-bearer on the king's right hand, the royal scribe, the overseer of the treasury, overseer of works in the place of

Fig. 46. The burial chamber and sarcophagus of Tuthmosis IV.

eternity and leader of the festival of Amun in Karnak, Maya ..., be charged to renew the burial of King Menkheperure (Tuthmosis IV), true of voice, in the noble mansion upon the west of Thebes.

His assistant, the steward of the southern city, Djhutmose.

This Maya is the same man whose superb tomb was found at Saqqara in 1986 by an Anglo-Dutch expedition, and whose career spanned the reigns of the last three or five kings of the Eighteenth Dynasty.

Whatever damage was done and made good under Horemheb, Tuthmosis' tomb was later completely ransacked, Carter finding broken equipment strewn throughout the tomb. Nevertheless, many fine objects were recovered, including the excellently carved body of a chariot and panels from the royal throne. The location of other, more mundane, finds give a good clue as to the disposition of such objects in a royal tomb. Large pottery jars containing provisions, including grain and water, were placed in the annex opposite the foot of the sarcophagus. Preserved joints of meat lay in the room directly on the other side of the burial chamber. In this position they were closest to the corpse's head, a location seen for such

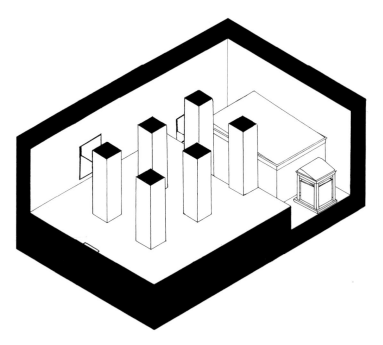

Fig. 47. The sepulchral hall of a typical royal tomb of the late Eighteenth/early Nineteenth Dynasty, showing the enshrined sarcophagus and canopic chest.

foodstuffs since the earliest times. The annexes opening off of the pillared section of the chamber seem to have been intended for funerary vases and shabtis. This pillared area was occupied by many of the larger items of equipment, with the crypt occupied by the enshrined sarcophagus, the canopic chest at its foot, and probably the enshrined figures of various funerary deities (fig. 47).

Apart from the pieces relating to the king's own interment, canopic jars belonging to two of his children indicate that they were buried with their father. Indeed, the mummy of one (Prince Amenemhet?) stood in one of the annexes, with other mummy debris in another. The king's body, however, was moved from the tomb in the Twenty-first Dynasty, and was found in the tomb of Amenophis II.

Apart from those members of the royal family who seem to have been buried with Amenophis II and Tuthmosis IV in their own tombs, very little is known of the burials of minor royalties of the middle of the Eighteenth Dynasty. The mummies of two of the latter king's daughters were found in a reused tomb-chapel on Sheik Abd el-Qurna in the mid-nineteenth century, but this was a Twenty-first Dynasty reburial, and tells us nothing of their original tombs. Canopic fragments from the southern part of the necropolis may point to tombs in that area, but the matter is very uncertain.

Fig. 48. The Western Branch of the Biban el-Moluk, showing the entrance to the tomb of Amenophis III, WV 22.

Besides KV 43, in which he was actually buried, Tuthmosis IV was responsible for the foundation of a second tomb in the Valley of the Kings. Foundation deposits found by Howard Carter, and now in Highclere Castle, show that he had begun a tomb now numbered WV 22. This does not lie in the main part of the wadi (the Kings' Valley), but some way up a second valley that branches off of the access road just before reaching the first of the principal tombs (fig. 48). This great wadi, now termed the West Valley, is in many ways even more impressive than the Kings', but seems not to have been touched prior to Tuthmosis IV's time. It is possible that the king had contemplated being buried there, but after initial work had switched back to the necropolis of his immediate ancestors. This could explain the unfinished state of the burial chamber of KV 43, since a ten year reign would normally be regarded as adequate to complete such a tomb. Alternatively, Tuthmosis could have intended to use the West Valley as the burial place of some of his family. This was indeed what it became, since WV 22 was continued by his eldest son and successor, Amenophis III, and was used to contain his burial at the end of his forty year reign.

In basic plan (fig. 49), the tomb follows that of its immediate precursors, with the principal exception that, uniquely for a kingly tomb, the entrance to the burial hall is not on the main axis, but at one end of a side-wall. In addition, it has two pillared chambers opening off the crypt, each with its own annex. That at the end of the chamber seems to have been part of the original plan of the tomb, and seems likely to have been

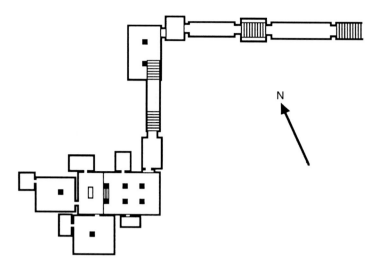

Fig. 49. Plan of the Tomb of Amenophis III (WV 22).

intended for the burial of Queen Tiye, although, as we shall see, she appears ultimately to have been buried with her son, King Akhenaten, at Tell el-Amarna. The second complex, on the other hand, preserves traces that show that it was enlarged out of what had been one of the standard four store-rooms found in earlier kingly tombs. As a late addition to the tomb plan, it would seem reasonable to attribute it to Sitamun, Amenophis III's eldest daughter, who obtained the dignity of Queen in the last decade of the king's reign.

The burial chamber is the last such room to carry a 'hand-written' version of the Amduat, although its style differs somewhat from that found in the tombs of Tuthmosis III and Amenophis II, since the upper parts of the figures are properly drawn, and only the legs left as 'sticks'. The remaining chambers follow Tuthmosis IV's lead in being decorated with fully coloured paintings. In the antechamber, the king receives 'life' from Hathor, Nut, the Goddess of the West, Anubis and Osiris, in two cases being accompanied by his ka. This being also accompanies him in the well-room, where Amenophis III appears before the same selection of deities. The MLPH remains undecorated.

The crypt of the burial chamber still contains the broken lid of the king's granite sarcophagus - the first king's example of the material known since the time of Ammenemes III, back at the end of the Twelfth Dynasty, and once gorgeously decorated in gold foil. Of its coffer, however, no trace has ever come to light. It is most likely that it was removed for reuse during the Third Intermediate Period, when many tombs were stripped of salvageable material. Pieces of the accompanying calcite canopic chest

62

Fig. 50. The black-varnished and gilded wooden sarcophagus of Yuya, father-in-law of Amenophis III, from KV 46. It is of the usual form for private New Kingdom sarcophagi and contrasts with the usual cartouche-form of kingly examples. It provides, however, the prototype for the stone sarcophagi of Akhenaten and his late-Eighteenth Dynasty successors.

were found in 1915 and by the Japanese excavations of the 1990s, together with the broken remnants of one or more of Amenophis III's coffins. These were of *rishi* design, but unlike earlier examples, they were heavily inlaid with coloured glass, as well as being gilded. In this they anticipate the rich use of inlay on the statuary and coffins of the succeeding Amarna Period. Various other pieces of funerary equipment have found their way into collections and include a number of once-fine shabti figures, the hub of a chariot wheel, some fragmentary statues in wood, together with pieces of inlay and stone vessels. Particularly interesting are shabti fragments which belonged to Amenophis III's wife, Tiye; these may suggest that she could have been reburied in WV 22 after the dismantling of the Amarna necropolis towards the end of the Eighteenth Dynasty (q.v.).

Tiye, like most chief queens of the dynasty, was of non-royal birth. Her parents, the Master of Horse, Yuya, and the Lady Tjuiu, were granted burial in a small tomb in the main Kings' Valley. When opened by James Quibell in 1905, much of its contents remained intact, providing a good idea of the contents of a high status private tomb of the time (fig. 50). They were by no means the first or only private individuals granted burial chambers in the wadi during the Eighteenth Dynasty, large numbers of small sepulchres clearly having been assigned to favoured subjects. Among

Fig. 51. The left-hand colossus of the pair that are among the only substantial remnants of the mortuary temple of Amenophis III: the 'Colossi of Memnon'.

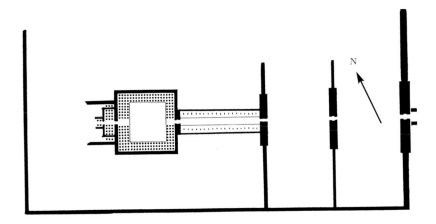

Fig. 52. Plan of the mortuary temple of Amenophis III.

those whose names are known are to be numbered the Standard-Bearer Maihirpri (temp. Amenophis II/Tuthmosis IV), the Overseer of the Fields of Amun, Userhat (TT 47 or 56), and the Vizier Amenemopet (TT 29, temp. Amenophis II). At least the last two named had tomb-chapels on the Sheikh Abd el-Qurna hill alongside the burial places of their peers, making it likely that other well-known grandees of the age were laid to rest close to their monarchs. A particular case is that of the celebrated vizir Rekhmire (temp. Tuthmosis III/Amenophis II), whose beautifully decorated chapel (TT 100) lacks any trace of a burial chamber.

For his own mortuary temple, Amenophis III selected a site south of that of his father. Originally of dimensions broadly in keeping with those of the temples of his predecessors, for his Jubilee in his thirtieth year, the building was enlarged to breathtaking size, filled with literally hundreds, if not thousands, of superbly carved statues in soft and hard stones. By far the largest of its genre ever built, its entrance was flanked by a pair of huge quartzite colossi, dubbed in classical times the 'Colossi of Memnon'. The northern, after earthquake damage, became famed for emitting a singing sound at dawn; this however, ended following its restoration under the Roman emperor, Septimius Severus, circa 202 AD. (fig. 51)

Three successive pylons were followed by an avenue lined with great recumbent jackals. The cut-up bodies of many of these were found to have been used in the construction of the nearby temple of Merenptah, much of the material for which seems to have been supplied by the demolition of the older monument. Beyond the jackal-avenue lay a great peristyle court, behind which was the inner temple (fig. 52). Its scanty remains form today's Kom el-Hatan, but it has proved impossible to even trace the plan of the sanctuary.

The temple teemed with three-dimensional divine images, some of less-than-common figures. This, together with the sheer scale of the structure, was doubtless predicated upon the status of the king, whose divinity becomes more and more pronounced as the reign proceeds. A large number of figures were carved specifically for the Jubilee, some seemingly forming parts of a large-scale astronomical representation, and buried at the conclusion of the ceremonies. Others date somewhat later, to a period in which Amenophis III became a living hypostasis of the sun-god. It has now been recognized that statues discovered throughout the Theban area, many of them usurped by later kings, derive from Amenophis III's mortuary temple. On this basis, it must have been the repository of a collection of art without parallel for its quantity and quality.

In its heyday, the building will thus have been an awe-inspiring sight, decorated with superbly carved and coloured reliefs, with statuary of a consistent excellence rarely found. A contemporary description, carved on a stela originally from the temple, but reused by Merenptah, talks of it as:

> an august temple on the West of Thebes, an everlasting temple of sandstone, wrought with gold throughout. Its floor is adorned with silver, its doorways with electrum, very wide and large, established for ever, adorned with this very great monument. It is rich in statues of granite, quartzite and every costly stone.... It is supplied with a 'Station of the King' wrought with gold and many costly stones. Flagstaves are set up before it, covered with electrum, like the horizon in heaven when Re rises within it...

All gone. Only the guardian Colossi of Memnon remain, staring faceless into eternity.

IV   Amarna and After

The accession of Amenophis IV was one of the most momentous events in the religious history of Egypt. It is still unclear whether he first came to the throne as his father's coregent, or as a sole ruler after Amenophis III's death, but, by his fifth regnal year, Amenophis IV had changed his name to Akhenaten. He had also moved his capital to the virgin site of Tell el-Amarna, in Middle Egypt, and made paramount his monotheistic cult of the Aten. The latter, a personification of the physical globe of the sun, had first appeared as a fully-fledged god back in late Tuthmoside times. In the initial years of Amenophis IV reign, he was depicted as a falcon-headed man, with a sun-disk on his head – essentially following the form of Re-Harakhty, of whom he had been considered an aspect. Soon, however, the god had assumed a more abstract appearance, a solar disk from which descended rays, ending in hands which held the sign of life to the noses of the king and queen. The royal family were central to the whole Aten-cult, for it was only through them that the people could address the god. Thus, the status of Akhenaten and his wife, Nefertiti, was further enhanced above even the existing divinity of kingship.

In addition to their politico-religious implications, Akhenaten's changes extended to the realm of art. Individuals were henceforth depicted in a distorted manner, modelled after the king himself. The latter is shown with a hanging jaw, swelling breasts and broad hips; the significance of this has been exhaustively discussed, with little unanimity. It may represent an exaggeration of some pathological condition, or have some cosmic meaning; one can only speculate in the current state of knowledge.

Normal royal practice seems to have been the foundation of the pharaoh's tomb soon after the completion of work on his predecessor's sepulchre. Accordingly, one would assume that Amenophis IV will have adopted the same procedure. During Amenophis III's time, we have already seen that the royal tomb had been moved from the Kings' Valley to the previously-unused West Valley, possibly accompanied by an increased employment of the former for other high-status interments. On this basis, any tomb begun for Amenophis IV will presumably also have lain there. The most likely candidate for such a beginning is now numbered WV 25, discovered by Giovanni Belzoni in 1817 and cleared by Otto Schaden in the mid 1970s.

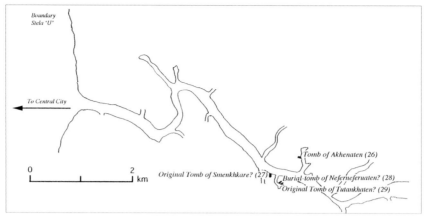

Fig. 53. Plan of the Wadi Abu Hasah el-Bahari: the royal necropolis of Tell el-Amarna.

It comprises a staircase and descending corridor, beyond which work had been abandoned. The form of the corridor clearly indicates royal ownership. No Eighteenth Dynasty remains were found in or near the tomb, which contained eight intrusive burials of the Third Intermediate Period.

Having moved to Amarna, Akhenaten founded a new royal necropolis. On the earliest of the boundary stelae that were carved into the cliffs on either side of the Nile to delimit the territory of the new capital, the king makes the following proclamation:

> May a tomb be made for me in the eastern mountain of Akhet-Aten; may my burial be made in it, in the millions of jubilees which my father, the Aten, decreed for me. May the burial of Queen Nefertiti be made in it, in the millions of years that my father, the Aten, decreed for her. May the burial of the Princess Meryetaten be made in it, in these millions of years.

> If I die in any town in the north, south, west or east in these millions of years, let me be returned, so that I may be buried in Akhet-Aten. If Queen Nefertiti dies in any town in the north, south, west or east in these millions of years, let her be returned, so that she may be buried in Akhet-Aten. If Princess Meryetaten dies in any town in the north, south, west or east in these millions of years, let her be returned, so that she may be buried in Akhet-Aten.

The tomb of which Akhenaten speaks was built far up the Wadi Abu Hisah el-Bahari, a canyon that opens out of the centre of the eastern cliffs that lie behind the capital city (fig. 53), and is numbered 26 in the register of tombs at Tell el-Amarna. Five kilometres down the wadi, and ten from

Fig 54. The entrance to the tomb of Akhenaten.

the heart of the city, a high and broad corridor, 3.2 metres square, was cut into the cliffs (figs. 54, 55). It leads to a flight of steps, beyond which is a well-room, its floor sunk three metres below the sill of the doorway. The stairway, and that which lies at the tomb entrance, are interesting in being the earliest to have a ramp down the centre, to aid the introduction of a sarcophagus. A doorway at the back of the well-room gives access to a square chamber; in its final form, it had only two pillars, but seems to have been designed for four. Two were, however, apparently cut away when a sarcophagus-plinth was cut from the floor; it is likely that the original plan

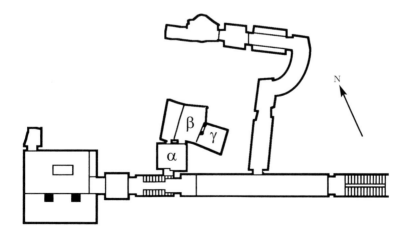

Fig. 55. Plan of the tomb of Akhenaten, TA26.

*Fig. 56. The burial chamber of the tomb of Akhenaten,
showing the rock-cut plinth for the king's sarcophagus.*

was for a further passage to lead beyond it to a definitive burial chamber (fig. 56).

The main corridor of the tomb is undecorated, but the well-room has badly damaged depictions of the worship of the Aten. For the first time in a royal tomb, relief was employed for its scenes; previously, paint alone had been used. The technique is fairly unusual, however, with most of the carving being done into a thick layer of plaster, rather than directly into the stone itself; the technique is found in most Amarna tombs, reflecting the quality of the local rock. The pillared room, the principal burial chamber, was decorated with scenes of sun-worship, and others so severely mutilated that their exact nature remains difficult to decipher. However, the two side-walls both show a scene of mourning. The subject being mourned on the right wall cannot be readily reconstructed, but may be Akhenaten himself. However, intriguingly, the left wall shows an apparently-female figure, being mourned by Akhenaten, Nefertiti and others. It would appear most likely that this is a representation of the Queen-Mother, Tiye, since from the debris of the tomb were recovered fragments of a sarcophagus that almost certainly belonged to her.

Tiye is known to have visited Amarna, and was also provided with a gilded wooden funerary shrine by Akhenaten in Atenist style. It seems therefore that Akhenaten planned a double-burial with her in his own sepulchral chamber; this conclusion derives from the fact that only the main chamber of the tomb is suitably decorated, and high enough to have contained her shrine. In this, Akhenaten will have followed the example of

Fig 57. The sarcophagus of Akhenaten, bearing the figure of Queen Nefertiti on its corners.

Amenophis II and Tuthmosis IV, who also shared their tombs with their families. Tiye's sarcophagus may have lain between the pillars on the left of the room, in front of her putative mourning-scene. The aforementioned sarcophagus-plinth, in the centre of the room, must have been occupied by the coffer of Akhenaten.

As restored from fragments, Akhenaten's sarcophagus is wholly unlike the cartouche-form norm of the earlier part of the dynasty. Of granite, it takes the form of a rectangular shrine, its lid incorporating a curved roof and cavetto-cornice. This shape had been common in private burials of the dynasty, but constructed in wood (see fig. 50). Apart from its shape, the sarcophagus of Akhenaten also differs from its royal predecessors in its decoration. Rather than the traditional figures of the funerary deities, the sides were dominated by great representations of the Aten; the corners were protected by in-the-round images of Queen Nefertiti (fig. 57). This motif of a divine female on the corners of a box of course derives from the kingly canopic chests which had been made since the reign of Amenophis II; the depiction of the queen in a position and role formerly held by Isis and her sisters indicates the status arrogated by the royal family in the nominally monotheistic religion of Atenism.

From the writings of the god's name on the monument, it is clear that its decoration was being carried out either side of the ninth year of Akhenaten's reign. Another of the major elements of the funerary outfit, the canopic chest had, however, been made rather earlier. Once again restored from fragments, this calcite item has divine figures at its corners, but in this case they are of the early hawk-form of the Aten, phased out of use by the fourth year of the reign. The object otherwise followed the usual form, with cylindrical cavities to receive the viscera, each topped by a stopper bearing the king's head. Queen Tiye's sarcophagus was of a similar shape to Akhenaten's, but lacked Nefertiti's figures on the corners and included a scene of the deceased royal lady receiving the homage of her son and daughter-in-law.

Aside from Tiye, intended to be buried alongside her son in the main chamber of the tomb, other members of the Amarna royal family were provided with burial places within the king's sepulchre. Nearest to the king's chamber, on the right wall of the second staircase, a doorway lead to a suite of three rooms, (α), (β), and (γ). The first and last are fully decorated; (β) is unfinished. The right- and left-hand walls of (α) bear great scenes of the king, queen and entourage, respectively greeting the rising Aten, and marking its setting. The right-hand wall includes representations of the birds and animals wakened by the coming of the new day.

It is the wall on the right-hand side of the entrance which contains some of the most significant decoration. It shows, twice, Akhenaten and Nefertiti standing at the head of a bier, on which lies the body of a deceased lady. Directly outside the doorway of the room in which the corpse is seen to lie is a baby in the arms of a nurse. Although various other explanations have been put forward, the most likely seems to be that the deceased has died in child-birth. Overturned offering tables seem to suggest the conversion of a time of celebration into tragedy. No indication of the identity of the dead woman survives on the damaged relief, but Geoffrey Martin has suggested that she might be Kiya, Akhenaten's junior wife, and perhaps mother of Prince Tutankhaten. She was, however, apparently disgraced during the latter part of Akhenaten's reign, in which case she is hardly likely to have received burial in a specially-decorated room of her estranged husband's sepulchre. The location of this representation suggests that its inclusion in chamber (α)'s decorative scheme was an after-thought; a similar motif in room (γ) dominates its left wall.

Numerous registers of adoring figures (to the left) and harnessed chariots (to the right) flank the principal doorway that leads from (α) into (β). The latter is devoid of any adornment and appears unfinished. Two doorways, one partly blocked, leads into chamber (γ). Unlike the anonymous occupant of (α), the owner of this room is clear, being Akhenaten's second daughter, Meketaten. The end wall bears a scene of the dead girl (or her statue) standing in a bower, mourned by her mother, father, sisters and household; the anguish of lesser folk is continued on the right wall. The cause of the princess' demise is shown on the left-hand wall, where a larger-scale version of room (α)'s death-chamber scene was carved. The body is clearly labelled as that of Meketaten; another label accompanies the figure of a baby which is being carried away by a nurse. Unfortunately, the latter is largely destroyed, with both the child's name and that of its mother lost; the latter is definitely said to be a daughter of Nefertiti, and there can be no doubt that we have here a depiction of the aftermath of Meketaten's death in child-birth.

She would appear to have hardly reached her 'teens at the time, and the father of her baby has been hotly debated. Since no husband is known for Meketaten, Akhenaten himself may have been the father; he has also been put forward as the father of apparent daughters of the Princesses Meryetaten and Ankhesenpaaten. However, the maternity of these latter babies is still not wholly certain, let alone their paternity.

Half way back up the main corridor, a further suite of rooms opens. Although unfinished and undecorated, it is far more extensive than the other set of rooms, and, if straightened out, closely follows the plan seen in royal tombs of the period. It would seem most likely that these galleries were intended to be the sepulchre of Queen Nefertiti, but there are no indications of their having been used as such. This lady would appear to have predeceased her husband, but no certain items of her funerary equipment are known to have come from the tomb. Indeed, the only such item is one of her shabti-figures, split between the Brooklyn and Louvre Museums; it may or may not have come from TA 26.

There seems no doubt, however, that Akhenaten was buried in the sepulchre: apart from his sarcophagus and canopic chest, large quantities of material, including shabti figures, have been recovered in and around the tomb. All had been smashed, and it is clear that the tomb suffered wholesale ransacking soon after Akhenaten's death. The extent of the damage, with sarcophagi reduced to the tiniest fragments, makes it certain that the vandalism was officially sponsored. Taking all evidence into account, it seems likely that the tomb was desecrated soon after the death of the last representative of the Amarna line, Tutankhamun. A wrecked mummy, possibly partly burned, was allegedly found around the time of the tomb's modern discovery; now lost, it may represent the last mortal remains of Akhenaten.

For the last three or four years of his reign, Akhenaten shared his throne with an individual who has been the subject of much debate. Suggestions that this person was Nefertiti in a different guise seem less likely than a view that Akhenaten's coregent was a son, originally bearing the name Smenkhkare. Initially based at Amarna, the new king will presumably have begun a tomb there; this sepulchre is probably represented by the unfinished beginning on the south side of the Royal Wadi, TA 27, which comprises a ramped staircase and part of a corridor. The curious thing about the new coregent, however, is that he appears not to have been an Atenist or, rather, did not believe in the Aten in a monotheistic way. He had begun work on his funerary equipment perhaps a year or so after his installation, and this group of material contrasts with that of Akhenaten in being wholly-traditional in its texts, invoking the age-old deities such as Osiris and Isis.

These items included a coffin, jewellery and canopic coffinettes; while the latter were being made, the royal name was changed: rather than Smenkhkare, he was now Neferneferuaten. This re-naming appears to coincide with the young king's residence at Thebes: certainly by his third year he had an Amun-dedicated religious foundation there, perhaps a mortuary temple. Whether he also was now building a tomb there is less clear, although he may have intended to continue WV 25, or begun a new West Valley tomb, WV 23. A restoration of the old religious regime was thus apparently underway while Akhenaten yet lived and worshipped his sole god at Amarna.

The tensions that must have existed in this situation were apparently relieved shortly by the death of Neferneferuaten. This outcome is indicated by the burial of the latter, devoid of amulets, in an Atenist coffin, originally made for Kiya, but extensively modified to receive the body of a king. Parts of the inscriptions were altered, and presumably a new gold mask was affixed to the face. Other 'borrowed' items made up the rest of the core deposit, the old canopic jars of Kiya losing their inscriptions and gaining the lids made for one of Akhenaten's daughters, while a shrine made for Tiye's Amarna burial was employed to shelter the coffin. This group, augmented by smaller items, was presumably buried at Amarna, perhaps in TA 28, the only sepulchre in the Royal Wadi (apart from TA 26 itself) suitable to contain the shrine. TA 28 is reminiscent of later monuments in the Valley of the Queens: perhaps it had been intended for one or more of Akhenaten's daughters? It is apparently finished, the walls and ceilings of all three rooms having been plastered, suggesting preparation for a burial. Either of the two main chambers would seem to have been large enough to take the ex-Tiye shrine.

Ultimately, however, the deposit was moved to Thebes, mutilated to remove the names/images of Neferneferuaten and Akhenaten, and interred in KV 55, an intended-private tomb in the Kings' Valley. This event may have coincided with the burial of Neferneferuaten's brother, Tutankhamun, in the neighbouring KV 62. The latter king's death may have marked the opportunity to remove the last traces of the now-discredited Atenist rulers. The demise of Akhenaten followed fairly closely on that of Neferneferuaten. Whether skulduggery was involved in one or both of their deaths is wholly unknown.

The founder of Atenism was definitively followed on the throne by his surviving son, Tutankhaten; within a few years, the latter had changed his name to Tutankhamun and endorsed a formal return to the ancient

Fig. 58. Plan of the unfinished Amarna tomb of Tutankhaten(?), TA 29.

religion. For quite some time, however, he appears to have intended burial at Amarna; the workmen's village on the way to the Royal Wadi was expanded, and a huge tomb begun in the South Wadi, next to TA 28 and some considerable way from Akhenaten's TA 26. Now numbered TA 29, work must have continued there for a fair proportion of the reign, since the tomb was no less than 45 metres long when work terminated at the commencement of what was probably to have been the first pillared hall (fig. 58).

The tomb which replaced TA 29 as the king's prospective sepulchre seems most likely to have been WV 23, but it was never used for Tutankhamun's burial. Instead, after sudden death in the tenth year of his reign, the king was buried in a modestly-extended private tomb in the Kings' Valley (KV 62: fig. 59). Perhaps begun for Ay, a general who had been prominent at the court of Akhenaten, and may have been the father of Nefertiti, the sepulchre had a sunken crypt added to the north end of its chamber, plus two small store-rooms. Into the new burial chamber was inserted the king's fine quartzite sarcophagus. Its form resembles that of Akhenaten, but with the female figures on the corners representing Isis,

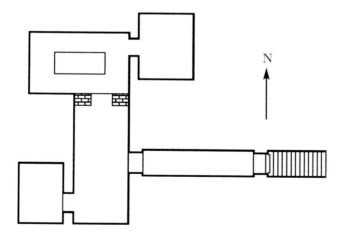

Fig. 59. Plan of the final, improvised, tomb of Tutankhamun, KV 62.

Nephthys, Neith and Selqet, rather than the queen. The decoration had been largely recut at some stage, with wings added to the arms of these figures, perhaps to convert them from royal ladies to goddesses. The occasion for these alterations was probably the amendment of the king's nomen from Tutankhaten to Tutankhamun, with the addition of epithets that would have made simple re-cutting of cartouche-contents difficult; it should be noted, however, that Marianne Eaton-Krauss has suggested that it reflects the sarcophagus having been made for Neferneferuaten, and later appropriated for the interment of Tutankhamun.

There is no doubt that a considerable number of items used in Tutankhamun's funerary outfit were derived from the unused equipment of his elder brother. Most notably, the middle coffin, canopic coffinettes and a number of pectorals had certainly been made for him, not to mention a considerable number of minor pieces. In addition, other items probably from the earliest years of Amenophis IV were used, including at least one of the shrines that enclosed the royal sarcophagus. Since it was found almost intact by Howard Carter in 1922, the tomb of Tutankhamun provides us with much information concerning the furnishings of a New Kingdom royal tomb, although its improvised plan makes it probable that their distribution was less than typical.

The quartzite sarcophagus was closed by a granite lid, broken while being lowered into place. The occasion for this accident was probably the discovery that the toes of the outermost coffin of the king were higher than the rim of the sarcophagus-coffer, and needed adzing down. This coffin was part of a set of three, and was of wood, covered with carved gesso and gilded, and depicted the king wearing the *khat*-headdress. The aforementioned middle coffin was again of wood, this time elaborately inlaid as well as gilded, and bearing the *nemes*-headdress. Its heavy inlay marks a continuation of the style seen on the coffin-fragments of Amenophis III, and the coffin used by Akhenaten for the actual burial of Neferneferuaten.

The innermost coffin was made of solid gold, like the outer examples covered with a feathered, *rishi*, pattern that represented the king as though a human-headed bird. Wearing the *nemes*, it also bore inlaid representations of the vulture-bodied goddesses, Nekhbet and Edjo, and contained the king's mummy. This was adorned with a gold portrait mask, gold hands and inlaid golden bands, containing religious formulae. Some additional trappings had been made from odd pieces of Neferneferuaten scrap. The mummy wrappings contained huge quantities of jewellery, but the cloth was found to be in a very poor state, having carbonized through the chemical reaction of the unguents with which the royal body had been drenched at the funeral. These had also badly damaged the flesh of the mummy itself, which had also been stuck to the floor of the gold coffin by them; this latter fact led to it being necessary to dismember the body to extract it for examination by Professor Douglas Derry.

The sarcophagus was surrounded by the now-usual series of four gilded wooden shrines, each covered with representations from the various funerary compositions of the Egyptians. A linen pall was also incorporated into the nest, supported on a frame and embellished with gilded rosettes.

The walls of the burial chamber were the only ones of the tomb to be decorated, with scenes painted on a yellow background; it is clear that they were applied after the interment, since they cover the partition-wall that can only have been erected after all the items had been placed within. The walls to the left of the doorway contain fairly usual scenes of the king and gods, plus part of the *Amduat*, but the rest bear much more unusual motifs. Firstly, the royal catafalque is shown being dragged by nobles to the tomb on the right wall, a scene common in private contexts, but unknown in royal ones. Then, on the end wall, alongside more usual figures of the dead king before Nut and with his ka before Osiris, one finds the Opening of the Mouth ritual, in which we see Tutankhamun's successor, Ay, carrying out the last rights. While the Opening of the Mouth motif is commonly found in royal tombs, the new king is never shown as the officiant. Clearly we have here a political statement, since the carrying out of predecessor's burial was a means of legitimating an accession. Ay was not of royal blood and can only have obtained the throne by virtue of *realpolitik*. The appearance of this motif may also relate to the known difficulties concerning the succession that occurred after Tutankhamun's death, and seem to have delayed his burial until eight months after his demise.

The style of the decoration, painted on plaster, marks the return to orthodoxy seen in most of the art of the reign, although with certain elements recalling the art of Akhenaten. The depictions are somewhat stocky, and hurried. The latter is doubtless a function of their having been applied after the burial, since they cover all the interior walls of the burial chamber, including the area of the blocked doorway. This follows the pattern seen in the Tuthmoside royal tombs, where the application of the decoration seems to have formed part of the funerary ceremonies. The artists will have made their exit via a hole near floor-level.

A doorway opposite the foot of the sarcophagus led into a small room, dubbed the 'Treasury'. A large shrine-shaped chest, upon which rested a canine image of the god Anubis, lay at the threshold of the chamber. The most important item within the room was Tutankhamun's square canopic shrine, of wood, guarded on each side by an image of a tutelary goddess, each one apparently adapted from the gilded-wooden figure of an Amarna Period queen. Within the shrine was the calcite canopic chest, of a similar design to that of Amenophis II, but with the design of the interior somewhat rationalised.

The gold coffinettes found within were of identical design to the full-size middle coffin; the texts inside their troughs clearly show the successive superposition of royal names, Smenkhkare, Neferneferuaten, and finally Tutankhamun. They each held a linen-wrapped bundle of embalmed viscera, and had been heavily anointed with unguents.

The Treasury also held a large number of resin-varnished shrines, containing wooden figures of the king and deities, overlaid with gold leaf; some of these were also left-overs from earlier reigns, including possibly the early years of Amenophis IV. They compare with the similar figures recovered from other royal tombs, but merely covered with black varnish. Other containers in the room held many shabti figures, while also present were a model granary, two chariots, model boats and various other items.

Amongst the latter were three miniature nests of coffins. The largest set, comprising what may have been intended as shabti-coffins of Tutankhamun, contained a gold figure of a king and a lock of the hair of Queen Tiye, Tutankhamun's grandmother. This has been matched with the hair of a mummy found in the tomb of Amenophis II, which was thus proclaimed that of the queen. Unhappily, as already noted, the archaeological evidence concerning the find-context of the corpse is very much against this, and the scientific basis has been shown to be possibly flawed. The other two nests, of designs appropriate to private persons of the later Eighteenth Dynasty, contained the mummies of two premature infants; both were female, and one had suffered from spina bifida. They almost certainly represent the offspring of Tutankhamun and his (half?-) sister and wife, Queen Ankhesenamun (previously Ankhesenpaaten).

The burial chamber was separated from the antechamber by a false wall and sealed doorway, the latter guarded by a pair of wooden, gilded and varnished statues; these are of a type familiar from royal tombs of the Ramesside Period (cf. fig. 72). One wall of the antechamber was taken up by three gilded wooden couches, each with a different pair of animal heads, under and on top of which were piled all kinds of food-containers and furniture, including a richly gilded and inlaid throne. Half of the other side of the room was taken up by four dismantled chariots.

A door under one of the couches gave access to the so-called 'Annex', a storeroom crowded with all kinds of funerary equipment, badly disturbed by tomb robbers and those who had cleared up after them. The tomb had been entered by robbers on two occasions, not long after the funeral, perhaps in the reign of Horemheb, when the tomb of Tuthmosis IV was certainly plundered. A considerable amount of damage had been done, but the innermost shrines and sarcophagus remained intact, the thieves being

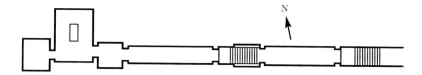

Fig. 60. Plan of the tomb of Ay, WV 23.

perhaps caught in the act. After the last robbery and subsequent resealing of the sepulchre, the tomb, which lay in the very bottom of the valley, was progressively covered by debris, in part from the construction of neighbouring tombs, until the huts of the artisans working on the tomb begun by Ramesses V, and continued by Ramesses VI (KV 9), were erected directly above its entrance. Accordingly, the tomb was passed by and missed in the orgy of tomb-robbing which accompanied the troubles of the late Twentieth Dynasty and was only discovered by Carter on 4 November 1922.

General Ay was clearly an old man at his accession, and used as his tomb WV 23, Tutankhamun's putative original Theban sepulchre (fig. 60). He occupied it only four years after mounting the throne, being interred in a burial chamber that had clearly been begun as the MLPH. The decoration of the room, on a yellow ground, is in similar style to that of the burial chamber of Tutankhamun, and also contains unusual depictions. The most striking are representations of the king and queen hunting in the marshes, a vignette otherwise used on the walls of private tomb-chapels (fig. 61): it is never otherwise found in a royal tomb. The remaining walls

Fig. 61. East Wall of the burial chamberr of the tomb of Ay, with the unique scene of the king fowling in the marshes.

Fig. 62. South-west corner of the burial chamber of the tomb of Ay, showing divine barks, surmounting texts from the Book of the Dead.

of the chamber are more conventional, comprising the First Division of the Amduat (fig. 62), and depictions of the king before the gods.

A granite sarcophagus was installed in the centre of the room; the coffer of Tutankhamun had reverted to quartzite, but Ay's change back to the granite favoured by Akhenaten was to be followed by future kings. It carried on the 'corner-goddess' motif, although with additional texts and a winged sun-disk placed on the long sides; an arched lid, lacking the usual end-boards was employed. One side of the coffer was smashed in antiquity, but the remainder stayed whole until 1896, when a Moroccan broke it to pieces, in the belief that he would thereby liberate hidden gold. Subsequently brought to Cairo and reassembled, the sarcophagus was returned to WV 23 in 1994, the hitherto-missing side being restored from the fragments found during the tomb's clearance in 1972.

These excavations, by Otto Schaden, also revealed the sarcophagus lid, buried in debris on the floor of the burial chamber, and various other fragments of funerary equipment. However, no sign of any canopic material, nor shabti-figures, came to light, the sum of recovered items giving the possible impression that the king's interment may have been rather summary. If correct, this may tie in with the later destruction of the names and faces of the king and queen on the walls of the burial chamber, and the damage suffered by some of the cartouches on the sarcophagus coffer. The date of this occurrence is unclear, but would presumably not have taken place too many years after the king's demise: Ay shared in the posthumous opprobrium suffered by the Heretically-tinged successors of Amenophis III.

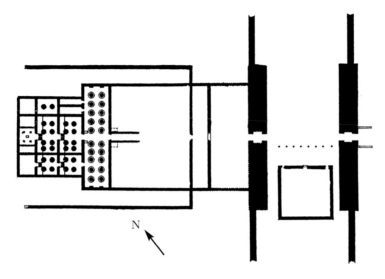

N

Fig. 63. Plan of the mortuary temple of Ay, later usurped and rebuilt for Horemheb.

Items recovered from the tomb included a gilded rosette that may have come from a pall, fragments of wooden statuettes, pieces from a ceremonial bed and pottery. Other pieces (of a chariot?) that may have originally come from the sepulchre were found in KV 58, a pit tomb a kilometre away in the East Valley. Some bones were also found in WV 23, but their date and ownership remains unclear.

We have no definite traces of the mortuary temple that Tutankhamun must have begun; however, Ay certainly founded such a monument, south of the huge temple of Amenophis III, in the area now known as Medinet Habu. Featuring a great colonnaded open court, the building was usurped, enlarged and completed by Horemheb, another general, who succeeded Ay on the throne (fig. 63).

In its final form, the temple was fronted by three pylons, a massive gateway giving access to the great court (fig. 64). A palace was constructed between the third pylon and the gateway, a feature that became standard in Ramesside temples. Behind the court was a broad hypostyle hall, two columns deep and ten wide, giving access to further, smaller, pillared courts and the three-fold cult complexes beyond. The temple was razed to the ground in antiquity, although excavations by the University of Chicago in the 1930s recovered indications of much of its plan and elevations. The only substantial finds were of fragmentary statuary, the best known examples of which are a pair of quartzite colossi, one each in Cairo and Chicago. Both were usurped by Horemheb, but are usually ascribed to Tutankhamun, although a recent view makes Ay their original author.

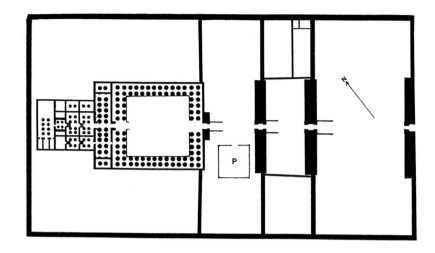

Fig. 64. The mortuary temple of Horemheb, rebuilt from that of Ay.

While commander of the army under his predecessors, Horemheb had built an impressive tomb at Saqqara, comprising an above-ground chapel, with sepulchral apartments opening off shafts below. It conformed to the normal pattern for Memphis-based dignitaries of the period, although amongst the most magnificent of its genre, with a particularly elaborate substructure.

However, although a uraeus was added to the brow of the new king's figures where they appeared on the walls of his chapel, a new sepulchre had to be constructed to hold the now-divine body of Horemheb. This was cut in the old, eastern, branch of the Biban el-

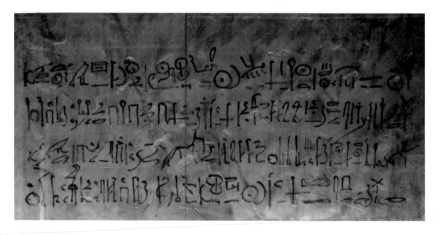

Fig. 65. Maya's restoration graffito in the antechamber of the tomb of Tuthmosis I.

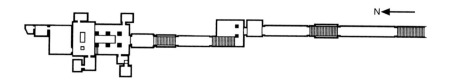

Fig. 66. Plan of the tomb of Horemheb, KV 57.

Moluk, thus marking an end to the experiment of the West Valley. Horemheb very much put himself forward as the true restorer of traditional values in Egypt, and it is possible that this move to tomb-site should be viewed against this light. Additionally, there may have been security considerations, since the reign saw the necessity for a number of tomb restorations, including that of the tomb of Tuthmosis IV (fig. 65). It may have been felt that it was easier to guard a tomb in the main valley, rather than the remoter West Valley.

The tomb (KV 57, fig. 66) is interesting in being the first structurally complete royal tomb known since the time of Amenophis III. In many ways, its plan closely follows that of WV 22, but with the crucial difference that it is laid out along a straight axis. This is usually explained as being a reflection of Atenist practice, since Akhenaten's tomb certainly lacks a turn. On the other hand, the latter's plan is clearly abbreviated, as is that of WV 23, not to mention that of the unfinished Amarna tomb, possibly attributable to Tutankhaten. Thus, the motivation for the layout of KV 57 must remain uncertain.

The outer galleries are undecorated, with the exception of the well-chamber, which shows the king before the usual Theban mortuary deities. The fundamental difference between these scenes and the corresponding ones in earlier tombs is that, as well as being painted, they are carved in low relief. Thus, unlike earlier practice that required some, if not all, the decoration to be applied after the burial had taken place, the adornment of the tomb had to be carried out at the same time as its cutting. The changes in scheduling following on from this innovation may explain why the decoration of the tomb was still incomplete at the king's death, after nearly three decades on the throne.

The antechamber (fig. 67) is the next room to possess decoration, with the well-room motifs repeated once again. The reliefs in the burial chamber are unfinished, comprising parts of the Book of the Gates, replacing the Amduat of earlier tombs. Their unfinished state is interesting in that they show every stage of their preparation, from initial red sketch, through black outlining, to exquisite carving (fig. 68). Other indications of the incomplete state of the tomb were the quantities of masons' debris that littered the rooms.

Fig. 67. Right-hand wall of the antechamber of the tomb of Horemheb.

Many fragments of the royal funerary equipment remained in the tomb when it was discovered by Edward Ayrton in 1908. Principal amongst the items found were the granite sarcophagus and its lid. This is

Fig. 68. Unfinished relief from the wall of the burial chamber of Horemheb. The scene, from the Book of Gates, has been outlined in red, then black, but has only been partially carved, including the figure of the sun-god on his bark.

84

Fig. 69. The red-granite sarcophagus of Horemheb. It is the last of the 'corner goddess' type, and additionally bears the figures of a number of the funerary genii.

the last of the 'corner goddess' type known, adding figures of the funerary genii to the elements seen on the sarcophagi of Tutankhamun and Ay (fig. 69). The broken pieces of the canopic chest, perhaps once sunk in a pit at the foot of the sarcophagus, were sufficient to show that it followed previous practice, but with wings added to the arms of the protective goddesses.

Other material included guardian figures of the kind seen outside the door of the burial chamber of Tutankhamun, a corn-Osiris, and statuettes of various deities, of kinds that were also found in a number of other royal tombs. Some of these statuettes later surfaced in the British Museum, clearly having been spirited away from the excavation by certain workmen (fig. 70).

A quantity of skeletal material was found in the tomb, although its present location appears unknown. Four skulls and various mixed post-cranial bones were found, suggesting to Nicholas Reeves that the tomb had been used as a cache during the Third Intermediate Period. Certainly, graffiti in the sepulchre show that there was official activity there around the beginning of the Third Intermediate Period. On the other hand, the additional bodies may represent members of the royal family, although the Queen, Mutnodjmet, seems to have been buried in her husband's old Saqqara tomb. The remains in question would show her to have been in middle age and in poor health on death, probably in child birth: the bones of a tiny infant were found with hers.

Fig. 70. Varnished wooden figure of a goat-headed funerary deity, from the tomb of Horemheb.

V   The First House of Ramesses

Horemheb appears to have died without a direct heir, his successor being his former vizier, Paramesse, an army officer and scion of a military family from the eastern Delta. Probably of advanced years, he reigned as Ramesses I for less than two years, before being succeeded by his son, Sethos I. Ramesses founded a tomb, now numbered KV 16, in the central area of the Kings' Valley, of which only two flights of steps and the corridor joining them appear to have been cut by the time of his death (fig. 71). Beyond them, a small square burial chamber was hurriedly cut, its rough walls covered with thick plaster and painted. The decoration is very similar in style to that of the reliefs in Horemheb's sepulchre, the same Deir el-Medina artists being probably responsible for both. It features the Book of Gates and the common motif of the king before the gods.

The king's granite sarcophagus discards the elaborate rectangular 'Amarna' design in favour of the cartouche form of Amenophis III and his predecessors. However, like the tomb, it is clearly unfinished, the lid only roughly shaped and the decoration never cut. The latter, similar to that of mid-Eighteenth Dynasty sarcophagi, is instead crudely applied in yellow paint. The scheme differs from its prototypes essentially in giving the goddesses at the head and foot outstretched wings, which they retain until the end of the dynasty. It seems likely that the sarcophagus' decoration actually took place in the tomb, given its poor style and at least two major errors in its texts: the speech of the human-headed Imseti accompanies a jackal-headed god, while that of the hawk-headed Horus accompanies an ibis-headed one.

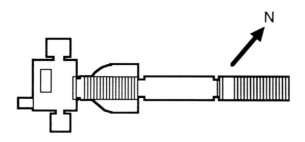

Fig. 71. Plan of the tomb of Ramesses I, KV 16.

Fig. 72. one of the guardian figures found in the tomb of Rameses I; similar figures guarded the entrance to the burial chamber of Tutankhamun.

Three annexes lead from the burial chamber. When entered by Belzoni in 1817, the left hand cubical held many wooden statuettes of deities, that on the right a life-sized wooden figure of the king. With its companion, found in the burial chamber itself, the latter formed a pair of guardians such as flanked the entrance to the burial chamber of Tutankhamun (fig. 72). Many of these figures are now in the British Museum.

Belzoni found two intrusive mummies in the sarcophagus; that of the king seems to have been moved to the cache at Deir el-Bahari, where an improvised coffin, and fragment of another were found. However, the mummy itself seems never to have been identified in modern times. Before being moved to Deir el-Bahari, a hieratic docket on Ramesses' coffin-

Fig. 73. Face of the coffin probably begun for Ramesses I but never finished. Later separated from his mummy, it was ultimately used for the reburial of his grandson, Ramesses II.

fragment notes that it lay for a time in the tomb of Sethos I along with that sepulchre's owner and the mummy of Ramesses II. It was perhaps at this time that the latter acquired what originally seems to have been the inner coffin of the first Ramesses, in which he was found lying at Deir el-Bahari. Of cedar, the coffin resembles the gold coffin of Tutankhamun, but is unfinished, the bare wood still preserving traces of the ink marking out the never-cut *rishi*-pattern (fig. 73).

Ramesses I appears to have been unable to complete a mortuary

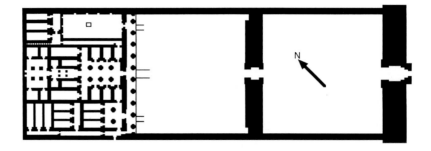

Fig. 74. Plan of the mortuary temple of Sethos I.

temple for himself, and provision for his cult seems restricted to the 'paternal' section of that of his son. Sethos I's mortuary temple was built at the opposite end of the necropolis from his late-Eighteenth Dynasty predecessors, in front of Dira Abu'l-Naga, at Qurna. The building (fig. 74) was incomplete at its founder's death, and was ultimately completed by his son, Ramesses II. The decoration applied by the latter, in sunk relief, is far inferior to Sethos' own work, in bas-relief of the very highest quality.

The temple was fronted by two courts and pylons, now almost totally destroyed, but much of the main temple remains intact. The ten-columned portico (fig. 75) gives access to three parallel sets of rooms, dedicated respectively to the royal cult, Amun and Re. The southernmost set comprises two groups of chambers; the first is the chapel of Ramesses I, with a pillared vestibule decorated by Ramesses II, and a central cult-room with a false-door decorated by Sethos. The latter king is shown before the barque of Amun and his deified father. Behind the chapel, and reached by a corridor to the south, is a further chapel whose sanctuary and flanking rooms are destroyed, with a vestibule decorated by Ramesses II. It is probable that this served the cult of Sethos himself.

The central complex begins with a hypostyle hall, flanked by a series of annexes containing scenes of Sethos and Ramesses II before the gods. Similar vignettes adorn the walls of the hall itself. The ceiling is supported by six columns with capitals imitating papyrus buds and across which carved vultures spread their wings. Alongside them are carved winged sun-disks and the names of the king; together they form a combination commonly found on the ceilings of monuments of the period. Beyond the hall, a vestibule leads into the sanctuary and its subsidiary rooms, behind which is to be found a four-pillared apartment adorned with fine reliefs. The final set of chambers is that associated with the open altar of Re, decorated in poor quality sunk-relief by Ramesses II. In Christian times,

Fig. 75. Facade of the mortuary temple of Sethos I at Qurna.

the altar-court was used as a church, the work including the cutting of seven niches into its walls.

Sethos I built his tomb directly next to that of his father; it was rediscovered by Belzoni only a few days after he had entered the elder king's sepulchre. Now numbered KV 17 (fig. 76), his sepulchre has long been regarded as amongst the finest in the Valley, its relief decoration being unsurpassed there. In its plan, it represents a logical development of Horemheb's KV 57, with the major innovation of being decorated throughout, rather than having paintings and reliefs restricted to the well-room, antechamber and burial chamber.

At the bottom of the entrance stairway, figures of Re-Harakhty are followed by the full text of the Litany of Re, followed, from the second stairway of the tomb, by the Book of Amduat. The decoration of the well-room is conventional, but the MLPH uses the Book of Gates, first encountered in Horemheb's burial chamber.

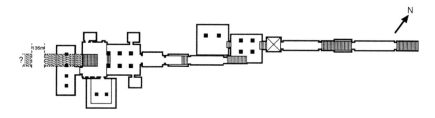

Fig. 76. Plan of the tomb of Sethos I, KV 17.

91

The chamber beyond, the first ever found in such a position, is interesting in that the decoration, comprising the *Amduat*, remains drawn in line only, as if never finished. It has been suggested that this was intentional, the chamber being a dummy to mislead robbers into believing that the tomb was unfinished and unused. However, no parallels are known amongst royal tombs of the New Kingdom, and it seems more likely that the chamber was a late addition and still incomplete on the king's demise. As with the pillars of virtually all royal tombs, those in these two chambers carry carved scenes of the king before various deities, though some of the latter make their first appearance in a royal tomb here.

Below the MLPH, a stairway and corridor descend, on whose walls appear depictions of ceremonies up to and including the Opening of the Mouth, and accompanying texts. The jambs of the doorway into the corridor were sawn away in the 1830s, and now repose in the Louvre and the Museo Archeologico, Florence.

The corridor ultimately leads into the antechamber, with reliefs of the king in the company of Hathor (thrice), Anubis, Isis, Horus (twice), Ptah, Osiris and Nefertum, and itself opening into the burial chamber. Of the same basic form as all such completed chambers since the time of Amenophis II, it is innovative in that its crypt has a vaulted ceiling, covered with a huge depiction of the night sky, bracketed by the body of the sky-goddess Nut, shown in the act of swallowing the evening sun, to pass through her body to be reborn at daybreak. The decoration of the burial chamber is, unlike that of the rest of the tomb, upon a yellow ground, recalling the room's designation in Egyptian texts as the 'Golden Hall'. That of the pillared section is taken from the Book of Gates, but that of the crypt comes from the *Amduat*, supplemented by motifs which include the opening of the mouth by Anubis.

Five annexes open from the burial chamber. Two of them lead from the pillared portion; that on the left contains part of the Book of Gates, that on the right the Book of the Cow, a composition relating the myth of the rebellion of mankind against the sun-god, hitherto only found on the outer shrine of Tutankhamun. These rooms contained funerary statuettes some 120 cm in height and equipped with cylindrical cavities which may have contained papyri.

The remaining annexes open from the crypt. The two-pillared chamber has been dubbed the 'Sideboard Room' after the rock-cut benches which surround its walls. These were presumably intended to support funerary equipment, such as those items depicted on the wall below them; the remaining wall-space is occupied by sections of the *Amduat*. The other annexes are devoid of decoration, but the four-pillared example held a sacrificed bull and a large number of shabtis in wood and

Fig 77. The calcite coffin-trough of Sethos I.

faience, which have found their ways into various collections.

No trace of a stone sarcophagus has ever been found in KV 17; however, in the crypt, Belzoni found the trough of the king's superb calcite outer coffin (fig. 77). Decorated with the Book of Gates and a figure of the goddess Nut, this fine anthropoid monument today stands in Sir John Soane's Museum, London. Fragments of the lid, on which the king was depicted wearing the *nemes* headdress, were found strewn throughout the tomb and are now in the Soane, the British Museum and the Institut d'Egyptologie, Strasbourg. The Soane also holds a piece of the king's calcite canopic chest, similar in design to that of Horemheb, but with additional figures of the four genii.

Since no king granted proper burial since the inception of the Eighteenth Dynasty appears to have been without a sarcophagus, it seems highly unlikely than Sethos I will have lacked one. On the other hand, the intact state of the calcite coffin-trough shows that it can never have been removed from a stone coffer. It would thus seem most likely that a wooden sarcophagus had been employed, lacking a bottom and assembled around the calcite coffin, just as was done to shelter the coffins in a number of private tombs of the previous dynasty, in particular that of Yuya and Tjuiu (see fig. 50). This sarcophagus will then have been enclosed in the series of gilded shrines that were a standard element of a royal burial from the time of Amenophis II down to at least the burial of Ramesses IV. Of the, probably, two inner coffins, only the larger survives, having been used for Sethos' reburial at Deir el-Bahari. Little can be discerned of its original decoration, the gilding having been stripped off, with the face and headdress partly re-cut to conceal the damage inflicted by robbers.

From the floor of the crypt, a rough tunnel, once paved over, dives steeply into the rock for over one hundred and twenty metres; its end has

Fig. 78. The Osirion, the cenotaph of Sethos I at Abydos.

not yet been reached. Its purpose has never been properly explained. Romer suggested that the intention might have been to place the coffin at the end of it as a substitute for a sarcophagus, but the much more likely view is that it was intended to reach the water table, which is certainly not far below the point where the most recent clearance stopped.

This hypothesis, that it provided a physical link with the primordial waters, derives some support from part of the design of the cenotaph which Sethos constructed at Abydos (figs. 78, 79). The tradition of erecting a royal 'tomb' at the sacred city of Osiris seems to have been initiated by Sesostris III, and resurrected by Amosis, although many private individuals had done so from early in the Middle Kingdom. Sethos I's 'tomb' lay behind the finely decorated temple that he had built, dedicated to seven of the gods of Egypt, including his deified self, and was discovered by Margaret Murray in 1903. Completely cleared by the Egypt Exploration Fund/Society between 1911 and 1926, its entrance lies just outside Sethos' temple-temenos. A pit descends to a brick-vaulted passage, although after 6 metres, the vaulting has collapsed. 32 metres from the entrance, however, a sandstone facing begins, decorated with extracts from the Book of Gates (west wall) and lists of denizens of the underworld (east) (fig. 80). This latter work was carried out by King Merenptah, over seventy years after his grandfather's death: while structurally complete at Sethos' death, little of the cenotaph's decoration had been carved, leaving the majority to be done by Merenptah. Its style is markedly inferior to that executed under the earlier king. A similar situation has been noted at Qurna, where Ramesses II was responsible for much of the

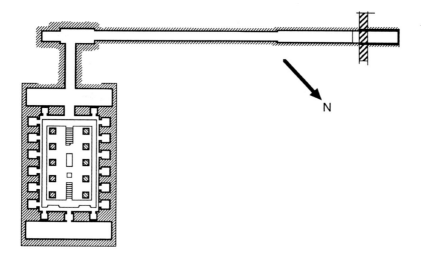

Fig. 79. Plan of the Osirion.

decoration, and also occurs in Sethos' Abydos temple.

From the antechamber, a sloping passageway, decorated with scenes from the Book of the Dead - the standard 'guidebook' to the hereafter frequently found in private burials - leads into a large transverse room, its roof preserving traces of swimming figures and an image of Nut.

Beyond is to be found the great hall, its roof supported by granite pillars and formerly covered by an earthen mound surrounded by trees.

Fig. 80. The west wall of the antechamber of the Osirion, decorated by Merenptah.

*Fig. 81. The ruins of the second court and hypostyle hall of the Ramesseum,
the mortuary temple of Ramesses II.*

The resemblance of the granite work to that of the Old Kingdom Valley Building of Khephren at Giza led early scholars to suggest that it was actually an ancient structure remodelled by Sethos I. This idea has recently been revived. Its east wall was decorated by Merenptah in poor sunk-relief, but is otherwise devoid of decoration. The central part of the hall is surrounded by a channel, intended to be filled by subsoil water so as to take the form of an island, on which cavities suggestive of a sarcophagus and canopic chest are cut. This use of water might provide evidence in favour of explaining the subterranean tunnel of KV 17 in terms of reaching the water table, though the correlation is by no means clear. The 'island', now permanently covered by the rise in the water table over the past three thousand years, was perhaps intended to represent the 'primeval mound' (*urhügel*) which features in creation myths as the place where the creator-god was first manifested amid the waters of Chaos.

The whole hall is surrounded by small annexes, a doorway opposite the entrance giving access to a final transverse chamber. It is possible that this was intended to be isolated from the rest of the cenotaph, the access passage being for use during construction only. Its ceiling is decorated in fine relief of the time of Sethos I, including an obscure, but important 'dramatic' religious text. Other texts relate to the heavens.

The length of Sethos I's reign is uncertain, but seems to have amounted to around a dozen years. He was succeeded by his son, Ramesses II, who was destined to rule for sixty-seven years. During those decades, Ramesses became easily the greatest builder of his era; few sites in the Nile Valley are without some sign of his activities, from his name carved on an existing building to huge temples some, like that at Abu Simbel, in Nubia, carved out of living rock. However, their artistic quality is extremely variable, rarely reaching the standards established by his father's artists.

One of his most important single works was his West Theban mortuary temple, known in Classical times as the Memnonium and today as the Ramesseum. Lying between the Eighteenth Dynasty temples of Amenophis II and Tuthmosis IV, its great enclosure contains, besides the temple itself (figs. 81, 82), a chapel possibly dedicated to his mother, Tuy, and wife, Nefertari and a large number of brick vaulted store-houses, some of which were used for burials in the Third Intermediate Period (fig. 83).

The temple's plan is considerably more elaborate than earlier examples of the genre, additionally being built of stone throughout as against the extensive use of brick for the outer elements of temples down to that of Sethos I. However, the basic layout of three cult complexes, of the king/his father, Amun and Re, is retained from earlier monuments.

Beyond the pylon, its inner face decorated with reliefs, lies the ruined First Court, flanked by colonnades, that on the right supported by Osirid columns, that on the left fronting a small palace (P), probably for the use of the king during festivals. A ramp leads from the First Court to the Second, at a higher level, and to its right lie the shattered remains of what was once the second-largest statue in Egypt. The largest was also the work of Ramesses II, erected at Piramesse, the new capital-city which he built in

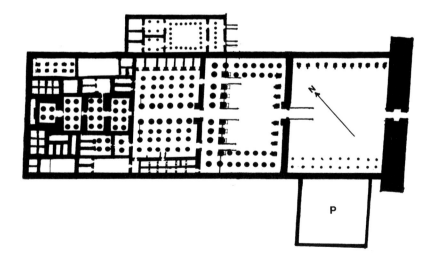

Fig. 82. Plan of the Ramesseum.

97

Fig. 83. Vaulted brick store-chambers at the Ramesseum, some of which were re-used as burial places during the Third Intermediate Period and later.

the Delta, and was found, cut up for building stone, at the near-by site of Tanis. The Ramesseum statue was carved from granite and represented the king seated; when complete, it towered seventeen and a half metres above the courtyard and weighed over one thousand tonnes.

The Second Court was surrounded on three sides by colonnades of which only portions survive, particularly the osiride pillars of the east and west sides. It formerly contained a number of granite colossi; the upper part of one was recovered by Belzoni in 1816, and is now in the British Museum (the so-called 'Young Memnon').

A section of the wall separating the two courts survives, part of its decoration dealing with the Battle of Qadesh, which occurred between the armies of Ramesses and Muwatallis, King of the Hittites, c. 1274 BC. This clash, in which the Egyptians narrowly avoided disaster, is to be seen depicted on many of the temples erected by Ramesses, and is also found on the pylon of the Ramesseum.

The west colonnade of the Second Court is elevated above the level of the courtyard itself. It is a feature of Egyptian temples that as one proceeds towards the sanctuary, the level of the floor rises and that of the ceiling falls, the amount of light admitted also being progressively reduced, until the sanctuary is reached, in total darkness. Reliefs upon the back wall of this colonnade include depictions of the king in the company of the gods, as well as of eleven of his many sons; in all, Ramesses sired over one hundred children.

Beyond lies the Great Hypostyle Hall, its roof formerly held up by forty eight columns, of which a considerable number still stand. Those flanking the aisle are rather more massive than the rest, supporting a clerestory which provided the only light for the hall. The columns all display reliefs of the gods and the king; the east wall has scenes of war in

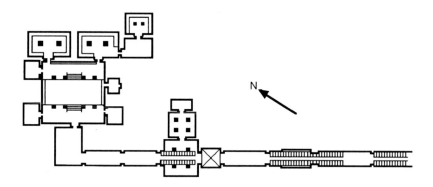

Fig. 84. Plan of the tomb of Ramesses II, KV 7.

Syria, the West, princes and gods.

Three complexes lead from the hall, of which only the centre is in any state of preservation. That on the left probably represented the chapel of the royal cult; that on the right, the chapel of Re. The central axis, of Amun, features a series of small hypostyle halls, decorated with ritual scenes, but the area of the sanctuary is almost entirely destroyed.

Ramesses II cut his tomb, KV 7, in the Kings' Valley, some 80 metres from those of his father and grandfather. Unlike them, it has suffered badly from flooding, leaving its decoration in a very poor state. Its plan (fig. 84) is unique for a Ramesside royal tomb in that the tomb turns to the right at the antechamber to the sepulchral hall. In addition, the form of the latter apartment changes, the layout current since Amenophis II's time being replaced by one in which the long axis is across the room, with eight (rather than six) columns placed in front and behind the sunken area. Elsewhere in the tomb, there are more subtle changes from the previous standards, with the MLPH straddling the tomb axis, rather than marking a lateral shift, and the stairways gaining the central ramp previously seen in the tomb of Akhenaten.

Decoratively, the sepulchre continues the pattern established by KV 17 in being adorned from the entrance onwards. The Litany of Re is once more prominent in the first two corridors, the Opening of the Mouth text preceding the antechamber, just as in the tomb of Sethos I. The burial chamber walls were adorned with sections of the Books of Gates and *Amduat*, compositions that were continued in the side-rooms, with the exception of one, which holds the Book of the Cow. This is the same chamber that holds this work in KV 17, further demonstrating the close kinship between the two sepulchres.

A further similarity between the tombs lies in KV 7 likewise lacking any sign of a stone sarcophagus, only calcite fragments from a coffin and a canopic chest having been known. The collapse of the back wall of the burial hall also suggests the existence of a subterranean passage of the same kind as that of Sethos I, although no definite proof of its presence yet exists. Like a large proportion of the tomb, the inner chambers were for many years heavily encumbered with debris, which certainly conceal the remains of any surviving funerary equipment. Until excavations by Christian Leblanc began in the middle of the 1990s, very little of the latter had come to light, being essentially restricted to a canopic-chest fragment in the British Museum (singular for being inlaid with blue glass) and a few shabtis, including a most unusual bronze example, now in Berlin. However, more of the chest has now been found, sunk in the floor of the burial chamber in a pit closed at half-depth by a limestone trap-door. It seems that the chest had occupied the upper section, other items being concealed below, perhaps items used during the king's mummification. Additionally, further pieces of the calcite coffin have come to light. The royal mummy found its way to TT 320, ultimately enclosed in the coffin of his grandfather. Previously it had lain temporarily in KV 17 and the tomb of Queen Inhapy, before being moved to its final resting place under Shoshenq I.

The reign of Ramesses II also saw the construction of a whole series of tombs for his extensive family. For a probably-large number of his sons, including the eldest, Amenhirkopshef A, Ramesse A, and Sethy, KV 5 was cut in the Valley of the Kings. The largest underground tomb in Egypt, and cleared under the direction of Kent Weeks since 1987, it comprises a pair of antechambers, leading into a sixteen-pillared hall. From the rear wall of this extends a T-shaped set of corridors, with small chambers along their sides: a figure of Osiris was carved in the wall at the end of the axial corridor. Large chambers also open from the pillared hall, along with a pair of passages which lead back out of the tomb, beyond the line of the entrance, in the general direction of Ramesses II's KV 7. Fragments of mummies, sarcophagi and canopics have been found scattered around the tomb, and much is doubtless concealed under the debris that still fill much of the sepulchre. Well over a hundred chambers have thus far been opened, and more clearly still await discovery.

For his womenfolk, Ramesses II took over a wadi south of Deir el-Medina, which had been employed for burials of the early Eighteenth Dynasty, and also for the interment of his grandmother, Sitre, the wife of Ramesses I. A whole series of tombs were cut in what is now known as the Valley of the Queens, including those of the king's mother, Queen Tuy (QV 80), one of his chief wives, Nefertari (QV 66), and at least three daughters (QV 60, 68 and 71). The glory of the series is the tomb of Nefertari, with exquisite painted reliefs that underwent a prolonged period

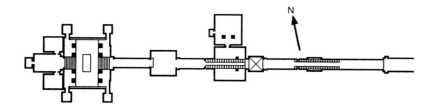

Fig. 85. Plan of the tomb of Merenptah, KV 8.

of restoration in the 1980s and 90s. A miniature version of a kingly tomb, it contained a rectangular granite sarcophagus, now largely destroyed. Various other parts of the burial were recovered by Ernesto Schiaparelli in 1905, including many shabtis and the knees of the queen's mummy, all now in the Turin Egyptian Museum.

A number of other tombs of royal ladies in the Valley are fully decorated, but have never had names inserted in their texts. These had clearly been 'mass-produced', with the intention that names would be added when the tombs were used. They all date to the Ramesside Period, and some, if not all, should probably be attributed to the time of Ramesses II.

The tomb of Ramesses II's successor, Merenptah (KV 8, fig. 85), is of essentially the same plan as KV 7, with the exception that the burial chamber regains its position on the main axis, and adopts a more regular layout for the rooms beyond the MLPH. The entrance to the tomb is particularly finely decorated with a scene of the king before Re-Horakhty, before giving way to the Litany of Re. The remainder of the tomb's decoration centres on the *Amduat* and Book of Gates, although that beyond the MLPH is badly damaged, this part of the sepulchre having been largely filled with flood debris until cleared by Howard Carter in 1903/4.

One of the most notable features of the tomb is the number of sarcophagi employed in the royal interment. The apparent abandonment of stone examples by Sethos I and Ramesses II is reversed with a vengeance, no fewer than three granite cases being employed, along with the calcite outer coffin. The innermost sarcophagus had actually been made for Merenptah while he had been Crown Prince. It is rectangular, and is unusual in having its lower margin adorned with panelling, seemingly imitating certain coffers of the late Twelfth Dynasty. Aspects of its internal decoration also recall the Middle Kingdom, although the lid, dating to the period after Merenptah's accession, is purely New Kingdom in its form. It is the first of a new royal design that features a three dimensional Osirian image of the deceased upon the top surface. A figure of the sky-goddess Nut kneels at the king's head, and is also to be found underneath the lid, stretched out over the contained body in the same way that the goddess stretches out from one horizon to the other. Nut's image is regularly found in such a location, but this example is the first in which she is carved in three dimensions.

This sarcophagus was contained within one of the traditional royal cartouche plan, but once again the lid is adorned with a recumbent figure of the king, this time wearing a *nemes* headdress, rather than the tripartite wig of the inner sarcophagus. The underside also bears a three-dimensional image of Nut, although rather flattened at each extremity, to provide sufficient clearance for the raised end-pieces of the inner lid. The second sarcophagus was decorated with extracts from the Books of Gates and *Amduat*, but its coffer was reduced to fragments in antiquity, only parts of the upper margin surviving to be reassembled by Edwin Brock, who has been working in KV 8 since the 1980s.

The reason for this destruction seems to have been the desire during the Twenty-first Dynasty to recycle much of the material left behind after the plundering of the royal tombs, and the consequent removal of the mummies, from the late Twentieth Dynasty onwards. A number of royal tombs lack their sarcophagus coffers, and it seems clear that they were removed at this period for the sake of their thick floors - ideal for the production of stelae and similar items. In Merenptah's case, however, the inner sarcophagus was coveted for its own sake since, once extracted, it was moved to the city of Tanis, in the Delta, where it was employed for the interment there of King Psusennes I (fig. 117).

Also demolished at the same time was the coffer of the gigantic (410 x 220 x ~200 cm) outermost sarcophagus in KV 8. It had rested on a calcite base made up of two blocks, one of which is now destroyed. The sides of this base bore the outline of a funerary bier, an actual example of which was found within the sarcophagus of Tutankhamun, supporting his coffins. Merenptah's outer sarcophagus was rectangular, with a lid of simple, slightly vaulted, form. Only about of a third of the coffer survives, showing the sarcophagus to have been decorated once again with a Gates/*Amduat* combination. The lid presently rests in the antechamber, presumably where it had been deposited by the Twenty-first Dynasty workmen.

It seems that a sarcophagus of such huge dimensions had not initially been planned, since various decorated door-jambs had had to be cut away to allow its passage down the tomb. These were later replaced by sandstone blocks; other, limestone, blocks were used to patch large holes that had to be cut into passage walls to hold wooden balks that allowed the use of ropes to check the progress of the sarcophagi down the steeply-sloping tomb.

Aside from the remains of the sarcophagi, only a few items have

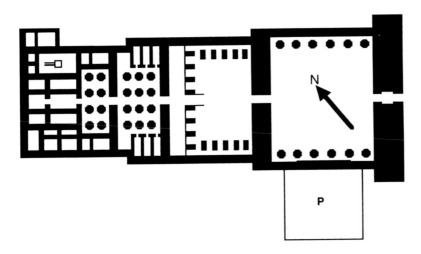

Fig. 86. Plan of the mortuary temple of Merenptah.

survived from Merenptah's burial. Of his calcite outer coffin, only a fragment in the British Museum (bought in 1911), and some pieces found in recent years in the tomb, are known. Likewise, his canopic chest is only represented by a few disparate fragments which show, however, that the protective goddesses are now no longer to found on the corners, as they had been from Amenophis II to Ramesses II. Some shabtis are extant, as are a set of thirteen calcite vessels, found just outside the tomb by Carter in 1920. The king's mummy was ultimately reburied in KV 35, resting in the trough of the coffin of Sethnakhte.

Merenptah's mortuary temple lay between those of his predecessor and Amenophis III. The basic plan (fig. 86) followed that of the temple of Sethos I, the temple's dimensions being rather more modest than those of the Ramesseum, although offset by the gigantic size of the pylon that fronted the building. The construction of the temple had been carried out in at least two phases, one presumably beginning at the opening of the reign, and one commencing after Merenptah's fifth regnal year, in which he had defeated a hostile Libyan-led coalition. The latter included the replacement of the First Pylon - originally of brick - with one of stone and an enlargement of certain elements of the temple structure.

Much of the material used in the structure was salvaged from earlier monuments, in particular those erected by Amenophis III. A number of colossal statues in various stones had been usurped from the earlier king, and others cut up for building material, not to mention straightforward building blocks. The structure had, however, been denuded down to the foundations, and only elements of its decoration have been recovered by the Swiss expedition that has worked at the site since 1971. Nevertheless, a

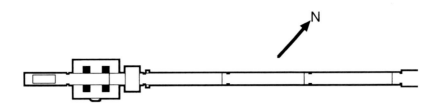

Fig. 87. Plan of the tomb of Sethos II, KV15.

considerable number of blocks have now been replaced in their original locations, while scenes from Amenophis III's donor building(s) have also proved possible to restore.

Merenptah reigned for approximately a decade. His heir was a Prince Sethy-Merenptah, who was to take the throne as Sethos II, but there has been much discussion as to whether he directly followed his father, or whether another king, Amenmesse, interposed between them. In the first case, Amenmesse will have been a 'counter-king', ruling in Upper Egypt during the middle years of Sethos II's reign. A key piece of evidence is that no dated records seem to exist at Thebes from Year 2 down to Year 5 of Sethos' six-year tenure, at a time when almost every year of a king's reign is usually attested in the archives recovered from the workmen's village at Deir el-Medina. Conversely, the dated material related to Amenmesse would very nicely fill the gap.

Also suggestive is the fact that the tomb constructed for Sethos II (KV 15, fig. 87) shows two separate phases of decoration. The very start of the first corridor is superbly decorated in raised relief, which swiftly switches to the sunk variety for further scenes, and the usual Litany of Re. While the left-hand wall is complete, the right changes from painted relief to initial sketches in red ink close to its end; the succeeding two corridors, with the Litany and extracts from the *Amduat*, display these ink drafts only. These become more and more sketchy as one proceeds, and also show at least one change of design. Two figures of the king have been summarily finished, with only the eyes marked out in paint. The cartouches in this outer part of the tomb display erasures and reinstatements.

The well-room beyond marks a major change in style, completely divorced from what had been begun before, with rather crude, simple paintings of various divine statuettes and images. Largely coloured yellow, they clearly depict the kinds of gilded statuettes that were actually found in the tomb of Tutankhamun. The MLPH is decorated in painted relief, but now of fairly poor quality, featuring parts of the Book of Gates, and the usual figures on the pillars. Only one figure is shown on each face of these pillars, however: in most earlier tombs one finds two images per side.

The tomb was certainly intended to be of a similar design to KV 8, but instead it comes to an abrupt halt not far beyond the slope that leads out of the MLPH. This unfinished corridor was turned into an improvised burial chamber and coarsely painted with a figure of Nut on the ceiling and elements taken from the Book of Gates on the walls. Into this was inserted a small rectangular sarcophagus, only the incomplete lid of which survives today. It is very similar to that of the inner sarcophagus of Merenptah, and it would seem likely that it was supposed to be enclosed in one or more outer boxes. The lack of such items is probably due to either their unfinished state, and/or the inability of fitting them into the confined space of this substitute for a burial hall. There is a possibility that the 'missing' outer sarcophagus was ultimately used for the burial of Ramesse III. As will be noted later, the latter's lid and coffer exhibit features that make them far more akin to the sarcophagi of Merenptah than those of Ramesses III's immediate predecessors and successor.

The pattern of decoration seen in KV 15 - good quality work suddenly stopped and its cartouches erased, followed by inferior work obviously carried out in a hurry, perhaps after a gap - would thus fit in well with a scenario in which Sethos II was overthrown, and later restored, although closer study indicates that the scenario may be rather more complex than that. A number of other strands of evidence pointing in this direction lead the author to support such a view, although much Egyptological opinion still seems to favour the opposite reconstruction of Amenmesse's usurpation preceding Sethos II's accession.

Amenmesse would seem to have been a grandson of Ramesses II, and on the view taken here may also have been Sethos II's own son as well. There is also evidence to suggest that Amenmesse had served under Merenptah as Viceroy of Kush (Nubia) under the abbreviated name, Messuy; the reasons behind any quarrel with his putative father remains unknown. Material naming Amenmesse as king is found principally at Thebes, although items have been found as far north as Riqqa, just east of the Fayoum. As already mentioned, all four of his known regnal years are recorded at Deir el-Medina, and nearby he was responsible for founding a sanctuary on the pass between the village and the Valley of the Queens, the so-called 'Oratory of Ptah'.

A tomb (KV 10) was begun in the centre of the Valley of the Kings, and seems to have been pushed ahead with some despatch. The plan adopted was almost identical to that being used in Sethos II's sepulchre (fig. 88), and the decoration was largely in the same high-quality sunk relief seen in the latter's first corridor. The main exception was on the facade, where raised relief was employed for the adornment of the lintel and jambs.

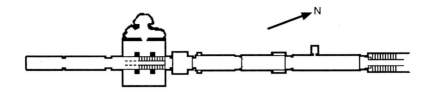

Fig. 88. Plan of the tomb of Amenmesse, KV 10.

During the four years of Amenmesse's rule, the tomb progressed past its MLPH into two corridors, at which point work stopped. Decoration had by then covered the walls of all parts of the tomb, down to at least the MLPH, which gave access on the left to an unfinished side room. The termination of the tomb's construction was doubtless the result of the ending of its author's rule and the restoration of Sethos II. Whether this restoration was accompanied by the death, exile or otherwise of Amenmesse is wholly unknown.

The subsequent treatment of the tomb was most singular. In most cases where a monarch had become *persona non grata*, their names and figures were excised from their monuments, but other decorative elements left intact. In KV 10, however, the entire decoration was sliced from the walls, often leaving ghostly outlines on the surface, especially in those places where raised relief had been employed (fig. 89). The effect of this technique was that in many cases the king's cartouches remained readable on the tomb's walls and pillars. This enables one to observe that the form of his names evolved while the tomb was being decorated.

The reasoning behind this treatment of the tomb has been the subject of considerable debate, including a suggestion that the king might have been buried in the 'religionless' tomb as a means of isolating him from the magical 'machinery' that would have eased his passage into the next world. However, the confirmation in excavations carried out in 1994 that the tomb ends in an unfinished corridor lessens the chance of this. It has also been suggested that the removal of the decoration might have been done with a view to redecoration for a new owner. However, since the decoration of a New Kingdom tomb is rather generic, surely it would have been far more reasonable to simply cover and re-carve the area of Amenmesse's figures and names in honour of the new owner. Alternatively, as is seen at many sites in Egypt, a simple plaster layer over the existing walls would have provided a perfect ground for new decoration.

Indeed, this is what was actually done in two of the rooms of KV 10, the MLPH and the preceding 'well' room. The latter received decoration in honour of a 'God's Mother and King's Mother', Takhat, and the former for a 'King's Great Wife', Baketwernel. The layer of plaster was badly

damaged by the flooding of the tomb in antiquity, and only the upper parts of the top register in both rooms survived when copied by Eugène Lefébure in 1883. By the twentieth century, the whole rear of the tomb was blocked by debris, and by the time that Otto Schaden's team re-entered the apartments in 1992-3, almost all traces had been lost, save a single portrait of Baketwernel on the back wall of the MLPH. Various fragments have been recovered from the debris, including part of a granite coffin and a canopic jar of Takhat, with more material likely to be found by the ongoing work in the tomb.

The affinities of the two ladies in KV 10 are uncertain. Older writers assumed them to be the wife and mother of Amenmesse, but this has become impossible with the confirmation that their decoration is secondary. Takhat is a not-unusual name, and was certainly borne by a wife of Sethos II - who seems also to have been Amenmesse's mother. However, the titles of the KV 10 Takhat do not include 'King's Wife', her particular titular formulation being of the kind implying that her royal son's father was not himself a king. Accordingly, the suggestion has been made that she could have been the mother of the Twentieth Dynasty king Ramesses IX, who may only have been the grandson of a pharaoh. Since the redecoration of both chambers seems to have been contemporary, Baketwernel would thus also have to be dated to the Twentieth Dynasty, perhaps as the otherwise-unknown wife of Ramesses IX himself.

No mortuary temple of Amenmesse has thus far been noted, nor

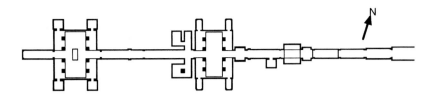

Fig. 90. Plan of the tomb of Tawosret and Sethnakhte, KV 14.

anything attributable to his rival, Sethos II. Since the original ownership of the temples of their immediate successors is guaranteed by foundation deposits found *in situ*, the foundations of the temple(s) presumably remain hidden under the sand of Western Thebes.

Sethos II only survived his restoration by a short period, dying in his sixth regnal year, and was succeeded by a prince named Siptah. The new king was barely a teenager at his accession, and thus under the tutelage of the dowager Queen, Tawosret. The latter's enhanced status is shown by the scale of the tomb which she now pushed forward in the Valley of the Kings (KV 14). As revealed by a Cairo ostracon, the sepulchre had been begun during the second year of her husband's reign, but was soon stopped, and not resumed until the beginning of Tawosret's regency. This clearly parallels the break in the construction of Sethos II's KV 15, presumably caused by Amenmesse's revolt.

As begun, and resumed, the tomb was intended as a reduced version of a 'standard' royal tomb. Close to the end of Siptah's reign, with Tawosret apparently already claiming pharaonic status, a new, larger, burial chamber (fig. 90) was begun just beyond the eight-pillared hall that had been initially intended to hold the queen's sarcophagus, a quasi-anthropoid affair that would never actually be used for her.

Work on this new room was cut short after a fairly short while, graffiti showing that it ceased soon after Year 6, II *Akhet*, day 18 in Siptah's reign. This must be close to the date of the young king's demise, and the accession of Tawosret as female pharaoh. As king, a more ambitious enlargement of the tomb was begun, a long corridor being cut beyond the unfinished room to a final eight-pillared burial hall.

In the decoration, Tawosret was everywhere prominent, occupying pillars and the usual positions in offering scenes; however, figures of a king were also initially incorporated into the scheme (fig. 91). The overall decorative scheme of the tomb comprises, apart from the usual vignettes, extracts from the Book of the Dead in the outer corridors, and the Book of Gates in the queenly burial chamber. The rear corridor contained the *Amduat*, and the pharaonic burial chamber the 'Gates'. One would assume that the distinction between the latter and the   Book of the Dead in the

Fig. 91. Siptah, from the outer corridor of KV14; his cartouches show signs of having been over-written by those of Sethos II.

queenly burial chamber was intentional, marking Tawosret's elevation to the divine status of king. The quality of workmanship in this rear room and its approach corridor is far inferior to that seen in the outer parts of the tomb, and probably indicate a degree of haste: Tawosret's two years of independent rule were not without opposition. Elsewhere in the tomb,

Fig. 92. Tawosret, from the left wall of the first corridor of KV 14. The figure shows heavy re-cutting from its changes to reflect her changing status, from queen-consort to sole pharaoh.

Tawosret's enhanced status was indicated by modifications to her figures, to incorporate a uraeus and double cartouches; in certain cases at least, a further change gave her a blue crown as well (fig. 92).

KV 14's initial decoration seems to date to the regency, since the figures of kings who appear on the walls of the first corridor were inscribed with the cartouches of Siptah (fig. 91). However, deeper inside, including the first burial chamber, on a pillar, the king was named as Sethos II, the images of Siptah being later re-labelled with Sethos' names. Some earlier writers took this as an indication that Sethos II was a successor of Siptah, but external evidence makes the true order of succession quite certain. The situation within KV 14 was clearly a result of Tawosret wishing to dissociate herself from her former ward, whose regnal years she also arrogated. This inevitably leads to suspicions concerning the demise of the young Siptah, although no further evidence is presently available.

A graffito in the entrance to KV 14, dated to the first year of an unnamed king, seems to record the burial of Sethos II in the tomb. Hartwig Altenmüller, who discovered the notation, is of the opinion that it records the primary interment of the recently-deceased king there in the first year of his successor's reign. He further considers that the body was then moved to the king's own KV 15 after the end of the Nineteenth Dynasty. Such events would echo those surrounding the mummy of Tuthmosis I under Hatshepsut and Tuthmosis III. Nicholas Reeves, on the other hand, would attribute all the graffiti in Tawosret's tomb to the activities of the reburial commissions of the late Twentieth/Twenty-first Dynasties. A further option is that the notation merely records the KV 14 workmen's presence at the funeral of Sethos II in the directly adjacent KV 15.

It is unclear whether Tawosret was ever buried in her tomb. Her last regnal year (eight) was apparently ended by a successful rising led by one Sethnakhte, founder of a new, Twentieth, dynasty. Shortly afterwards, as will be related in the next chapter, the sepulchre was taken over for the victor's burial, implying that the queen had at very best been evicted. Given that we know nothing of the precise way in which Tawosret's was reign ended, nor whether or not she survived it, little more can be said on the matter. It should be noted that there is no real evidence for the identification of a mummy from KV 35 ('Unknown Woman D') which is sometimes attributed to Tawosret.

In parallel with the initial construction of KV 14 proceeded that of another tomb, now numbered KV 13, at the opposite corner of the bay in the rock from that occupied by that of Sethos II (fig. 93). Of essentially the same initial design and dimensions as that of Tawosret, it was nevertheless not intended for a royal figure; instead, the texts that accompany the images of Isis and Nephthys over the main entrance name a Chancellor of

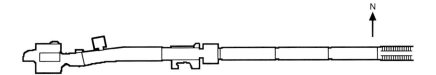

Fig. 93. Plan of the tomb of the Chancellor Bay, KV 13.

the Whole Land. His name has been mutilated, but can only be Bay, a man of probably Syrian origin who played a key role in the accession of Siptah, and may have briefly exercised personal control over at least part of Egypt at the very end of the dynasty. Bay is also mentioned on a surviving label text further into the tomb. The overall decorative scheme seems to have closely followed that of KV 14, although it is now in a very badly damaged condition, as a result of the flooding suffered by the tomb over the centuries. The first corridor opened with figures of kneeling goddesses spreading their wings, followed by a series of images of Bay, before various gods and, on both walls, the king: although his name is lost, he was almost certainly Bay's protegé, Siptah. The second and third passageways were largely taken up with sections from the Book of the Dead, although very little could be positively identified in the latter corridor. Any decoration that might originally have been applied to the following chambers has long since vanished. The original constructional work in KV 13 seems to have been stopped at the end of the corridor after the MLPH.

The tomb is unfinished and was choked with debris until its excavation by Hamburg University, carried out under the direction of Hartwig Altenmüller from 1989 onwards. It is unclear whether Bay was ever buried in the tomb. During the Twentieth Dynasty, a rough extension was cut, terminating in the burial chamber of a Prince Amenhirkopshef. Subsequently, the burial of a Prince Montjuhirkopshef was inserted into the corridor, five metres in front of the chamber doorway. From each of these interments derived a stone sarcophagus and canopic fragments, plus shabti figures belonging to Montjuhirkopshef. That the appropriation of the tomb dates to the reign of Ramesses VI is suggested by a fragmentary inscription naming his wife, Queen Nubkhesbed. As part of the Twentieth Dynasty take-over of the tomb, the figures of Bay in the outer passages had been changed into those of women.

The precise affiliations of the two princes are as yet unproven, but Montjuhirkopshef was perhaps the son of Ramesses III of that name, and possibly the father of Ramesses IX. On the other hand, based on the representation of Queen Nubkhesbed in the altered reliefs, which would seem to be contemporary with the extension of the tomb to house the burial of Amenhirkopshef, the latter may have been an offspring of

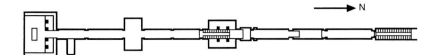

<figure>*Fig. 94. Plan of the tomb of Siptah, KV 47.*</figure>

Ramesses VI. In this scenario, the prince's uncle could have died shortly after him, and for convenience been buried in the same sepulchre.

The container in which Amenhirkopshef was buried is of some interest, since it had been made for Tawosret while queen (or regent). It had then been modified, with altered texts, and the female headdress cut away and altered to show a princely side-lock. Its overall form combines features of contemporary anthropoid coffins with those of sarcophagi with recumbent figures on their lids. The latter have already been seen in the tombs of Merenptah and Sethos II, and were used for kings at least down to the time of Ramesses IV; they also appear in certain princely tombs of the reign of Ramesses III.

The last of the Nineteenth Dynasty royal tombs to be begun was that of Siptah (KV 47, fig. 94). Originally named Ramesses-Siptah, but renamed within a year of his accession as Merenptah-Siptah, the king's parentage is somewhat obscure, but it seems most likely that he was the offspring of the late, disgraced, King Amenmesse. His accession was clearly engineered by Bay, a number of whose inscriptions give him the epithet 'who establishes the king in the seat of his father'. The new pharaoh's tomb was cut at the same end of the Valley of the Kings as those of Sethos II and his contemporaries, but somewhat nearer the central area.

In plan, the tomb essentially follows Merenptah's prototype, and came far closer to structural completion than any of the intervening royal sepulchres. It is, however, unclear how far decoration had progressed, since the tomb has suffered severely from flooding, the entire stone surface of the floor, walls and ceiling beyond the MLPH being destroyed. The outer galleries are, however, in almost perfect condition (fig. 95). A very fine quality sunk relief of the king and Re-Harakhty is on the left wall of the first corridor. The remainder of the first two galleries is taken up by the Litany of Re, with a number of divine vignettes at the end of the second passage. The ceiling of the first part of the tomb is also in a good state, but from the third corridor onwards, all is ruin. Some fragments of the *Amduat* survive near its roof, but little more: much of the remainder of the tomb has the aspect of a natural cave.

Vaulting and a row of pillars may be distinguished in the burial hall, which contained a granite, cartouche-form, recumbent-figure

Fig. 95. Figure of Maet, from the left-hand door-jamb of the tomb of Siptah, showing the erased and re-installed cartouches.

sarcophagus, plus vast quantities of calcite fragments. The latter included two anthropoid coffins and two canopic chests. One of each belonged to the king and his mother, Tia, who had clearly been buried with her son. The precise arrangements for this installation are unclear, but presumably included the unfinished side-passage that leads off to the left, just before the doorway of the burial chamber. It had been brought to an abrupt stop when it had inadvertently run into an early Eighteenth Dynasty tomb, KV 32, cut in the flank of a branch of the valley that runs parallel to the tomb's axis.

A particularly interesting aspect of the decoration of the tomb of Siptah is that on its walls, and on the king's sarcophagus, his cartouches have been erased, and then reinstated. The ramifications of this are unclear, but certainly reflect the political turmoil that continued down to the end of the Nineteenth Dynasty. In the present state of knowledge, it would seem that the cartouches were excised by the Regent Tawosret when she replaced Siptah on the throne, and then replaced by Siptah's old mentor, Bay, who appears to have exercised control over Upper Egypt for a brief period at the very end of the dynasty. These erasures clearly tie in with the treatment of the depictions of Siptah within KV 14 already noted.

The mortuary temple of Siptah lay between the Eighteenth Dynasty monuments of Tuthmosis III and Amenophis II, north of the Ramesseum at Western Thebes. Excavated by Flinders Petrie in 1896, nothing survives

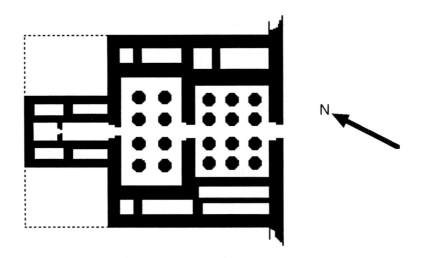

N

*Fig. 96. Plan of the rear part of the mortuary temple of Siptah:
no trace of the outer courts could be found by Petrie.*

apart from the foundation trenches of its rear part (fig. 96). A number of
foundation deposits were revealed, including a series of plaques in
sandstone, faience and gold foil, bearing the names of Siptah and,
significantly, the Chancellor Bay. Jar sealings from the site indicate that
work was going on during the king's third and fourth regnal years. The
portion of the plan that survives shows that two hypostyle halls were
intended to precede the usual threefold sanctuaries, but little else can been
said, given the loss of the outer parts.

At Siptah's demise, Tawosret became the fourth known female
pharaoh of Egypt. The major changes that were instituted in her tomb, to
change it into a fully-fledged king's tomb have already been described, but
in addition a mortuary temple was founded, just south of the ancient
sanctuary of Tuthmosis IV. Like Siptah's, only the outline of the
foundations survived to be traced by Flinders Petrie (fig. 97). Once again,
foundation deposit plaques were fairly plentiful, in sandstone and faience.
The plan showed the temple to have been fronted by a pylon, with a first
court probably colonnaded on the right and left. Beyond were three rooms
that should be interpreted as hypostyle halls, and the sanctuaries, including
a sun-court to the north.

A stela of Sethnakhte from Elephantine, and the prologue of the
Great Harris Papyrus, written in the reign of Ramesses IV, make it clear
that the Nineteenth Dynasty ended in conflict. The main protagonists were
Tawosret, the Chancellor Bay, and Sethnakhte, a man of unknown
antecedents, but most probably a scion of the royal family to judge by his

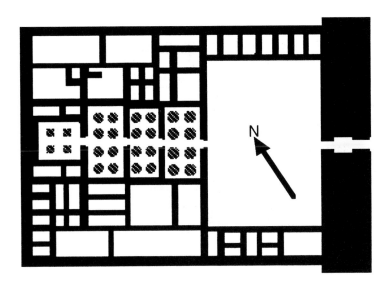

Fig. 97. Plan of the mortuary temple of Tawosret.

name: Seth was clearly regarded as a sponsor of the Ramesside house. Sethnakhte was the victor in this conflict and was subsequently regarded as founder of the Twentieth Dynasty, a period which saw a rally, and then steady decline of royal power, ending in the effective division of the country.

VI   The Last Years of the Valley

Sethnakhte's enjoyment of victory was short-lived, his reign lasting for no more than two years. During that time he began a tomb in the central area of the Valley of the Kings, somewhat to the right of the location earlier adopted by Amenmesse for his sepulchre, KV 10.

The entrance to the tomb (KV 11, fig. 98) has a pair of apparently unique cow-headed columns on either side, the conventionally-adorned doorway giving on to a pair of corridors containing the Litany of Re: the basic scheme thus accorded exactly with Nineteenth Dynasty prototypes. Work proceeded until the third corridor was being cut. Standard procedure was to remove stone step-wise from the ceiling of the tomb down to the floor; thus the working face would always have an upper tongue jutting into the mountain, while at floor level the excavation was considerably less advanced. In KV 11's case, a hole suddenly appeared in the flat surface half way down the work-face. This turned out to lead into the ceiling of the side chamber of the tomb of Amenmesse. Not for the first (or last) time, a tomb had run into a neighbour.

The tomb could not continue in this direction, and accordingly the first section of the intended third corridor was cut away to the right, forming a rectangular chamber. This allowed the axis of the tomb to be shifted away from the obstruction, and continued parallel to its intended course, albeit with a slight positive slope for a short way to ensure that it cleared KV 10 cleanly. Decoration of the tomb had reached this room when Sethnakhte died.

The tomb was thus far from being in a state to receive a body. This was by no means unusual and, following the precedent of the tomb of Ramesses I, Sethnakhte's son, the third Ramesses, could easily have had an improvised burial chamber constructed out of the 'well room'.

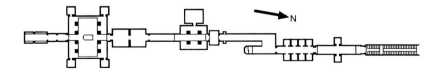

Fig. 98. Plan of the tomb of Ramesses III, KV 11.

Fig. 99. Parts of the Opening of the Mouth ritual, as depicted in KV 14. Figures of Tawosret were originally the object of the ceremonies, but all have been obliterated by plaster and replaced by the roughly-painted cartouches of Sethnakhte.

However, an alternative was available, in the form of the probably unused tomb of Tawosret. It was formerly thought that Sethnakhte's work on KV 11 had been terminated as soon as KV 10 had been hit, and that he had subsequently constructed the entire rear part of KV 14. More recent study has shown, however, that Sethnakhte had instigated the axis-shift, with the intention of carrying on KV 11, and also that the extension of KV 14 should be attributed to Tawosret as pharaoh. Thus, it would appear to be Ramesses III who usurped the latter, and that only changes to decorative detail changes should be attributed to the Twentieth Dynasty.

These were simple, aimed at substituting Sethnakhte for all the royal figures depicted in KV 14. This was straightforward in the cases where Siptah or Sethos II had been included in the decoration: the cartouches were readily overwritten. The figures of Tawosret were much more problematic, since even when equipped with pharaonic headgear, the images were still clearly female. Large-scale re-carving was obviously ruled out by the need to carry out the work without unduly delaying the late king's funeral. Thus, the female pharaoh's depictions were simply covered over with plaster and something new added in ink. In most cases, nothing more than Sethnakhte's cartouches and titles were added, written at such a scale that they completely filled the space formerly occupied by Tawosret's figure (fig. 99). In others, an ink drawing of the king was substituted, very occasionally made polychrome.

Sethnakhte was interred in a granite sarcophagus of typical Nineteenth/Twentieth Dynasty type. It remains unclear whether or not it had been usurped from Tawosret, its study being hampered by its smashed state, and numerous missing fragments. Its exterior decoration is very similar to that of the sarcophagi of Siptah and Ramesses IV. The lid arrangements of these sarcophagi represented a development of those seen on the inner two covers of Merenptah, the recumbent figures being now more three-dimensional, wearing the elaborate *atef* crown, and flanked by Isis, Nephthys, crocodiles, and some curious snake-bodied deities.

Although the fate of the king's body is uncertain, his inner coffin was found in KV 35. It is of the age-old rishi design, but including on the side of the trough four kneeling genii and winged goddesses, and contrasts strongly with contemporary private cases. It is also unusual in being made of cartonnage, the combination of linen, glue and plaster, rather than the usual fine wood, or even gold. The use of such a cheap material, and the poor modelling of the royal features, is most curious, but the surviving inscriptions make it quite clear that the coffin is the king's original. The only explanation would seem to be that it was made in a hurry following the king's premature demise.

No mortuary temple has been identified for Sethnakhte, not unsurprisingly, given the shortness of his reign. It is possible that he could have taken over one of the temples of Siptah and Tawosret, but the total loss of their structures makes a judgment impossible. On the other hand, no question mark surrounds the monument of Sethnakhte's son, Ramesses III, whose mortuary chapel is the best preserved of all such buildings. This came about partly by accident, in that during the latter part of the Twentieth Dynasty its precincts had become the headquarters of the Theban necropolis administration, and later a popular place of burial for high-status individuals. It also lay close to a favoured Eighteenth Dynasty cult temple, which continued to be altered and extended into the Roman Period. Thus, the entire precinct, now known as Medinet Habu, was preserved from the demolition suffered by so many of the other great mortuary sanctuaries along the front of the Theban necropolis.

A feature of Ramesses III's personality appears to have been a great desire to imitate Ramesses II. His titulary was modelled upon that of the earlier king, while his children were named for those of Ramesses II. The latter trait was taken so far as to include the naming of new-born sons to 'replace' prematurely-deceased siblings. This desire to imitate also came

Fig. 100. The mortuary temple of Ramesses III at Medinet Habu.

to the fore in the design of his mortuary temple (fig. 100), which is in essence an enlarged copy of the Ramesseum.

One unique feature, however, was the High Gate that gives access to the Medinet Habu complex, surrounded by a massive brick wall. The gateway is of a fortified type, incorporating features of Syrian migdol-fortresses, and is adorned by images of the king smiting his enemies (fig. 101). Inside, the rooms within its towers were decorated with domestic

Fig. 101. The temple complex at Medinet Habu, viewed from the west; to the left is the Small Temple, in the middle the gateway of Ramesses III, partially built in the form of a Syrian fortress, or migdol. The mortuary temple occupies the whole of the right-hand side of the photograph; the scanty remains outside the brick enclosure walls are those of the mortuary temple of Horemheb.

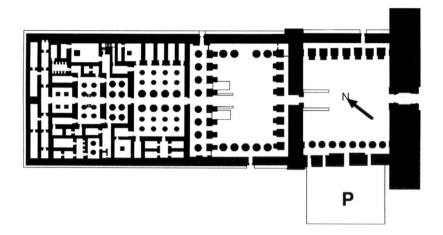

Fig. 102. Plan of Ramesses III's mortuary temple.

scenes of the king and his womenfolk engaged in leisure activities.

The temple itself conforms to the 'standard' New Kingdom temple design, with a series of pylons and courtyards leading to a set of pillared halls, and finally the sanctuaries (fig. 102). The First Pylon bears the usual 'smiting' scenes, and was formerly adorned with flagpoles, as were the portals of most temples. Together with the brightly-painted reliefs, such facades presented in former times an almost garish splendour, contrasting with their solemn aspect of today.

The First Court, beyond, is asymmetric, since its southern side formed the front wall of the palace that lay beyond, thus reflecting the plan of the Ramesseum, the temple of Merenptah, and other mortuary sanctuaries since Horemheb's time. The focus of this south wall is the 'Window of Appearances', at which the king made his official manifestation (*khau*) at festival-time. The palace was not intended for long-term occupation, rather as the king's lodging during the great festivals of Thebes, in particular the Opet and the Feast of the Valley. During the latter, Amun visited a whole range of West Bank sanctuaries, centring on Deir el-Bahari.

The opposite side of the courtyard is dominated by seven piers, each fronted by a colossal statue of the king (fig. 103); although wearing the *Atef* crown, the figures wear the dress of the living, and are thus not strictly osirid. The wall decoration features scenes showing the celebratory aftermath of battles depicted on the exterior of the temple, along with those referring to festivals that took place in the temple.

The Second Pylon bears 'historical' texts and scenes of captives. The Second Court to which it gives access is colonnaded on all four sides. Its

Fig. 103. The Second Pylon of the mortuary temple of Ramesses III, from the top of the First Pylon and showing the engaged staues that are a feature of only the right-hand side of the First Court.

walls, their colours protected by layers of whitewash applied by those who constructed a Coptic church in its midst, are in the vast majority of cases adorned with scenes of divine festivals. Principal amongst them are those of Min, the fertility god, and Sokar, the Memphite god of death.

The portico on the west side of the court is fronted by two rows of pillars, the outermost originally bearing engaged figures of the king as Osiris. The upper parts of its walls are decorated with scenes taken from the royal coronation ritual, but the lower sections contain almost mirror-image processions of the king's children, on either side of the doorway leading into the First Hypostyle Hall. This latter motif was explicitly copied from the Ramesseum; until the time of Ramesses II, depictions of royal children, and in particular sons, had been rare. A change of policy clearly came about early in the Nineteenth Dynasty, and such processions continue down to the early Twenty-first Dynasty.

The processions were carved during Ramesses III's reign, the children being depicted worshipping deep-cut cartouches of their father; label-texts were, however, only added in subsequent reigns. Ramesses IV inscribed his kingly cartouche below his princely titles; the rest seem to have been left untouched until after the accession of his brother, Ramesses VI, whose royal cartouches and former titles as king's son were placed on the next two figures. His still-living sibling, Sethhirkopshef, had the next figure on each side named for him, with junior and long-dead brothers commemorated by labels affixed to some of the remaining figures. However, some figures were never 'named', including all of those of the princes' sisters. The final addition to the procession occurred after Sethhirkopshef's accession as Ramesses VIII, when his cartouches were placed alongside his image.

Beyond the two open courts, the temple was essentially a roofed building, with rising floor and lowering ceiling levels, leading towards the Holy of Holies. However, this part of the building has suffered badly, and although some rooms survive, the principal (hypostyle) halls have been denuded down to the lowest drums of their supporting columns.

The First Hypostyle Hall had a series of small shrines along its northern side and in the south-west corner, apparently dedicated to deities including Ramesses III himself, Ptah, Sokar, and Amun-United-with-Eternity - i.e. of the Medinet Habu temple, the deified Ramesses II, and Montju.

The Second Hypostyle Hall gives access to the three principal cult-complexes of the temple. The left (south) set of rooms were dedicated to Osiris, and contain extensive scenes, including an astronomical ceiling. The northern complex belonged to Re-Harakhty, occupying the position allocated to the solar element of the royal mortuary temple since the early Eighteenth Dynasty. Like them, it included an altar open to the sky; the western end of this area had a single-columned portico.

The central complex had as its vestibule a third hypostyle hall. Small chapels were dedicated to manifestations of Horus and Amun, and also to the Great Ennead - Amun, Shu, Tefnut, Geb, Nut, Osiris, Isis, Seth and Nephthys, plus the later additions, Montju, Horus, Hathor, Sobk, Tjenenet and Iunyt. However, on the central axis of the temple was the sanctuary of Amun-Re himself, flanked by those of his consort, Mut, and their child, Khonsu, the focus of the whole monument. This entire rear section represents the ultimate completed development of the classic New Kingdom mortuary temple: some of Ramesses III's successors attempted to build a monument even larger, but were frustrated by life and circumstance.

The exterior of the building bears scenes almost exclusively depicting Ramesses III's physical prowess, either on the hunting field or in battle. Their sequence begins on the rear wall of the building, where one finds an account of a Nubian campaign. Then follows one of the most important series of war reliefs on an Egyptian temple. The northern exterior walls of the temple depict the campaigns in which the king defended Egypt from a succession of foreign aggressions. The first was against a Libyan coalition in Ramesses' fifth regnal year; the success of the action is shown by the huge piles of hands and penises - cut off enemy corpses by the Egyptians to keep tally.

The next set of reliefs depict the actions of three years later against the invasion of the 'Sea Peoples'. They had probably originated in the Aegean, and had effectively eliminated the states of the Hittites (Anatolia), northern Syria and Cyprus, before advancing against Egypt. A land battle in Palestine was followed by one on the sea, depicted in great detail, with the victory celebration and presentation of captives to Amun concluding the episode.

The series of battle scenes is brought to a close by those associated with a second Libyan war; these lie on the outside wall of the temple's first court, along with those showing attacks on certain north-Syrian strongholds. It has been questioned whether the latter recall real events, or stereotyped rehearsals of what an Egyptian king should do: they may be copied from earlier sources, an occurrence not unknown on Egyptian monuments.

The decoration of the southern exterior of the temple starts at the First Pylon with a series of scenes of the king hunting antelope, wild asses and bulls. Then, covering almost the whole length of the temple is a vast festival calendar, surmounted by figures of the king kneeling before various deities, each of which is identified with a specific locality. The whole ensemble is of the greatest importance for the study of the organization of Egyptian cults, listing as it does the various daily feasts and services celebrated in the temple, together with the offering involved on each occasion.

In parallel with the construction of Medinet Habu, work went ahead with the royal tomb. Most economically, Ramesses took over Sethnakhte's unfinished KV 11, replaced his father's cartouches where they appeared in its decoration, and pushed on into the hillside. Overall, the tomb is a logical enlargement of the tomb-type instigated by Merenptah. The main area of variance is the series of small chambers cut in the first and second corridors. These rooms are decorated in a manner alien to other royal tombs, beginning with the first pair, which respectively show the preparation of food and boats under sail. Those opening from the second corridor display a variety of motifs, including fecundity figures, militaria, jars of wine and produce (including imported Aegean vessels), the incarnations of Osiris and, best known, the images of harpists. The latter have been famous since their recording by James Bruce in 1768: the tomb was long known colloquially as 'Bruce's Tomb' or that 'of the Harpers'.

The division of the work within the tomb between Sethnakhte and Ramesses III is fairly difficult to establish, given the broad unity of the style. This is, of course, not surprising given the minimal probable gap between each monarch's work in the sepulchre. The painted relief is notable for the brilliant white background seen through the outer part of the tomb, contrasting with the more subdued impression given by most other tombs of the period. Its quality does not come up to that seen in earlier Ramesside tombs, but nevertheless provides excellent examples of the final state of the decorative compositions of that period. Succeeding tombs would see important changes in overall decorative scheme.

Thus, following from the Litany of Re in the outer corridors, the Book of *Amduat* is found in the stretch from the axis-shift to the well-room, scenes of the king and gods in the latter, the Book of Gates in the MLPH, and representations of the Opening of the Mouth in the passage leading to the twin antechambers. Unlike the outer parts of the tomb, which are very well preserved, the parts below the MLPH are in a very poor state, the result of flooding around the turn of the nineteenth century. Only fragments of the scenes on the walls of the passage, antechambers, massive pillared burial hall and rooms beyond survive, debris still littering the innermost parts.

A large granite sarcophagus was installed in the burial chamber, along the axis of the apartment, rather than across it, as had been standard practice since the early Eighteenth Dynasty. The only previous exception had been in KV 15, where the improvised sepulchral room had been too narrow to allow the sarcophagus to be placed athwart it. The new orientation would become standard.

The sarcophagus displays a number of features that do not fit easily into the sequence of such monuments during the middle Ramesside Period. Firstly, the coffer's external decoration (fig. 104) is entirely taken from the Sun-god's nocturnal journey, rather than employing the different motifs used on the sarcophagi of Ramesses III's immediate predecessors. Interestingly, these other motifs are, however, to be found inside the box: no internal decoration is to be found in other coffers of the period. Secondly, the sceptres grasped by the figure of the king on the upper surface of the lid are held vertically, contrasting once again with the arrangements on the monuments of Siptah and Sethnakhte. All these misfits also apply when comparing the sarcophagus of Ramesses III with that of his successor, Ramesses IV.

All of the exceptional features, however, are to be found on the sarcophagi of Merenptah, and it might be suggested that the sarcophagus represents the missing outer casing of Sethos II. The fact that, apart from its height, the dimensions of the sarcophagus of Ramesses III are smaller than those of Siptah and Sethnakhte's monuments, thus reversing the expected trend, would also favour such a placement. Indeed, the greater height could be explained by the presence of Sethos II's inner sarcophagus - an element not present in Siptah and Sethnakhte's assemblages. The coffer and lid were removed from KV 11 by Belzoni,

Fig. 104. Sarcophagus-coffer of Ramesses III.

the former now being in the Louvre, the latter in the Fitzwilliam Museum, Cambridge.

Some recently-identified fragments of calcite may represent what remains of Ramesses III's outer coffin, continuing the tradition, begun by Sethos I, of using this material. The badly battered trough of the inner coffin was found in KV 35, holding the mummy of Amenophis III. The violence of its former treatment had been such that the removal of the lid had torn the very sockets for the lid-tenons out of the edge of the trough. Decorated with precisely the same motifs as the cartonnage coffin of Sethnakhte, Ramesses III's is, however, carved from a single log of cedar, contrasting with the usual system of construction from separate planks. This allowed the particularly thin walls to be executed, overlaid with gilded stucco; as a contrast, the exterior divine figures were filled with coloured paste.

Aside from the work being carried out in KV 11, the necropolis workmen were also employed in the excavation of a series of tombs for some of the king's sons. Apart from one built in the Valley of the Kings (KV 3) - now anonymous - the others lay in the Valley of the Queens, and seem to have all been decorated at much the same time, early in Ramesses III's reign: a dedication text refers to the 'King's Children', rather than the specific tomb owner. Princes interred included Amenhirkopshef B (QV 55), Khaemwaset C (QV 44) and Prehirwenemef B (QV 42), all of whom predeceased their father. On the other hand, tombs also existed for the future Ramesses IV (QV 53) and Ramesses VIII (Sethhirkophsef C: QV 43).

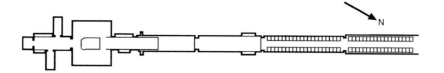

Fig. 105. Plan of the tomb of Ramesses IV, KV 2.

Ramesses III would appear to have been murdered as the result of a harim conspiracy, to judge from a number of surviving judicial documents. His mummy was restored in Year 13 of the reign of Smendes I of the Twenty-first Dynasty, and ultimately came to rest in TT 320. At some point, perhaps during its restoration, the mummy had become separated from its coffin, and was actually found inside a cartonnage case, in turn resting within the giant coffin of the Eighteenth Dynasty queen, Ahmes-Nefertiri.

The thirty-two year reign of Ramesses III was followed by the half-dozen of his son, Ramesses IV. The latter king's tomb (KV 2, fig. 105) has long been famous through the survival in the Turin Egyptian Museum of a damaged papyrus plan of the sepulchre, apparently produced for some ritual purpose: it is certainly not a constructor's working plan. This is made obvious by any close study of the tomb's design, which is certainly the result of a major attenuation of the traditional royal tomb plan: the burial chamber occupies the location of the intended MLPH. The beginning of the tomb had been delayed into the second regnal year, and the relatively advanced age of the king may have suggested some recasting of the design as time went by. There also seems to have been an increase in the size of the Deir el-Medina workforce, which may also have been intended to avoid the possibility of the tomb remaining unfinished.

As it was, haste and abbreviation may still be seen in the inner parts of the tomb, all of which are, however, decorated to a fairly good standard, on an unusually-yellow background. The arrangement of the decoration begins, as usual, at the entrance, with the Litany of Re. The third corridor, however, introduces a new Book of Caverns to the repertoire; the antechamber follows the tomb of the king's father in including the Book of the Dead, the burial chamber being adorned with the traditional Book of Gates.

The burial chamber is dominated by a gigantic granite sarcophagus, its decoration basically following late Nineteenth Dynasty patterns. The interior is shaped to receive the trough of the outer coffin of calcite, anciently reduced to fragments. This latter container is apparently mentioned in a Turin papyrus, along with wooden items being produced for the royal burial. Ramesses IV reverted to the employment of separate

126

canopic jars, after the long-time use of integral boxes by kings. His surviving vase, in Berlin, is one of the largest known, and it is possible that the set were buried in the floor of the chamber, two on each side of the sarcophagus, if the they followed the pattern seen in the later tomb of Ramesses VII. Otherwise, only a few shabtis and minor fragments have survived from the burial; the royal mummy ended up in TT 320.

The tomb of Ramesses IV is externally impressive, with a great entrance-way cut into the side of the hill that would have been almost impossible to conceal after the burial. In this, it marks a culmination of a trend that begins during the Nineteenth Dynasty, when there is a perceptible shift from the inconspicuous, easily hidden, tombs of the Eighteenth Dynasty. The latter may be seen generally to have been cut in odd corners of the Valley, sometimes under waterfalls, which would rapidly obliterate all trace of the sealed tomb. In contrast, there are indications that from the time of Ramesses II, royal sepulchre entrances were not necessarily buried after the interment, and by the latter part of the Twentieth Dynasty it is possible that 'pylons' of rubble were arranged to flank gateway-entrances that lay several metres above the contemporary ground level: today's tourist paths are bedded upon very great quantities of redistributed debris. The difficulty in hiding the entrances of these Ramesside tombs is shown that while the royal tombs down to and including Sethos I were all only revealed by archaeological investigation, later tombs (with the exception of Siptah's) have stood open since antiquity.

The tombs seem to have been closed by simple wooden doors, no evidence of the sealed blockings found in earlier tombs being present in those of Ramesses II and his successors. Indeed, Catharine Roehrig has suggested that the doors of royal tombs may have been on occasion opened ceremonially subsequent to the burial. In this situation, the security of the tombs will have relied paradoxically on their visibility, and the reliability of the necropolis police - the latter perhaps an unwise approach in the troubled times of the late Twentieth Dynasty.

The situation concerning Ramesses IV's mortuary temple is somewhat complex, since three unfinished structures have revealed the king's names. Two lie in the area of the lower end of the causeways leading up to the temples of Deir el-Bahari (the Asasif). Of one, found by Howard Carter, only two column bases and a single foundation deposit survived. Ramesses IV changed his prenomen in his second year, and the use of both forms in the deposit allow it to be dated around the change - incidentally, also approximately the time of the foundation of the royal tomb.

The second temple lies some way to the south, the plan of a huge forecourt, second court and fronting pylons being recovered by Winlock in

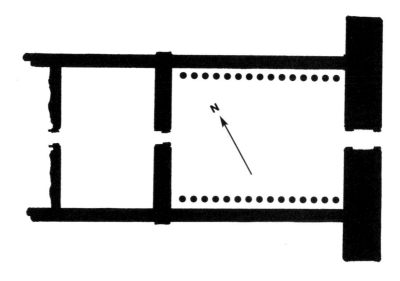

Fig. 106. The unfinished Ramesside temple on the Asasif, begun by Ramesses IV, continued by his successors, but never finished.

1913 and Ambrose Lansing in 1934-5. The intended temple (fig. 106) was one and a half times the size of Ramesses III's Medinet Habu edifice, and on the evidence of the foundation deposits had been laid out by Ramessess IV in the latter part of his reign. Little of the structure remained, and what did yielded only the names of Ramesses V and VI. The latter had clearly taken over their predecessor's unfinished monument, which had not progressed far above ground level.

Yet a third mortuary temple was begun just south-west of the by-now demolished mortuary temple of Amenophis III. Its scanty remains have never been excavated, but its modest dimensions suggest that it could have been completed to serve as the cult-centre of Ramesses IV that we know to have functioned soon after his death. One might speculate that the decision to abandon the gigantic Asasif temple coincided with one to scale down the royal tomb, to ensure that a complete burial complex was available to the king.

As just noted, Ramesses V, the son and successor of Ramesses IV, took over his father's unfinished mortuary temple, most probably with the intention of making it into his own memorial. He also began a large tomb in the Valley of the Kings, now numbered KV 9 (fig. 107). The basic plan followed tradition, but was cut short not far beyond the well-room, which is the last part of the tomb to originally display the king's cartouches: from the evidence of his mummy, it has been suggested that the fifth Ramesses' demise in the fourth year of his reign was caused by smallpox. The

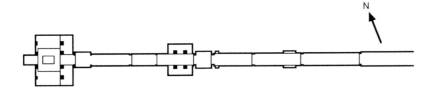

N

Fig. 107. Plan of the tomb of Ramesses V/VI, KV 9.

decorative scheme thus far shows a number of changes from previous examples, since instead of an extensive Litany of Re and extracts from the *Amduat*, the area decorated by Ramesses V is dominated by the Book of Gates, along with the recently-introduced Book of Caverns and the wholly-fresh Book of the Heavens. A fundamental change in thinking had obviously occurred, and heralds a series of tombs that appreciably diverge from earlier-Ramesside norms.

Such a premature royal death had previously usually resulted in an attenuation of the tomb, and the construction of an improvised burial chamber for the funeral. However, in this case (as with Ramesses III *vis à vis* Sethnakhte), the unfinished sepulchre was appropriated by the next king, a son of Ramesses III named Amenhirkopshef (C), usually known as Ramesses VI. A record survives on an ostracon of the interment of Ramesses V in his successor's second regnal year when 'Sekheperenre [Ramesses V] reached the West of Thebes in burial'. The delay in the funeral can only be explained by Ramesses VI's take-over of KV 9, and the consequent need to prepare a new tomb for the late monarch. This sepulchre, presumably fairly modest, has never been identified, although it almost certainly lay in the Valley of the Kings: there are a number of small tombs there which have never been completely cleared. In any case, the royal mummy was ultimately deposited in KV 35.

It is possible that other members of the royal family died in the same putative smallpox outbreak, since documentary evidence exists for six burials taking place at short notice in the Valley of the Queens. All this, and other possible problems, seem to have led to a considerable delay in starting Ramesses VI's own work in the Valley of the Kings.

His continuation of KV 9, beginning well into Year 2, carried on the revised decorative scheme initiated by his predecessor. All cartouches of Ramesses V were filled with plaster and re-cut for the new king; the old names are readable in places where the later filling has dropped out. The first chamber decorated from the outset by Ramesses VI was the MLPH, which contained extracts from the Books of the Gates and the Caverns, rather than the previously-expected series of depictions of the king and the gods; its ceiling bore astronomical representations, which had also been applied to the outer corridors as well. In earlier tombs, only the burial chamber had played host to such decoration. Moving deeper into the sepulchre, the *Amduat* occupied the walls of the passages leading into the antechamber: these had usually borne scenes of the Opening of the Mouth ritual. Although the antechamber followed the pattern of the immediately preceding royal tombs in containing the Book of the Dead, the burial hall is adorned with the Book of the Earth, previously only found on the sarcophagi of Siptah and following kings.

The hall, although entirely decorated, is unfinished, the rear row of columns not having been released from the matrix, and the rearmost parts of the chamber never begun. The exact form of the sarcophagus in the centre of the room is unclear: while clearly cartouche-shaped, the great box that lies there broken could be explained either as the coffer, or an extremely deep lid, once placed over a cutting in the floor - as was certainly the case in the next royal tomb. Whichever arrangement had been adopted, a greywacke anthropoid coffin, decorated with the Book of the Earth, like the calcite example of Siptah, had been placed within. This was smashed to fragments, the head of the lid now being in the British Museum, with the remainder still in the tomb.

The interest of KV 9, easily the most complete and best preserved of the later Ramesside royal tombs, is increased by the survival on a Turin Papyrus of what seems to have been the work-plan drawn up on Ramesses VI's appropriation of the sepulchre. Various dimensions are given, and from these it has been deduced that the intention seems to have been to create the largest of all royal tombs, with nearly 30 cubic metres of stone to be extracted by each working crew each day for 348 days a year. However, the effective loss of a year's working time at the outset led to the need to recast the plan; as we have already seen, at the king's death in his eighth regnal year, work had to be cut short.

The tomb was robbed early, within a generation or so of the interment, with an associated trial datable to Ramesses XI's reign. It is probable that thieves gained entry from the neighbouring tomb KV 12, which had been accidently penetrated by the quarrymen when excavating the corridor leading into the antechamber. Thus, while the necropolis police kept watch over the sealed gateway of the tomb, material was being removed surreptitiously deep underground: indeed, some shabtis of Ramesses VI were found outside the entrance to KV 12, where they had doubtless been discarded by robbers, leaving with more precious loot. In this, or later, robberies, the royal mummy suffered particularly severely, being largely dismembered, and rewrapped only with difficulty in the Twenty-first Dynasty. Little more than the legs were in their correct anatomical position, the whole facial skeleton had been broken away, and

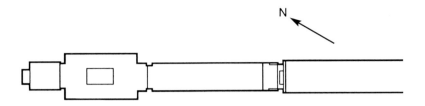

Fig. 108. Plan of the tomb of Ramesses VII, KV 1.

pieces of other bodies were found amongst the remains. So bad was its state that a piece of the king's broken coffin had had to be employed to hold the whole thing together. The sorry corpse was found in the tomb of Amenophis II, in a reused mid-Eighteenth Dynasty coffin.

A reign of under eight years was also the fate of the next pharaoh, Ramesses VII Itamun. By his accession, the central area of the Valley of the Kings was evidently becoming crowded, resulting in his sepulchre, KV 1, being constructed some way outside, beyond the site of Ramesses IV's tomb. As it stands today, it is one of the smallest of all the royal tombs (fig. 108). However, the dimensions of the entrance corridor show that it was intended to be as imposing as any other tomb of the Twentieth Dynasty.

The first corridor imitates KV 9 in containing elements from the books of the Gates and the Caverns, but instead of leading into a further corridor it opens directly into the vaulted burial chamber. The latter is long and relatively narrow, and is very clearly a lateral expansion of the intended second corridor: this may be observed from the better finish of the floor along the central axis. The room's decoration features the Book of the Earth, once again showing its affinity with KV 9, the tomb of Ramesses VII's father. A rear chamber may have originally been the start of the intended third corridor.

The sarcophagus arrangements comprise a cutting in the bedrock of the tomb 2.6 metres long, covered by a very deep lid, decorated in paint and relief. A hole had been cut in the foot of this cover by plunderers, who had evidently destroyed the contained coffins and mummy, since no trace of them has ever come to light. The lack of any elements attributable to a stone outer coffin, in spite of a careful clearance by Edwin Brock in 1983/4 and 1994, would suggest that such an item had now been abandoned.

An interesting feature of the sarcophagus arrangements is the fact that two niches are to be found flanking the coffer-cut on each side, just outside the perimeter of the lid. It seems very likely that these will have contained the canopic jars, a supposition possibly supported by the depiction of the four canopic genii on the adjacent surfaces of the sarcophagus lid. Nothing of the vases was recovered, but the pieces of a

Fig 109. The tomb of Prince Montjuhirkopshef (KV 19), showing the location of the Eighteenth Dynasty tombs of Tuthmosis I/Hatshepsut (KV 20) and Tuthmosis IV (KV 43).

number of shabti figures were recovered from the debris. A number of these came from so-called 'lost contour' shabtis, formed of summarily shaped pieces of calcite and decorated in wax paints. These crude images are ubiquitous in mid Twentieth Dynasty royal tombs, and supplemented the other, often very fine, figures that formed other parts of the outfit.

The enigma of the Valley of the Kings in the Twentieth Dynasty is the burial place of the final son of Ramesses III to occupy the throne, Ramesses VII's successor, Ramesses VIII Sethhirkopshef. Nothing deriving from his interment has ever come to light, and it has been questioned whether he was even buried away from Thebes, at the end of a reign which seems to have lasted only months. On the other hand, no fewer than two tombs have been attributed to him as a prince. One is in the Valley of the Queens, and dates like the other princely tombs there to the earlier part of Ramesses III. Numbered QV 43, it is very similar to the sepulchres of his siblings, and contains the usual scenes of Ramesses III introducing his son to the gods, albeit badly blackened by smoke.

The other tomb lies in the Valley of the Kings, and has only recently been recognized as having been initially decorated for a Prince Sethhirkopshef. Numbered KV 19 (fig. 109); it was discovered by Belzoni, and contains some of the finest paintings known from the Ramesside Period, depicting a prince together with various deities. The label-texts name a Prince Montjuhirkopshef, dated to the reign of Ramesses IX by the latter's cartouche being an integral part of the detail decoration of one of

132

the divine figures in the tomb. However, Brock has now noticed that the dedicatory text on the exterior doorjambs originally named Sethhirkopshef, the Seth-animal having been partially erased and replaced by the falcon of Montju. It would thus appear that the tomb was begun by Sethhirkopshef, but then taken over by Montjuhirkopshef before much of the decoration had been executed. KV 19 must then have been granted to Sethhirkopshef late in his princely career, when as the last surviving son of Ramesses III he had become the 'elder statesman' of the realm, and had 'outgrown' his juvenile Queens' Valley sepulchre.

When he succeeded Ramesses VII, it is possible that he intended to continue with KV 19, given that it lay in the royal valley, and that its dimensions were already commensurate with a pharaoh's burial place. However, no trace of a kingly decoration may be seen, and it may be that another tomb was begun - most probably continued after his demise by one of Ramesses VIII's successors. In any case, the brevity of Ramesses VIII's reign makes it impossible that any kind of true pharaonic tomb can have been prepared sufficiently to contain his burial. On this basis, unless he were buried away from Thebes, some small, improvised, tomb will have had to suffice; in this case, and since not a single fragment has ever been found, it is not impossible that Ramesses VIII's mummy still rests undisturbed somewhere in the Valley of the Kings.

Ramesses IX may have been a nephew of his predecessor, perhaps the son of the Prince Montjuhirkopshef who had been buried in KV 13. His tomb (KV 6, fig. 110) lies opposite KV 9, marking a return to the central area of the Biban el-Moluk. It is possible that it represents a continuation of a beginning made by Ramesses VIII. Although the king's reign lasted for nineteen years, only the first two corridors had been plastered eighteen years in, with only the first of them decorated in extremely fine-quality relief. This comprised the Litany of Re, together with the beginning of the Book of Caverns.

At this point, a major change in the planned decorative scheme took place, with elements of the Book of the Dead introduced. However, shortly afterwards, the king died and the remainder of the tomb was decorated in a great hurry, probably during the two and a half months occupied by the

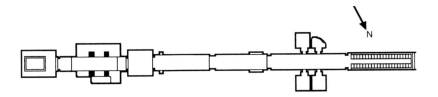

Fig. 110. Plan of the tomb of Rameses IX, KV6.

king's embalming. The scheme adopted for this work differed from either of the earlier plans, and also in many details from that seen in the preceding royal tombs. As may be expected from the haste with which the tomb was finished off, the quality of the decoration of the inner parts of the tomb fell far short of that in the outer corridors,

Architecturally, the tomb is fairly standard, most notably resurrecting the small chambers opening off of the first corridor otherwise found in Ramesses III's KV 11, although without their decoration. The first room on the right is unfinished, possibly because the quarrymen had heard an echo that suggested another tomb was near. By the Ramesside Period, the central area of the Valley of the Kings was becoming distinctly crowded, as the collisions between KV 10 and 11, 47 and 32, and 9 and 12 attest. As a matter of fact, the rear part of KV 55 lies directly below the first elements of KV 6. It seems probable that this inadvertent rediscovery of the Amarna tomb's location lay behind its final ancient opening, and an attempt to remove some of its remaining contents.

The burial chamber is yet another example of an enlargement of what had been intended to be a corridor. The precise form of the royal interment is uncertain, since the two-stepped cutting in the floor is surely far too large ever to have been covered by a stone lid of the kind seen in KV 1. In fact, no trace of any stone covering or container has ever been found associated with the tomb. Some wooden runners, found by Georges Daressy when he cleared the tomb in 1888, may come from a wooden sarcophagus, although little else has been identified. A number of shabtis are known, along with a life-size 'guardian' wooden statue of the king, removed by Henry Salt in the 1820s and now in the British Museum. This doubtless once stood at the entrance to the burial chamber, together with a now-vanished partner.

The king's body is the latest of the surviving New Kingdom royal mummies, being found in TT 320 in coffins originally made for Nesikhonsu, wife of the Twenty-first dynasty High Priest of Amun, Pinudjem II. It was apparently under Ramesses IX that the depredations of robbers around the Theban necropolis first reached crisis levels. A series of papyri - in particular P. Ambras, Leopold II-Amherst, Harris A, and Mayer A and B - provide the basis for a reconstruction of events during the reign, in particular the sixteenth regnal year.

Following various rumours of robbery, a commission was appointed to inspect parts of the Theban necropolis. Ten royal tombs in the el-Tarif/Dira Abu'l-Naga/Deir el-Bahari area were examined, of which two showed signs of attempted penetration, and one - that of Sobkemsaf I of the Seventeenth Dynasty - had been robbed and the royal mummies burnt. Furthermore, the sepulchres of two priestesses of Amun and many lesser individuals had also been thoroughly rifled. Forty-five persons were arrested, tortured, and after confessing, brought to trial. The trials' records provide much information concerning legal proceedings during that era, as well as some vivid accounts of the tomb robbers' experiences while breaking into sealed royal sepulchres. The punishment of the guilty was harsh: for violating a royal tomb a man could be impaled. The investigation seems to have been complicated by a feud between Paser and Paweraa, Mayors of Eastern and Western Thebes, respectively: when the number of robberies appeared to be less than alleged by Paser, he was tried and convicted of malicious exaggeration!

Making an example of the robbers did not stem the tide of robbery. Only a year later, there are records of thefts from sepulchres from the Valley of the Queens, notably that of Queen Iset, wife of Ramesses III, whose burial (QV 51) was wrecked: her smashed sarcophagus still lies in the burial chamber. The papyri continue to recount similar incidents through the reigns of Ramesses X and XI, while dockets on royal mummies record a series of peregrinations beginning in Ramesses XI's last years. Despite all efforts to staunch the flow of tomb robbing, the increasing number of robberies led to the need to continually restore the burials that were still worth saving. By the Twenty-first Dynasty, the pressure was such that the maintenance of individual tombs was increasingly abandoned in favour of caches, where groups of bodies could be brought together in remote locations for protection. This was accompanied by the salvage of items of funerary equipment - particularly if gilded - for recycling. The most important caches were those of royal mummies, the most significant of which, TT 320 near Deir el-Bahari, took its final form in the reign of Shoshenq I of the Twenty-second Dynasty.

The successor of Ramesses IX, the tenth king of the name, is particularly obscure, the very length of his reign being uncertain, although it seems most likely that it occupied little more than three years. His tomb (KV 18) was also long a mystery, since it has been blocked beyond the first part of its second corridor since at least 1739. Examination was greatly hindered by the tomb's long use as home to the Valley of the Kings electric generator. However, work by the University of Berne in 1998-9 finally began the removal of the flood debris, revealing that the tomb was never finished, ending in a quarry-face in the second corridor. Nevertheless, decoration had been begun, figures of the king appearing just inside the entrance, the pharaoh also being shown before Re-Harakhty a little further on. This scheme seems to be similar to that planned for the tomb of Ramesses XI, the two tombs thus forming a distinct unit. Unfortunately, most of the detail is concealed by a thick

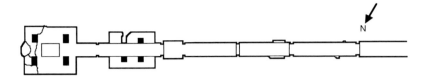

Fig. 111. Plan of KV 4, the tomb of Ramesses XI.

whitewash layer that was applied over the carvings at an as-yet-undetermined point in the past.

In addition, the conventional sun-disc and supporting figures were carved over the tomb doorway. Although in good condition in the early nineteenth century, it is now in a bad state, partly through staining by the exhaust of the old oil engine that drove the generator. No trace of royal funerary equipment has yet been found in the debris within the tomb, and combined with the sepulchre's unfinished state it seems clear that Ramesses X was not buried in the tomb, and may have been interred away from Thebes.

The next tomb, of Ramesses XI, last king of the dynasty (KV 4, fig. 111), is fully accessible, but incomplete. Sketched decoration is restricted to a conventional lintel and the first corridor. On the both walls one finds the king (fig. 112), followed by his image in a kiosk before Amun-Re-Harakhti (left) and the goddess of the West, the home of the dead (right). There is a north/south iconography employed in the depiction of the clothing of the king in this scene, which may also be present in KV 18. Beyond the kiosk scenes, guidelines suitable for eight columns of text have been laid out, perhaps to accommodate the section of the Litany of Re found in just this spot in the tomb of Ramesses IX.

No other decorative work seems to have been done under Ramesses XI, and a considerable amount of what little was done has been lost by the disappearance of plaster in many places, and the catastrophic expansion of a natural rock joint on the left wall, largely destroying the image of Re-Harakhty. This must have occurred during the tomb's construction, or shortly afterwards, since less than two decades after Ramesses XI's death the damaged area was drawn in a restored duplicate by the priest-king Pinudjem I, just a short way to the right, with the latter's names substituted for Ramesses'.

It has been suggested that this rock expansion was part of a complex of structural difficulties that led to the tomb's abandonment. Certainly, the unfinished state of the tomb is most odd, given that Ramesses XI's reign lasted for nearly three decades. One assumes that the tomb will have been begun soon after the king's accession, in which case, unless interruptions supervened, work was been halted within ten years. On the other hand,

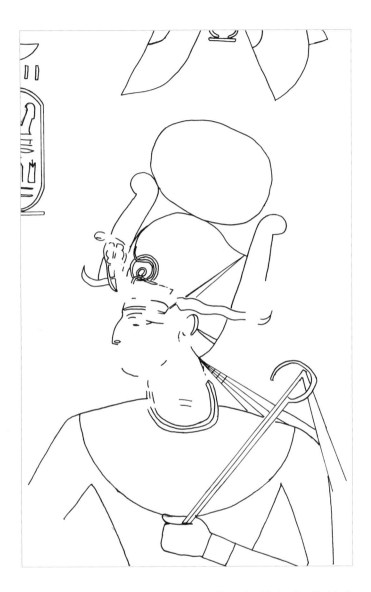

Fig. 112. Upper part of an unfinished figure of Ramesses XI, on the right-hand wall of the first corridor of his tomb. Note the unusual combination of the blue crown, horns, feathers and sun disc.

there is ample evidence for problems and conflict in the Theban area during the latter part of the Twentieth Dynasty, which led to the abandonment of the workmen's village at Deir el-Medina, in favour of residence at Medinet Habu: this could have contributed to the lack of progress. A final factor is that by the end of the Ramesside Period the pharaoh was firmly resident in the north, thus reducing any personal royal interest in the progress of the tomb.

When terminated, the entire plan of the tomb had been excavated, although the inner parts were decidedly rough, with certain elements not fully detached from the matrix, in particular in the margins of the two pillared halls. Masons' debris still lie in the tomb, and various workmen's tools have been found among them. The 'well' had not been cut, but in the centre of the burial chamber is a large shaft, 12 metres deep. That it was contemporary with the tomb's construction is shown by the discovery at its corners of foundation deposits of Ramesses XI, including a statuette of the king and the goddess Maet, two groups of baboons, all in beeswax, three mud baboons, and more conventional plaques of faience and gold with the king's cartouches.

From its position, the shaft would logically have been intended to contain the royal body: if filled with stone and carefully concealed, it might have afforded the mummy useful protection. However, it is clear that the shaft had never been finished, nor used for a primary burial. Nevertheless, when cleared by John Romer in 1979, large quantities of material were recovered, all deposited during the Third Intermediate Period. Apart from the partly-burned debris of a Twenty-second Dynasty cartonnage mummy case and coffin from an intrusive burial, most items derived from New Kingdom royal burials.

All were fragmentary, and included pieces of funerary statuettes, debris of other wooden items, and gilded gesso, chopped from the surface of anthropoid coffins. Some elements can be joined to objects found elsewhere - for example a wooden foot to a statuette of a goose, found in the tomb of Tuthmosis III - or have links with other known material. Accordingly, some of the gesso may be attributable to a coffin of Tuthmosis III, and a piece of wood certainly came from a coffin or item of furniture belonging to Hatshepsut. This would seem to imply that KV 4 was in some way employed as a workshop during the Twenty-first Dynasty, when most of the Theban royal burials were dismantled in the wake of the epidemic of tomb robbery that characterised the late Twentieth Dynasty. The details of this use remain for the present uncertain.

Since KV 4 was certainly not used for his burial, the actual tomb of Ramesses XI, the very last of the Ramesside royal line, is wholly unknown. The most likely location for it may be Tell el-Daba/Qantir, the location of Piramesse, the Delta residence-city founded by Ramesses II, and increasingly used during the later part of the Ramesside Period. In favour of this is the fact that by the last decade of Ramesses XI's reign, Thebes was essentially a state-within-a-state, initially occupied by the ultimately-renegade Viceroy of Nubia, and then by the military regime that had been charged with dislodging him. Combining military rank with the High Priesthood of Amun, the General Hrihor assumed quasi-royal titles in the last years of Ramesses' reign.

Accordingly, Ramesses XI may well have been interred in a built tomb sunk in the ground within the precincts of the temple of Amun at Piramesse. Such sepulchres are common in the Delta cities, where the flat, alluvial terrain was unsuited to deep and/or rock cut tombs. They would become standard for the kings that followed Ramesses XI on the throne, who would make the Delta city of Tanis (San el-Hagar) the new political and religious capital of Egypt. Any chance of finding the tomb of Ramesses XI is probably doomed by the large-scale robbing of the site for building stone in subsequent years, most of Tanis' later buildings being constructed from blocks recovered from Piramesse.

VII   Delta Finale

Ramesses XI's successor to the crown of the pharaohs was Smendes, formerly the governor of Tanis, the port associated with Piramesse. He seems to have been a son-in-law of the last Ramesside, and is regarded as the founder of Manetho's Twenty-first Dynasty. However, power in the south of Egypt lay in the hands of the latest of the soldier-priests, another royal son-in-law, High Priest Pinudjem I; later in Smendes' reign, the latter was to assume full royal titles, and sire a pharaoh of the whole of Egypt.

In view of the effective separation of Thebes, Smendes abandoned the Valley of the Kings as the royal burial place: after four and a half centuries no more pharaohs were to be laid to rest in that hallowed wadi. Instead, a fresh royal necropolis was established at Tanis, the new capital. Since it was not possible there to tunnel deep galleries into rock, the tombs, built from masonry, were sunk just below the surface within the

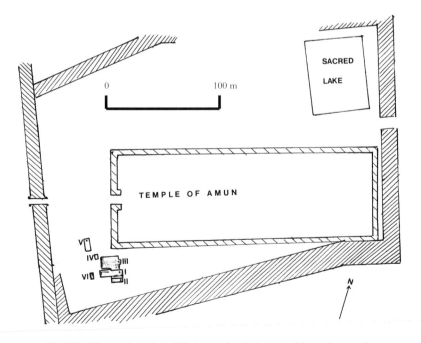

Fig. 113. The temple-precinct of Tanis, showing the location of the royal necropolis.

Fig. 114. The tomb of Psusennes I, NRT III.

enclosure of the Great Temple of Amun (fig. 113). Here, it was also perhaps hoped that the regular passage of temple staff nearby would help safeguard the tombs, as the Theban tombs' remoteness had not. The concept of burial in a temple precinct was well-established in the Delta; for example the necropolis of Bubastis lies close to the temple of the cat-goddess, Bastet.

That this stratagem had partial success was revealed in 1939-40, when Pierre Montet uncovered six royal tombs and, although five had been wrecked by thieves, found that all retained much equipment, and that one was still intact. No tomb preserved the name of the dynasty's founder, but the purchase at the beginning of the Second World War of one of his canopic jars in the vicinity suggests that he was buried there. This jar is now in the Metropolitan Museum of Art, New York. A second jar also emerged onto the antiquities market more recently, and is currently in the Aubert Collection in Paris. These jars are unusual in having wholly-unique texts upon them.

That Smendes' tomb was once the tomb now numbered NRT I, found decorated by Osorkon II of the next dynasty, seems quite probable, since it is clear that the basic structure had been built before the neighbouring tomb of Psusennes I (NRT III), Smendes' second successor: part of the north wall of NRT I had been cut back to make room for Psusennes' monument. That Smendes' burial had been cleared out by robbers, leaving his tomb for reuse some two centuries later is by no means unlikely, with ample parallels in the Egyptian tomb record.

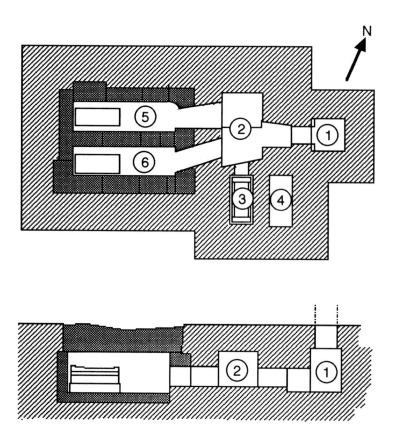

Fig. 115. Plan and section of the tomb of Psusennes I.

After a reign of some twenty-five years, Smendes was succeeded briefly by one Amenemnesu, and then by Pasebakhaniut, son of Pinudjem I of Thebes, and better known by the Greek form of his name, Psusennes. A gold bow-cap bearing the names of him and Amenemnesu may suggest a brief co-regency between the two kings. While Amenemnesu's burial-place remains an enigma, Psusennes I's Tanite tomb was almost unbelievably found intact (figs. 114, 115). Probably once surmounted by a brick chapel, the tomb is built largely of limestone, with the exceptions of two granite burial chambers. Entry was by way of a shaft (1) at the eastern end of the tomb, which leads into an antechamber (2), decorated in relief.

On the north and west walls, processions of genii surmount scenes of the king offering to Osiris and Isis, while on the east, Psusennes offers to Re-Harakhty, above which scene are to be found a series of demons. In the south wall, a doorway surrounded by bands of texts leads to a chamber almost completely filled with a sarcophagus intended for the king's son,

142

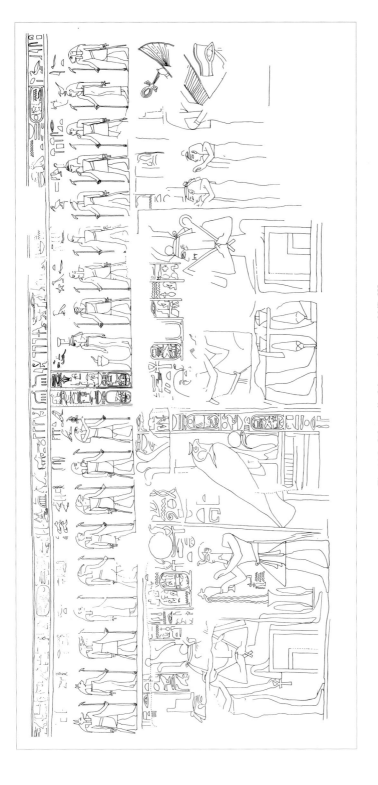

Fig. 116. West wall of the antechamber of NR III.

The blocks either side of the crowned hawk concealed the entrances to the two main burial chambers, the right-hand preserving the original scene of Psusennes I, offering to Osiris. The left-hand one, however, covering the doorway into the intended burial chamber of Mutnodjmet, has been replaced by one (re?)cut with a figure of Amenemopet, its ultimate occupant.

Fig. 117. The sarcophagus of Psusennes I. It had been made for Merenptah, but was removed from his tomb to Tanis in the Twenty-first Dynasty.

Ankhefenmut (3); this was evidently never used, the prince's disgrace being suggested by the erasure of his figures, names and titles from the walls of his chamber, where he had been depicted adoring the gods. Directly to the east lies another chamber, completely embedded in masonry and accessible only from above (4). Here was found the untouched burial of the General Wendjebaendjed, lying inside granite, gilded wood and silver coffins, a gold mask on his face. On the walls of the chamber, the favoured courtier is to be found doing homage to Osiris, Harakhty and Apis. The granite coffin had been made for a Nineteenth Dynasty Theban official, Amunhotpe, and like many such items found at Tanis, had been salvaged from a plundered tomb for re-use in the north.

Two concealed doorways in the west wall of the antechamber, sealed with granite plugs and then covered with limestone reliefs (fig. 116), lead to a pair of parallel chambers, prepared for Psusennes himself (5) and his wife, Mutnodjmet (6). The king was found just as the priests had left him nearly three thousand years before: his four canopic jars, and the debris of their chest, lay at the foot of the sarcophagus, together with shabtis, whose boxes had decayed in the humidity of the tomb, vessels of metal and stone, and the skeleton of an animal, whether a sacrifice or a pet. On the rear wall of the chamber, the dead king is depicted as a mummy, surveying his offerings. The great granite sarcophagus had been taken from the Theban tomb of Merenptah, dead for two centuries (fig. 117), while a black granite coffin found within proved likewise second-hand. However, the coffin which lay within this had been made for its king, beaten from solid silver; while in no way comparable in workmanship with Tutankhamun's gold coffin, it is still a fine piece of work, and shows that the ancient rishi pattern

Fig.118. Gold mummy-mask of Psusennes I.

still remained in royal use, six centuries after its introduction in the Second Intermediate Period, and nearly five centuries after its abandonment by private individuals. Within lay Psusennes' mummy, equipped with a gold mask (fig. 118) and cover and bedecked with jewellery. Unfortunately, the damp, inevitable in the wet Delta, had reduced the mummy to a mere skeleton, though enough remained to reveal that the very aged king had spent his last years a pitiful cripple, wracked with arthritis.

His wife, however, had not been permitted to sleep through the ages with her husband. Anciently, she had been evicted and replaced by Psusennes I's successor, Amenemope. This monarch had apparently been buried, after less than ten years on the throne, in NRT IV, a small tomb of but one chamber just to the west of that of his probable father, but seems to have been moved within a short while. One would assume that Queen Mutnodjmet's mummy and coffin were removed from her chamber, and Amenemope's coffins and equipment emplaced. The breach in the wall of the antechamber was filled with blocks carved with a scene of the king designed to fit in with Psusennes' old decoration. His name replaced the queen's on the lid of her sarcophagus and on her chamber's wall, where it now incongruously accompanies Mutnodjmet's carved female figure. Remains of a coffin found in Amenemope's old tomb would suggest that the queen was reburied there.

Once reinterred, Amenemope remained undisturbed until the chamber was opened by Montet. The burial was less rich than Psusennes', his coffin being of gilded wood, rather than silver, and a rather inferior gold mask covered the decayed mummy's face. Outside the sarcophagus lay the canopic jars and other vessels, along with the remains of a gilded coffin, with Amenemope's name, perhaps too large to fit into the borrowed sarcophagus, much as seems to have been the case when the attempt was made to place the outer coffin of Tuthmosis I in an old sarcophagus of Hatshepsut (see pp. 35-37, above).

Three other kings also found refuge in Psusennes' rather crowded sepulchre. In the antechamber lay three coffins; two of gilded wood, were totally disintegrated, but the third, a magnificent silver example, was largely intact. The wooden coffins contained the utterly decayed remains of bodies; one was pronounced that of a woman in 1939, but since both coffins seem to have worn the kingly nemes and a uraeus, this seems unlikely. One burial had an outer and inner coffin, but no trace of names survived. Between them, they possessed five canopic jars, all borrowed and bearing different names, together with shabti figures. The latter bore the names of Kings Siamun and Psusennes, thus making it most likely that these sad remains represent those of the last monarchs of the Twenty-first Dynasty. The silver coffin belongs to the Twenty-second Dynasty, and will be discussed later. Also in the antechamber were decayed wooden royal statues, clearly referrable to Psusennes' funerary equipment.

As already noted, during the reign of Smendes the Theban High Priest of Amun, Pinudjem I, obtained royal titles. He is accordingly found represented in full pharaonic regalia, and at one point may have contemplated burial in the Valley of the Kings. As seen in the previous chapter, a damaged scene and accompanying text in the unused tomb of Ramesses XI were copied, with Pinudjem's cartouches substituted, onto an adjacent wall. The form of the prenomen cartouche clearly dates the scene to the very first year or two of Pinudjem I's kingship. The whole exercise would seem to indicate an intention to finish the tomb for the priest-king's own use.

That the scene was no more than sketched, with no other work apparently carried out, points to any such plan being abandoned at an early stage. The idea of reusing existing monument(s) in putting the royal burial together was continued, however. Thus, the four hundred year old outer coffin of Tuthmosis I (fig. 26) was decorated anew in the contemporary style, to contain Pinudjem's mummy and adorning mummy-board.

Why a coffin of Tuthmosis I was taken over is uncertain, but must have been due to something more than expediency. Although some members of the high-priestly family used coffins originally made for others, these were simple cases of erasing one name and substituting a new one, rather than the laborious complete re-work to be seen on the Tuthmosis/Pinudjem coffin. An explanation may be a desire for a physical link with a valued element of the past: there are a number of earlier instances of reuse which can only be explained against such a background. The choice of Tuthmosis I's coffin in particular may have been prompted by two factors. The first could simply be that, desirous of an ancient coffin, Pinudjem I found that of Tuthmosis vacant and thus eminently suitable: Tuthmosis I's mummy is one of the few Eighteenth Dynasty kingly ones that seem to be missing. Secondly, and perhaps more significantly, Pinudjem seems to have felt a particular affection for the Tuthmosids: he named a son for Tuthmosis III (Menkheperre) and a daughter for Hatshepsut (Maetkare).

Pinudjem's primary burial-place remains unknown; the same is true for the other representatives of the Theban military/pontifical family of the earlier Twenty-first Dynasty. Romer has put forward reasons for placing them in the little-explored southern wadis at Thebes, and it is suggestive that no trace of the funerary equipment of many of the High Priests have yet come to light. However, the coffins and mummies of Pinudjem I and his elder son, the High Priest Masaharta, were found in the TT 320 cache, badly battered and clearly disturbed in their first resting place(s).

TT 320 had actually been (re)founded as the tomb of the High Priest Pinudjem II (grandson of Pinudjem I) and his family, and had been

Fig. 119. The canopic chest of Shoshenq I.

appropriated as a cache after the end of the Twenty-first Dynasty. Earlier, a number of caches had been set up in the Valley of the Kings and elsewhere, before further robbery and concentration had brought the majority of fugitive mummies together in Pinudjem II's spacious grave soon after Year 10 of Shoshenq I of the Twenty-second Dynasty.

Amenemope was followed on the throne by a king of Libyan extraction, Osokhor, only known from two fragmentary inscriptions at Karnak, and then by Siamun, whose two decades of rule are among the best attested of his dynasty. It was in his reign that many of the transfers of royal mummies took place, although not at this stage to TT 320, as was thought prior to Nicholas Reeves' work on the subject. It has been generally assumed that Siamun was followed as king by Psusennes II, who had served him as High Priest of Amun, but it now seems likely that Psusennes never ruled alone, like his great-grandfather, Pinudjem I, being only joint-king with a Tanite monarch. In this case, the latter was Shoshenq I, a nephew of Osokhor. As we have seen, Psusennes II was apparently eventually buried at Tanis in NRT III.

Shoshenq's reign featured a reassertion of Egypt's international position, a major campaign in Palestine being perhaps remembered in the Book of Kings, which relates how 'Shishak, King of Egypt' forced the surrender of the treasures of King Solomon's temple. Shoshenq I's tomb remains unidentified, but not so some of its contents. The most impressive is his calcite canopic chest, now in Berlin (fig. 119). It came to the museum from the collection of Julius Isaac in 1891, indicating the discovery and plundering of his tomb during the nineteenth century. It is the only stone canopic chest known to have been made since the time of Siptah, and follows the naos-form of the New Kingdom examples. The decoration is, however, rather coarser and somewhat differently arranged: instead of bending around the corners, the goddesses occur in pairs on each face, and are restricted to Isis and Nephthys. Texts are drastically reduced to the king's cartouches and brief titles, on the front only. On the lid is carved a vulture, with wings outstretched, to which a separate metal head was attached. The lid had been forcibly removed by robbers, who had broken a hole in the front edge to accept a pry-bar. Inside are the four traditional cylindrical compartments, but apparently never covered with the lids depicting the king's head that had been normal in earlier times. In his employment of a piece of funerary equipment of a type not used for nearly three hundred years, we may see a wish on Shoshenq I's part to emulate his Imperial predecessors in death as well as in his conquests in life.

The tomb of his son, the first Osorkon, likewise remains unknown; since the gap in the tomb-record comprises the first kings of the Libyan line, Osokhor, Shoshenq I and II and Osorkon I, it is possible that the new family moved their necropolis elsewhere, perhaps to Bubastis, whence Manetho derives the family. However, Shoshenq II was later reburied in the old Tanite burial ground, in NRT III, the abandonment of any new necropolis certainly having occurred by the beginning of the reign of Osorkon II, who took over the probable tomb of Smendes, for his father Takelot I, and himself. This may have followed the plundering of NRT I during our proposed break in the area's use. It is possible that it was while uncovering the tomb for reconstruction that the opportunity was taken to place Shoshenq II in Psusennes' antechamber.

Shoshenq II's silver coffin bore a hawk head, a distinguishing feature of kingly coffins of the Twenty-second Dynasty, together with a surface decoration reminiscent of contemporary private coffins: the old *rishi* design

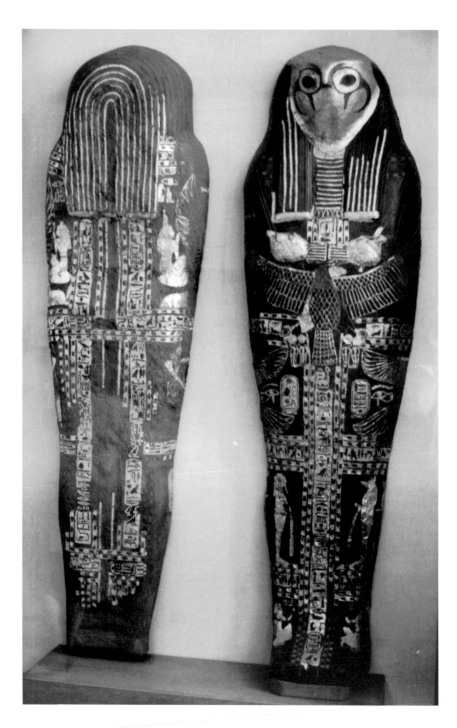

Fig. 120 The hawk-headed cartonnage of Shoshenq II.

was now dead. The trough was found to be broken, with earthy debris mixed with its contents, suggesting that it had been moved from elsewhere.

At the coffin's head lay a large number of shabtis and, mixed in amongst the others in the chamber, a set of four borrowed canopic jars. Each of the latter held a miniature silver coffin containing a dummy bundle of embalmed viscera. During the Twenty-first Dynasty, the practice had begun of returning the internal organs to the body after treatment, but the symbolic importance of canopics was by now such that empty, or even solid dummy, jars continue to be found in high-status burials. Shoshenq II's dummy bundles are the most extreme manifestation of this triumph of form over function.

The silver coffin had once been covered with linen pall, now totally decayed; likewise in a very poor state was the hawk-headed cartonnage that lay inside, now excellently restored in the Cairo Museum (fig. 120). Therein lay the mummy, a gold mask over its face and finely equipped. Reduced to a skeleton by humidity, death was found to have been due to a head wound which had resulted in meningitis.

The King's position in history has been much discussed. He has been variously identified as an ephemeral co-regent of Osorkon I, who had an eldest son Shoshenq; a short-lived independent king at about the same time; and as none other than Hedjkheperre Shoshenq I, a suggestion made by Sir Alan Gardiner and Helen Jacquet-Gordon, who felt that he might have adopted a variant prenomen in some of his funerary equipment. Against this is the fact that all funerary equipment definitely attributable to Shoshenq I bears his normal prenomen.

The full extent of Osorkon's rebuilding of NRT I is unclear, but certainly involved the tomb's complete decoration, and the probable provision of a new access. The original entrance would seem to have been what is now Chamber 2 (fig. 121), but that of Osorkon was on the west (5), probably approached by an earthen ramp, suggesting that the old pit was covered by some kind of superstructure. The left-hand jamb of the new entrance bears a curious lamentation-text in the name of the General Pasherenese; that a king should be mourned like a mortal is a new departure. Beyond the entrance lies what was initially a single antechamber, running north-south (1, 1a), its ceiling bearing a text and depictions of the celestial decans. The west wall of the chamber shows the sun's journey across the sky, bracketed by a figure of the goddess Nut, while on the south wall the dead king prepares to approach Osiris; the remaining wall surfaces are occupied by episodes from the Book of the Dead, the north by the weighing of the heart and the east by the so-called 'Negative Confession'. Such elements are new to a kingly tomb, and symptomatic of the declining prestige of the pharaoh seen at this time: no longer is he the

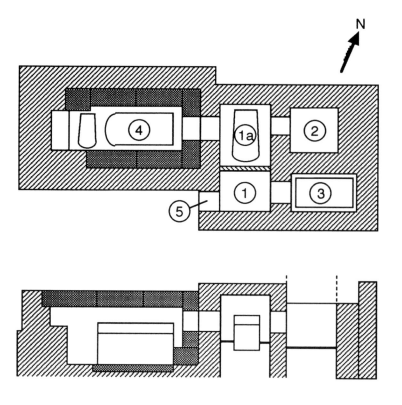

Fig. 121. Plan and section of the tomb of Osorkon II (NRT I).

god on earth gone to join his brothers in heaven, but one who must now submit to judgement like a mere mortal. Chamber 2 has more traditional royal scenes, the south and west walls the tenth to twelfth hours of the *Amduat*; the north Osorkon before Osiris and Isis; and the east, a double scene of the king adoring a djed-pillar, the hieroglyph for 'stability' and a fetish of Osiris. The neighbouring chamber 3 contains further depictions of the adoration of Osiris, as well as the king in the elysian 'Field of Rush Nuts'. While of good quality, many of the reliefs are in poor condition owing to high local humidity.

To the west lies the burial chamber, built of granite and almost completely filled with the similarly-composed sarcophagus of King Osorkon, his figure engraved is very slightly raised relief on the lid. Scenes of the regeneration of the sun feature on the chamber walls. When entered, the chamber proved plundered, but the sarcophagus still contained the damp-rotted remains of a gilded coffin, falcon-headed cartonnage and three skeletons. Two canopic jars lay within the coffer, two more outside.

At the head of the king's sarcophagus lay another, to accommodate

which a number of the chamber's lining blocks had been removed. A Middle Kingdom stone canopic chest also lay there, apparently reused as building material. The sarcophagus belonged to the king's young son, the titular High Priest of Amun at Tanis, Harnakhte, whose burial had been plundered through a hole in the side of the sarcophagus. The 9-year-old boy had been lavishly provided for by his grieving father, a silver coffin and numerous ornaments having been among the sarcophagus' contents.

In addition to his young son, Osorkon II also planned to share his tomb with his father, Takelot I. Chamber 3 was equipped with a late-Twelfth Dynasty sarcophagus of one Ameny, which then had its new owner's name crudely painted on its interior; also provided were canopic jars, jewellery and a large number of shabtis. The back wall received a relief showing Osorkon II worshipping Takelot in the guise of Osiris (fig. 122).

Like Psusennes I, Osorkon and his family did not retain sole occupancy of their tomb for long. A wall was erected across the antechamber under Shoshenq III and a large sarcophagus introduced into

Fig. 123. The burial chamber of the tomb of Shoshenq III (NRT V).

the northern half, either then, or at a later date (1a). On the wall, Osorkon II and Shoshenq III were shown doing homage to an unidentified figure. To a king Shoshenq belonged a number of broken shabtis which were found with the sarcophagus, none of them bearing a royal prenomen, thus making the king difficult to precisely identify. He cannot easily be the third Shoshenq, whose tomb lay elsewhere in the necropolis; however, Shoshenq V is without a known tomb, and thus may have been interred in the giant sarcophagus. This probably multiple reopening of the tomb might explain why, unlike the adjacent tomb of Psusennes I, it was extensively robbed: while attention was drawn to NRT I's location, surface work associated with its remodelling may have obliterated all trace of Psusennes' sepulchre.

The successor of Osorkon II, Shoshenq III, built his own tomb (NRT V) to the northwest of the earlier sepulchres (fig. 123). Compared with the tombs of Psusennes I and Osorkon II, it is of a much simpler design, comprising just an antechamber and a burial chamber. The entire structure is of reused blocks, its decoration largely derived from the *Amduat*, supplemented by various less-usual scenes. The south wall of the burial chamber is being adorned with scenes of the king's reawakening, including his welcome into the boats of the Sun God. At the top, a winged sun-disk presides over the whole. The cornices of the vaulted chamber bear vignettes from the Book of the Dead.

Two sarcophagi lay within the chamber, one belonging to Shoshenq III, and bearing his figure on the lid; the other was associated

Fig. 124. The burial chamber of the tomb of Pimay (NRT II).

with fragments of canopic jars, which belonged to a King Hedjkheperre Shoshenq (IV), whose very existence was only established in 1994.

Another anonymous sarcophagus is the limestone example found in NRT II, a sepulchre built up against, and sharing a wall with, the tomb of Osorkon II (fig. 124). In basic plan, the tomb is identical to Shoshenq III's, which suggests proximity in date, but the walls are devoid of decoration. It yielded the debris of a silver and two wooden coffins, plus canopic fragments, one in the name of a King Usermaetre-setpenamun. Three kings at this point in Egyptian history used this prenomen: Osorkon II, Shoshenq III, and the latter's second successor, Pimay. Since the latter lacks a known tomb, we are certainly justified in assigning NRT II to Pimay. His building of his tomb against NRT I could have provided an opportunity for pillaging that of Osorkon, given the venality displayed by Egyptian undertakers and tomb-builders on numerous occasions over the millennia.

During the reign of Osorkon II, the Tanite king, like Smendes and possibly Shoshenq I before him, was forced to concede kingly titles to the Theban High Priest of Amun. In this case the beneficiary was Harsiese, grandson of Osorkon I and great-grandson of Psusennes II. The Theban's tomb lies within the enclosure of the mortuary temple of Ramesses III at Medinet Habu, a sandstone structure probably once surmounted by a chapel (fig. 125). Uncovered by the expedition of the University of Chicago, it became apparent that while much of the eastern end of the tomb had been destroyed, the structure of the remainder was still

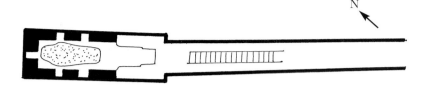

Fig. 125. Plan of the tomb of Harsiese at Medinet Habu.

reasonably intact. The priest-king had been laid to rest in the trough of the granite coffin which had once held the mummy of Ramesses II's younger sister, Henutmire, in her tomb in the Valley of the Queens (QV 75). Her name had been erased from the interior, but on the exterior it was intact, the coffin having been sunk up to its rim in the burial chamber floor. A rather rough hawk-headed lid had been added (fig. 126), while a set of canopic jars and two hundred and fifty shabtis had also been provided. Alongside the coffin were found a skull and arm-bone; probably belonging to Harsiese, the former exhibited a partly-healed hole in its brow, presumably the result of surgery.

After a short hiatus, the independence of Thebes was reasserted by Takelot II, whose latter years were clouded by a civil war, in which the main protagonists were his son, the High Priest of Amun, Osorkon, and one Pedubast, who was to seize the Theban throne. Ultimately, Osorkon triumphed and was able to ascend the throne as Osorkon III. While his tomb cannot be presently recognized, it probably lay at Medinet Habu, and is mentioned in Twenty-sixth and -seventh Dynasty papyri. A painted hawk-headed cartonnage formerly in Berlin may have come from his burial.

Apart from those members of the Tanite royal family who had been provided for in the royal tombs themselves - e.g. Queen Mutnodjmet and the Princes Ankhefenmut and Harnakhte - little is known of the burials of the families of the Twenty-first and -second Dynasty rulers. Almost the sole remains are those of the tomb of Shoshenq, heir to Osorkon II, who was High Priest of Ptah at Memphis and was buried with fellow office-holders in tombs within Ptah's enclosure on his premature death. On the other hand, the presence of a private necropolis at Tanis is suggested by fragments of the tomb-chamber walls of one Khonsuemheb and Ankhefenamun, recovered from the city's ruins.

In the latter part of the Third Intermediate Period, a number of petty kingdoms arose to join those already in place at Tanis and Thebes. One was at Leontopolis (Tell Moqdam), where a queen named Kama(ma) was buried in a stone-built tomb; she may have been related to a King Iuput II who is known to have ruled there around 725 BC. Her burial proved to be

Fig. 126. Lid of the granite coffin of Harsiese.

intact when examined by C.C. Edgar in 1921, but had been largely destroyed by water, although considerable quantities of jewellery were recovered from the mud which filled her granite sarcophagus.

This fragmentation of the country culminated in the invasion of the King of Kush, Piye, who had already become the effective overlord of the Theban polity. Kush, comprising Nubia and part of the modern Sudan, had once been an Egyptian possession, but was effectively lost at the end of the Twentieth Dynasty, when its Viceroy rebelled. Fully Egyptianised, this state increased its power until Piye (formerly read 'Piankhy') felt strong enough to invade the whole of Egypt, obtained the submission of the various rulers and then returned home, leaving them under a nominal overlordship that soon lapsed.

It was left to Piye's brother and successor, Shabaka, to return in 715 BC and actually take over the running of Egypt in the name of the Twenty-fifth Dynasty, although certain local rulers retained some power. The Kushites, formerly buried under tumuli and mastabas, adopted the pyramid shape for their tombs, built in the heart of their homeland, at El-Kurru and Nuri. Small and of high elevation, these monuments surmounted relatively simple substructures and continued to be constructed long after the end of the Kushite domination of Egypt.

The pyramid of Piye is wholly-vanished; however, the substructure still survives (Ku 17), consisting of a corbel-roofed room, approached by a stairway. Although sets of canopic jars and shabtis were provided, instead of a sarcophagus, a rock-cut bench lay in the middle of the burial chamber, with a cut-out in each corner, to receive the legs of a bed. Interment on a bier has been characterized as a typical feature of Nubian burials since Kerman (Second Intermediate Period) times.

Shabaka's tomb at El-Kurru (Ku 15) displays rather better workmanship than Piye's, both in its architecture and its funerary equipment, while also preserving a few traces of paintings in its burial chamber. However, a regression seems to be seen in the sepulchre of the following king, Shabataka (Ku 18). The workmanship of his canopics is poor, while the wholly-tunnelled substructure of Ku 15 is replaced by a corbelled pit of the same type as Piye's. In addition, the tomb lies apart from the other Twenty-fifth Dynasty sepulchres, located amongst the burial places of the ancestors of the royal line which date perhaps as far back as the early Third Intermediate Period.

Taharqa, on the other hand, as penultimate Nubian ruler of Egypt, constructed by far the largest and finest of the Kushite royal tombs (fig. 127). Rather than employ the now somewhat crowded family cemetery of El-Kurru, he made a fresh start at Nuri, a little way downstream. Although his pyramid there (Nu 1) contained large amounts of funerary

Fig. 127. The pyramid of Taharqa at Nuri.

equipment bearing his name, together with some fragments of a human skull, during the 1960s there were suggestions that Taharqa had possessed a second pyramid (numbered W T 1) at Sedeinga, nearly 350 kilometres away to the north, in which he had actually been buried. However, it has now become clear that the inscribed blocks upon which this attribution was based had been reused, leaving no question that Taharqa's only, and real, tomb was Nu 1.

Apart from its size, some 52 metres square, as against but 7.6 metres for the monument of Piye, Taharqa's pyramid has the most elaborate substructure of any Kushite royal tomb (fig. 128). A conventional stairway below the site of the mortuary chapel led into a small antechamber, which in turn gave access to a six-pillared burial chamber, the aisles of which were vaulted. A curious corridor completely surrounded the subterranean rooms, at a slightly higher level, accessible via a flight of steps at the far end of the sepulchral chamber, or a pair of stairways just outside the doorway of the antechamber. The usual bench lay in the centre of the burial chamber, upon which had lain a nest of coffins. These had been largely destroyed, but quantities of their gold foil and stone inlay remained. The canopic jars are of a very fine quality, and introduce new textual formulations, which become standard in subsequent Egyptian burials. A vast number of shabtis were recovered, in a variety of hard and soft stones, and many in remarkably large sizes - up to 60 centimetres in height.

The last Kushite to rule Egypt was Tanutamun. For his pyramid site, he moved back to El-Kurru, with a much simpler substructure,

159

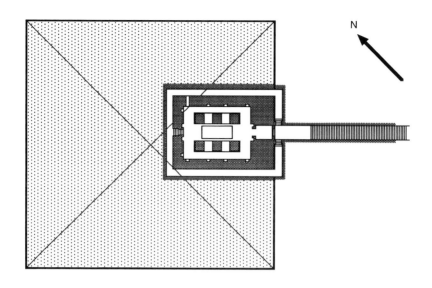

Fig. 128. Plan of the pyramid of Taharqa at Nuri.

curiously omitting the previously-obligatory coffin-bench. Like Shabaka's tomb, his Ku 16 had a burial chamber adorned with paintings, in his case sufficiently well preserved to identify the topics covered. The vignettes and texts essentially follow the age-old association of royal burials with solar matters, the entrance doorway being surmounted by painted apes adoring the sun-god in his bark, a similar motif also appearing on the rear wall.

Tanutamun's rule in Egypt was ended by an Assyrian invasion. However, his successors continued to rule in what is the modern Sudan for centuries more. Pyramids also continued in use, although their contents and ornamentation show a steady shift towards a distinctly Kushite interpretation of the ancient motifs. Canopic jars initially remained in use, supplemented for a short period by, for the first time in Kush, stone sarcophagi, but both types of container had disappeared soon after the reign of Melanaqeñ, sixth successor of Tanutamun. At first, the royal tombs were primarily built at Nuri, but they later shifted further south to Gebel Barkal and Meroë. It was at the latter site that the last Nilotic pyramid was built, around AD 350, three thousand years and 1,600 kilometres from the first such monument at Saqqara.

The Assyrians who drove the Kushites out of Egypt in 664 BC, were soon supplanted by a native dynasty (the Twenty-sixth), hailing from the Delta city of Sais. Following the practice of the Tanites, these kings' tombs lay within the enclosure of the local temple of the goddess Neith. Not thus far physically located by archaeologists, a record of them survives in the writings of Herodotus, who visited Sais c. 450 BC, and records that Apries, fourth king of this dynasty was

> buried in the family tomb in the temple of Athena [Neith], nearest to the shrine, on the left-hand as one goes in. The people of Sais buried all the kings who came from the province inside this area. The tomb of Amasis is also in the temple court, although further from the shrine than that of Apries and his ancestors. It is a great cloistered building of stone, decorated with pillars carved in the imitation of palm trees and other costly adornments. Within the cloister is a chamber with double doors, and behind the doors stands the sepulchre.

This implies that the earliest Saite kings were buried in a single tomb - or perhaps that each had a separate tomb below a single superstructure. The description of Amasis' monument seems to conjure up a standard Egyptian peripteral shrine, with a central cella surrounded by a colonnade. The cella would have contained the cult-image of the dead king; presumably, the burial chamber was sunk in the ground beneath.

The latter arrangement finds confirmation in the mortuary chapels of the God's Wives of Amun of the Twenty-sixth Dynasty buried at Medinet Habu. Their shrines differ in that they take the form of a miniature standard temple, with a pylon, rather than the peripteral type, but their burial chambers lie directly underneath, sunk no great depth into

Fig. 129. The monumental private tombs of the late Twenty-fifth/early Twenty-sixth Dynasties on the Asasif at Thebes.

Fig. 130. The tomb of Nepherites I at Mendes (Tell el-Rub'a).
The decorated limestone walls were reduced to fragments in antiquity,
leaving just the massive limestone sarcophagus.

the ground. In contrast to these modest royal tombs, the high dignitaries of the period at Thebes were buried in gigantic subterranean tombs on the Asasif, east of Deir el-Bahari. Amongst these sepulchres are some of the largest tombs ever built in Egypt (fig. 129).

A few items presumably intended to be placed into the Saite royal tombs are known, principally a number of shabtis, at least one of which was actually discovered at Saqqara, far from the Saite royal necropolis. Oddest are two canopic jars belonging to Apries: one was found in a Late/Ptolemaic catacomb at Saqqara containing the mummy of a hawk; the other came to light in an Etruscan tomb in far-away Italy. The dispersion of Apries' equipment may derive from the king's unfortunate mode of demise, killed in the aftermath of his overthrow by Amasis. Although Herodotus records that he was granted burial in his own tomb, it is possible that the interment was somewhat makeshift, and omitted certain items, which remained in store and were later reused in various contexts.

The Twenty-sixth Dynasty was driven from power by an invasion from Persia, and it was not until 404 BC that power was regained by Egyptians. Three dynasties ruled in succession, from Sais, Mendes and Sebennytos, which cities thus became royal necropoleis in the time-honoured manner.

The cemeteries of Mendes (Tell el-Rub'a) have long been known, and in 1869 Albert Daninos found within a large limestone sarcophagus lying on site some bones and a shabti figure of Nepherites I, founder of the Twenty-ninth Dynasty (fig. 130). However, it was not until 1991-3 that clearance of the area by a team led by Donald Redford discovered fragments of the walls of the chamber that had once surrounded the sarcophagus, which bore funerary texts in favour of Nepherites I, thus confirming its ownership. The tomb closely resembles those of Tanis. The limestone sarcophagus contains a smaller basalt inner container, closed by an angle-topped lid of a type typical of the Late Period. Another shabti of Nepherites I is also known, as well as two belonging to his second successor, Akhoris; presumably all originally came from Tell el-Rub'a.

Only the sarcophagi (and a few shabtis) survive from two Thirtieth Dynasty royal tombs, wholly divorced from their probable original location, Sebennytos (Sammanud/Behbeit el-Hagar). Belonging to Nektanebo I and II, first and last kings of the Thirtieth Dynasty, the sarcophagi found their ways to Cairo and Alexandria respectively - both sites devoid of contemporary pharaonic remains. That of Nektanebo I, of a very similar design to sarcophagi of the Eighteenth Dynasty, was recovered in fragments from various modern buildings, but a large proportion remains lost.

The other sarcophagus came from Alexandria's Attaria Mosque, the site of the Church of St. Athenasius, where it had been used as a ritual bath. It had for centuries occupied a small domed building in the mosque's courtyard, and was seen there by the traveller George Sandys as far back as 1611. Recorded by the Napoleonic expedition at the end of the eighteenth century, it was taken over by the British in 1800 along with other antiquities, including the famed Rosetta Stone, and came to lie in the British Museum. Of breccia, the sarcophagus is typical of its era, decorated externally with scenes of the Sun-God's journey through the night, essentially taken from the Book of *Amduat*, with the time-honoured figures of Nephthys and Isis at the head and foot (fig. 131). It was never used by its

Fig. 131. The sarcophagus of Nektanebo II.

163

royal owner, who fled to Kush before another Persian invasion.

Egypt rejoined the Persian Empire for a decade, before the onslaught of the young Macedonian king, Alexander III, brought that entity to a sudden end. Alexander, 'the Great', was hailed by the Egyptians as a liberator; the oracle of the god Amun at Siwa Oasis, deep in the Western Desert, went as far as to recognize him as legitimate Pharaoh. Amongst his acts in Egypt was the foundation of the city of Alexandria in the north-west Delta and the instigation of various works in sanctuaries around Egypt. However, within ten years, the conqueror was dead, and his followers were squabbling over his inheritance - and corpse.

The Satrap (governor) of Egypt was Ptolemy, son of Lagos, and it was he who managed to obtain the royal body during its journey through Syria, from Babylon, where Alexander had died, and transport it to Egypt. Although there is some confusion over the point, it would seem that the body was first interred at Memphis, but moved soon afterwards for definitive burial in Alexandria, mummified and enclosed in a gold coffin. The precise location of Alexander's tomb within the city has long been a matter of dispute, but certainly seems to have lain within the 'The Palaces', the residence-area of the Ptolemaic Dynasty that followed Alexander's short-lived brother and son on the throne in Egypt.

Although there is very little 'hard' evidence on which to base an assessment of the location of Alexander's tomb, most recent writers have concluded that it might have lain fairly near the waterfront in the general area of the city centring on the modern Ramleh Station; various myths and legends have grown up concerning the tomb's location. The most persistent theories concern the Mosque of Nebi Danyel, with Alexander allegedly lying deep below the mosque's crypt. Investigations carried out in and around the monument by Evaristo Breccia in the 1920s, and subsequently, have provided no evidence for pre-mediaeval structures in the area. Other legends link Alexander's body with the sarcophagus of Nektanebo II and the mosque in which it long stood, Edward Clarke publishing a book in 1805 to substantiate the identification. A modification of the view was put forward by A.C. Wace in 1948, speculating that the sarcophagus, unused following its owner's flight to Kush, might actually have been used as an appropriate shelter for Alexander's gold-coffined mummy. Another, not unconvincing, view, however, places the tomb considerably further east, in the area occupied by the modern 'Latin' Cemeteries.

Before 1914, there was found in the Terra Sancta Cemetery off Anubis Street, a massive calcite structure that had once formed the antechamber of a large tumulus-tomb of Macedonian type, the kind of tomb that held the interment of Alexander's father, Phillip II, at Vergina, back in Macedonia itself. While no inscriptions remain, with the innermost

Fig. 132. The main burial chamber of the catacombs of Kom el-Shuqafa in Alexandria, showing the combination of Classical and Egyptian motifs in that city.

chambers entirely vanished, Achille Adriani was led in 1966 to first suggest that the sepulchre might have been one of the two built for Alexander by the Ptolemies. In any case, the tomb must have belonged to an extremely important individual at Alexandria in the early Ptolemaic Period, whether or not a king.

Various other strands of myth, and modern speculation, exist, all without any firm basis. In 1995, yet another facet was added by the claim by a Greek archaeologist, Linana Souvaltzi, that she had found Alexander's tomb at Siwa. However, the architectural and textual evidence put forward was rapidly discredited, political considerations seemingly having contributed to an 'over-evaluation' of the discovery.

The burial places of the Ptolemaic Dynasty seem to initially have been constructed near, but separately from, Alexander's sepulchre. However, under Ptolemy IV Philopator a new royal mausoleum was constructed, known as the Sema, in which were buried the later Ptolemaic monarchs, together with their predecessors, including Alexander himself. Once again, little is known of the position of the sepulchre, although a description by the Roman writer Lucan suggests some form of pyramidal superstructure covering subterranean vaults. The latter will presumably have been decorated in the composite Egyptian/Classical manner found in various private Alexandrine tombs, for example those of Kom el-Shuqafa (fig. 132).

While it would seem that most of the Ptolemies were interred in the Sema, Kleopatra VII is reported to have had a separate tomb, 'adjacent to the Temple of Isis'. Unfortunately, our source for this, Plutarch, does not define which of the many Isis-shrines was involved, while the tomb's design remains obscure, a number of diametrically-opposed reconstructions having been proposed.

The Sema tomb-complex was visited by various figures of the Roman Imperial period, but was apparently destroyed, together with most of 'The Palaces' area as a result of rioting in the time of the Roman emperor, Aurelian, c. 273 AD. So, then, disappeared the last royal tombs to be built in Egypt while the old religion still reigned. Over a three thousand year period, holes in the desert had been replaced by brick mastabas; brick mastabas had given way to stone pyramids; stone had given way once more to brick; pyramids had shrunk and then been replaced by deeply cut rock tombs and then they had given way to small chambers buried under temple courtyards. Now, Egypt no longer had its own kings: no more royal mummies would be laid away on the banks of the Nile.

Epilogue: The House of Mohammed Ali

Between 30 BC, when the country became part of the Roman Empire, and 1922, Egypt was never formally independent. For various periods during the Middle Ages, Cairo was the capital of a number of dynasties, but in the context of regimes that embraced much wider geo-political territories. In 1517, however, the Sultan Selim I incorporated Egypt into the Ottoman Empire, where it nominally remained until 1914.

The Napoleonic expedition to Egypt in 1798-1801 was followed, on the other hand, by the assumption of power by Mohammed Ali, nominally as simply Ottoman governor, but with far greater real power. His desire for untrammelled authority led to a number of major conflicts with the Imperial government in Constantinople, resulting ultimately in the recognition of his family's hereditary right to the governorate. The dynasty's status advanced to that of Viceroys (Khedives) in 1867, and then to that of Sultans in 1914, when a British Protectorate was established, following Turkey's declaration for the Central Powers in the First World War. In 1922, a constitutional monarchy was finally established in the person of King Fuad I, formerly the Sultan Ahmad Fuad. His death in 1936 marked the establishment of the last of the Egyptian truly royal mausolea.

Mohammed Ali himself had been first buried in the Hosh el-Basha, in the Southern Cemetery of Cairo, a complex containing many tombs of members of the Pasha's family, including his immediate successor, Abbas I. However, in 1857, the body of Mohammed Ali himself was moved to the great mosque which he had built in the Cairo Citadel, where he rests under an elaborate monument. The Khedive Taufiq was buried in 1892 in the Qubbat Umm Waldah Basha, in Cairo's Eastern Cemetery, constructed as the mausoleum for Abbas I's mother, but enlarged to hold Taufiq's body. Also interred here was his son, Abbas II Hilmi, whose body was returned to Cairo after his death in exile in 1944. Various other members of the royal family found rest in the same mausoleum, including a number whose bodies were displaced from Alexandria's Nebi Danyel mosque by building work in 1984, including the Khedive Said, whose reign had seen the establishment of the Egyptian Antiquities Service, under Mariette.

King Fuad, however, was interred in the Rifai Mosque, built below

Fig. 133. The last Egyptian royal tomb: the Rifai Mosque.
To its left stands the mosque and mausoleum of Sultan Hasan (AD 1347-61); on the right of the
photograph is the madrasa and tomb of the Amir Qani Bey el-Sayfi (AD 1503).

the citadel, and begun in 1869 (fig. 133). Its foundress was the Princess
Khushiar (d. 1885), mother of Khedive Ismail, who wished to replace the
earlier Zawiyat el-Rifai, the burial place of two local saints, including el-
Rifai himself, with a much greater shelter for both the latter, and members
of Khedival royal family. In contrast to the Ottoman Turkish-styled
Mohammed Ali Mosque, the Rifai was constructed on the basis of the
ancient Mameluk traditions. This was clearly intended to make a point
concerning Egypt's reassertion of independence, the Mameluk era being
the golden age of Cairo's Islamic architecture, which directly preceded the
country's absorbtion into the Ottoman Empire.

Designed by Husein Fahmi, the building's construction was
interrupted following the abdication of Ismail in 1880, and was not
resumed until 1905, under the direction of the Austrian, Max Herz. While
still under construction, the mosque received the body of the Khedive
Ismail in 1895, work finally being completed in 1911. As it stands today,
most of the rooms on the southern, western and northern sides of the
structure are occupied by royal tombs. To the north, chambers hold the
bodies of Ismail and the Sultan Husein Kamil, together with members of
Ismail's family, including the Princess Khushiar. On the west side of the
mosque-proper is the tomb-chamber of Fuad I himself, which also holds
two other kingly bodies. The presence of both has a melancholy aspect.
One is that of Mohammed Reza Pahlevi, last Shah of Iran, who died in

exile in Cairo in 1980; his father, Reza, had also briefly rested in the mosque, following his own exiled demise in 1944. The other is that of Farouk I, last effective King of Egypt. Overthrown in 1952 by General Naguib's coup, he died in Rome in 1965; President Gamal Abd el-Nasser nevertheless allowed his burial in Egypt, Farouk being initially interred in the Hosh el-Basha, alongside Mohammed Ali's son, Ibrahim. In 1975, however, the corpse was translated to the Rifai, to lie beside his predecessor. Farouk's infant son briefly occupied the Egyptian throne as Fuad II, before the Republic was declared in 1953, thus bringing a definitive end to the history of the Egyptian monarchy and its necropoleis after no fewer than five millennia.

Chronology

NOTE: Full details are given for the kings of the period covered by this book, from the Middle Kingdom to the Ptolemaic Period. Only those earlier kings actually mentioned in the text are detailed. The first name quoted for each king is his *prenomen*; the second is his *nomen*, usually the name bestowed at birth.

		Conjectural Dates	Regnal Years
ARCHAIC PERIOD			
Dynasty I		3050-2813	
Dynasty II		2813-2663	
Horus and Seth			
Khasekhemwy	Nebwyhetepimyef	2690-2663	27
OLD KINGDOM			
Dynasty III		2663-2597	
Horus Netjerkhet	Djoser	2654-2635	19
Dynasty IV		2597-2471	
Horus Nebmaet	Seneferu	2597-2547	50
Horus Medjedu	Kheops	2547-2524	23
Horus Userib	Khephren	2516-2493	23
Horus Kakhet	Mykerinos	2493-2475	18
Dynasty V		2471-2355	
Dynasty VI		2355-2195	
Neferkare	Pepy II	2290-2196	94
FIRST INTERMEDIATE PERIOD			
Dynasty VII/VIII		2195-2160	
Dynasties IX/X		2160-2040	

Dynasty XIa   2160-2066

MIDDLE KINGDOM
Dynasty XIb

Nebhepetre	Montjuhotpe II	2066-2014	52
Senkhkare	Montjuhotpe III	2014-2001	13
Nebtawyre	Montjuhotpe IV	2001-1994	7

Dynasty XII

Sehetepibre	Ammenemes I	1994-1964	30
Kheperkare	Sesostris I	1974-1929	45
Nubkhaure	Ammenemes II	1932-1896	36
Khakheperre	Sesostris II	1900-1880	20
Khakaure	Sesostris III	1881-1840	41
Nimaetre	Ammenemes III	1842-1794	48
Maekherure	Ammenemes IV	1798-1785	13
Sobkkare	Sobkneferu	1785-1781	4

Dynasty XIII

Sekhemre-khutowi	Sobkhotpe I	1781-	
Sekhemkare	Amenemhatsonbef	:	
Nerikare	?	:	
Sekhemkare	Ammenemes V	:	
Sehetepibre	(Ameny-)Qemau	:	
Sankhibre	Ammenemes VI	:	
Smenkare	Nebnuni	:	
Hotepibre	Sihornedjhiryotef	:	
Swadjkare	?	:	
Nedjemibre	?	:	
Khaankhre	Sobkhotpe II	:	
?	Rensonbe	:	
Auibre	Hor	:	
Sedjefakare	Ammenemes VII	:	
Sekhemre-khutawi	Wegaf	:	
Userkare/Nikhanimaetre	Khendjer	:	
Smenkhkare	Imyromesha	:	
Sehotepkare	Inyotef IV	:	
Sekhemre-swadjtawi	Sobkhotpe III	:	3
Khasekhemre	Neferhotpe I	:	11
?	Sihathor	:	
Khaneferre	Sobkhotpe IV	:	
Merhetepre	Sobkhotpe V	:	4

Khahtepre	Sobkhotpe VI		4
Wahibre	Iaib	:	10
Merneferre	Aya	:	23
[4 kings)			
Merkaure	Sobkhotpe VII	:	
[18 kings]			
Swahenre	Senebmiu	-1650	

SECOND INTERMEDIATE PERIOD
Dynasty XV

-	Semqen?	1650-	
-	Aperanati		
-	Sakirhar		
Seuserenre	Khyan	:	
Nebkhepeshre/			
Aqenenre/Auserre	Apophis	1585-1545	40
?	Khamudy	1545-1535	

Dynasty XVI-XVII

Sekhemre-smentawi	Djehuty	1650-	
[3 kings]			
Swadjenre	Nebiriau I	:	
[8 kings]			
Seneferibre	Sesostris IV	- 1590	
Sekhemre-wahkhau	Rehotpe	1585-	
Sekhemre-shedtawi	Sobkemsaf I	:	
Sekhemre-wepmaet	Inyotef V	:	
Nubkheperre	Inyotef VI	:	
Sekhemre-heruhirmaet	Inyotef VII	:	
Sekhemre-wadjkhau	Sobkemsaf II	:	
Senakhtenre	Taa I	-1558	
Seqenenre	Taa II	1558-1553	5
Wadjkheperre	Kamose	1553-1549	4

NEW KINGDOM
Dynasty XVIII

Nebpehtire	Amosis	1549-1524	25
Djeserkare	Amenophis I	1524-1503	21
Akheperkare	Tuthmosis I	1503-1491	12
Akheperenre	Tuthmosis II	1491-1479	12
Menkheper(en)re	Tuthmosis III	1479-1424	54
(Maetkare	Hatshepsut	1472-1457)	

Akheperure	Amenophis II	1424-1398	26
Menkheperure	Tuthmosis IV	1424-1388	10
Nebmaetre	Amenophis III	1388-1348	40
Neferkheperure-waenre	Amenophis IV/		
	Akhenaten	1360-1343	17
(Ankhkheperure	Smenkhkare/		
	Neferneferuaten	1346-1343	3)
Nebkheperre	Tutankhamun	1343-1333	10
Kheperkheperure	Ay	1333-1328	5
Djeserkheperure-setpenre	Horemheb	1328-1298	30

Dynasty XIX

Menpehtire	Ramesses I	1298-1296	2
Menmaetre	Sethos I	1296-1279	17
Usermaetre-setpenre	Ramesses II	1279-1212	67
Banenre	Merenptah	1212-1201	11
Userkheperure	Sethos II	1201-1195	6
(Menmire-setpenre	Amenmesse	1200-1196	4)
Sekhaenre/Akheperre	Siptah	1195-1189	6
Sitre-merenamun	Tawosret	1189-1187	2

Dynasty XX

Userkhaure	Sethnakhte	1187-1185	2
Usermaetre-meryamun	Ramesses III	1185-1153	32
User/Heqamaetre—			
setpenamun	Ramesses IV	1153-1146	7
Usermaetre-sekheperenre	Ramesses V		
Amenhirkopshef I		1146-1141	5
Nebmaetre-meryamun	Ramesses VI		
Amenhirkopshef II		1141-1133	8
Usermaetre-setpenre-	Ramesses VII Itamun	1133-1125	8
meryamun			
Usermaetre-akhenamun	Ramesses VIII		
Sethhirkopshef		1125-1123	2
Neferkare-setpenre	Ramesses IX		
Khaemwaset I		1123-1104	19
Khepermaetre-setpenre	Ramesses X		
Amenhirkopshef III		1104-1094	10
Menmaetre-setpenptah	Ramesses XI		
Khaemwaset II		1094-1064	30
(Hemnetjertepyenamun	Hrihor	1075-1069	6)

THIRD INTERMEDIATE PERIOD
Dynasty XXI

Hedjkheperre-setpenre	Smendes	1064-1038	26
Neferkare-heqawaset	Amenemnesu	1038-1034	4
(Kheperkhare-setpenamun	Pinudjem I	1049-1026	23)
Akheperre-setpenamun	Psusennes I	1034-981	53
Usermaetre-setpenamun	Amenemopet	984-974	10
Akheperre-setpenre	Osokhor	974-968	6
Netjerkheperre-meryamun	Siamun	968-948	20
(Tyetkheperure-setpenre	Psusennes II	945-940	5)

Dynasty XXII

Hedjkheperre-setpenre	Shoshenq I	948-927	21
Sekhemkheperre-setpenre	Osorkon I	927-892	35
(Heqakheperre-setpenre	Shoshenq II	895-895)	
Hedjkheprre-setpenre	Takelot I	892-877	15
Usermaetre-setpenamun	Osorkon II	877-838	39
Usermaetre-setpenre	Shoshenq III	838-798	40
Hedjkheperre-setpenre	Shoshenq IV	798-786	12
Usermaetre-setpenamun	Pimay	786-780	6
Akheperre	Shoshenq V	780-743	37

'Theban Dynasty XXIII'

Hedjkheperre-setpenamun	Harsiese	867-857	10
Hedjkheperre-setpenre	Takelot II	841-815	26
Usermaetre-setpenamun	Pedubast I	830-799	30
(?	Iuput I	815-813)	
Usermaetre-setpenamun	Osorkon III	799-769	30
Usermaetre	Takelot III	774-759	15
Usermaetre-setpenamun	Rudamun	759-739	20
-	Iny	739-734	5
Neferkare	Peftjauawybast	734-724	10

Dynasty XXIII

Sehetepibenre	Pedubast II	743-733	10
Akheperre-setpenamun	Osorkon IV	733-715	18

Dynasty XXIV

Shepsesre	Tefnakhte	731-723	8
Wahkare	Bokkhoris	723-717	6

Dynasty XXV

Seneferre	Piye	752-717	35
Neferkare	Shabaka	717-703	14
Djedkare	Shabataka	703-690	13
Khunefertumre	Taharqa	690-664	26
Bakare	Tanutamun	664-656	8

SAITE PERIOD
Dynasty XXVI

Wahibre	Psammetikhos I	664-610	54
Wehemibre	Nekho II	610-595	15
Neferibre	Psammetikhos II	595-589	6
Haaibre	Apries	589-570	19
Khnemibre	Amasis	570-526	44
Ankhka(en)re	Psammetikhos III	526-525	1

LATE PERIOD
Dynasty XXVII

Mesutire	Kambyses	525-522	3
Setutre	Darios I	521-486	35
?	Xerxes I	486-465	21
?	Artaxerxes I	465-424	41
?	Xerxes II	424	1
?	Darios II	423-405	18

Dynasty XXVIII

?	Amyrtaios	404-399	5

Dynasty XXIX

Baenre-merynetjeru	Nepherites I	399-393	6
Usermaetre-setpenptah	Psamuthis	393	1
Khnemmaetre	Akhoris	393-380	13
?	Nepherites II	380	1

Dynasty XXX

Kheperkare	Nektanebo I	380-362	18
Irimaetenre	Teos	362-360	2
Senedjemibre-setpenanhur	Nektanebo II	360-342	18

Dynasty XXXI

-	Artaxerxes III Okhos	342-338	5
-	Arses	338-336	2
-	Darios III	335-332	3

HELLENISTIC PERIOD
Dynasty of Macedonia

Setpenre-meryamun	Alexander III	332-323	9
Setepkaenre-meryamun	Philippos Arrhidaeos	323-317	5
Haaibre	Alexander IV	317-310	7

Dynasty of Ptolemy

Setpenre-meryamun	Ptolemy I Soter	310-282	28
Userka(en)re-meryamun	Ptolemy II Philadelphos	285-246	36
Iwaennetjerwysenwy-setpenre-sekhemankhen-amun	Ptolemy III Euergetes I	246-222	24
Iwaennetjerwymenekhwy-setpenptah-userkare-sekhemankhenamun	Ptolemy IV Philopator	222-205	17
Iwaennetjerwy-merwyyot-setpenptah-userkare-sekhemankhenamun	Ptolemy V Epiphanes	205-180	25
Iwaennetjerwyperwy-setpenptahkhepri-irimaetamunre	Ptolemy VI Philometor	180-164	16
Iwaennetjerwyperwy-setpenptah-irimaetre-sekhemankhenamun	Ptolemy VIII Euergetes II	170-163	7
-	Ptolemy VI (again)	163-145	18
?	Ptolemy VII Neos Philopator	145	1
-	Ptolemy VIII (again)	145-116	29
Iwaennetjermenekh-netjeretmerymutesnedjet-sepenptah-merymaetre-sekhemankhamun	Ptolemy IX Soter II	116-110	6
Iwaennetjermenekh-netjeretmenekhsatre-setpenptah-irimaetre-senenankhenamun	Ptolemy X Alexander I	110-109	1
-	Ptolemy IX (again)	109-107	2
-	Ptolemy X (again)	107-88	19

-	Ptolemy IX (again)	88-80	8
(?	Ptolemy XI	80	1)

Iwaenpanetjerentinehem-
   setpenptah-merymaetenre-
   sekhemankhamun
	Ptolemy XII Neos Dionysos	80-58	22

-	Ptolemy XII (again)	55-51	4
-	Kleopatra VII Philopator	51-30	21
(?	Ptolemy XIII	51-57	4)
(?	Ptolemy XIV	47-44	3)

(Iwaenpanetjerentinehem-
   setpenptah-irimeryre-
   sekhemankhamun
	Ptolemy XV Kaisaros	41-30	11)

ROMAN PERIOD

BC 30-395 AD

BYZANTINE PERIOD

395-640

ARAB PERIOD

640-1517

OTTOMAN PERIOD

1517-1805

KHEDEVAL PERIOD

Mohammed Ali	1805-1849
Abbas I	1849-1854
Said	1854-1863
Ismail	1863-1879
Taufiq	1879-1892
Abbas II Hilmi	1892-1914

BRITISH PROTECTORATE

Husein Kamil	1914-1917
Ahmad Fuad	1917-1922

MONARCHY

Fuad I	1922-1936
Farouk I	1936-1952
Fuad II	1952-1953

REPUBLIC

1953-

The Royal Cemeteries of the Middle Kingdom and Later

NOTE: The following list includes all tombs used, or intended to be used, for the burials of rulers of Egypt from the Eleventh Dynasty onwards. The necropoleis in the Nile valley holding the tombs of reigning kings are listed in approximately geographical order, from north to south. Those known only from documentary sources, and as yet undiscovered are marked with an asterisk; those which have always been known are marked '‡'. A king later reburied either at Deir el-Bahari or in the tomb of Amenophis II is marked '†'. Under 'tomb type', the following codes are used:

TPB	True pyramid (brick)	T	Stone tomb chambers sunk in
R	Rock-cut tomb		temple-courtyard
SPS	Step pyramid (stone)		

The suffix 'u' indicates unused for burial, either through being incomplete, or some other reason.

Site	Tomb number	Tomb type	Owner/ occupant	Dynasty	Date of excavation or entry
Alexandria	-	?	Alexander	Mac.	*
	-	?	Ptolemy I-XIV	Mac.	*
	-	T?	Kleopatra VII	Ptol.	*
Sa el-Hagar	-	T	Apries	XXVI	*
(Sais)	-	T	Amasis	XXVI	*
Tell el-Rub'a (Mendes)	-	T	Nepherites I	XXIX	1992/3
San el-Hagar (Tanis)	NRT I	T	Osorkon II[1]	XXII	1939
			Takelot I	XXII	

[1] Probably usurped from Smendes.

179

Tanis (contd.)	NRT I	T	Shoshenq V (?)	XII	1939
	NRT II	T	Pimay	XXII	1939
	NRT III	T	Psusennes I	XXI	1939/40
			Amenemopet[2]	XXI	
			Siamun(?)	XXI	
			Psusennes II(?)	XXI	
			Shoshenq II[3]	XXII	
	NRT IV	Tu(?)	Amenemopet	XXI	1939
	NRT V	T	Shoshenq III	XXII	1945
			Shoshenq IV	XXII	
South Saqqara	L.XLIV	TPB	Khendjer	XIII	1929
	L.XLVI	TPBu	?	XIII	1929
Dahshur	L.XLVII	TPB	Sesostris III	XII	1894
	L.LI[4]	TPS	Ammenemes II	XII	1894
	L.LIV	TPB	Ammenemes V?	XIII	-
	L.LVIII[5]	TPBu	Ammenemes III	XII	1894
	L.LVIII/1	R	Hor	XIII	1894
South Dahshur	A.	TPB	?	XIII	-
	B.	TPB	?	XIII	-
	C.	TPB	Ameny-Qemau	XIII	1957
Mazghuna	N.	TPB	?	XIII	1911
	S.	TPB	?	XIII	1911
Lisht	L.LX	TPS	Ammenemes I	XII	1883
	L.LXI	TPS	Sesostris I	XII	1883
Hawara	L.LXVII	TPB	Ammenemes III	XII	1888
Lahun	L.LXVI	TPB	Sesostris II	XII	1890
Tell el-Amarna	TA.26	R	Akhenaten	XVIII	1880s
	TA.27	Ru	Neferneferuaten?	XVIII	1984
	TA.28	R	Neferneferuaten?	XVIII	1984
	TA.29	Ru	Tutankhaten?	XVIII	1984

[2] Reburial?

[3] Reburial·

[4] 'The White Pyramid'

[5] 'The Black Pyramid'

Western Thebes :					
El-Tarif	-6	R	Inyotef III	XIa	1970
	-7	R	Inyotef II	XIa	1970
	-8	R	Inyotef I	XIa	1970
Dira Abu'l-Naga	-	TPB	Inyotef V	XVII	*/1860s?
	-	TPB	Inyotef VI	XVII	*/1860s?
	-	TPB	Sobkemsaf I	XVII	*
	-	TPB	Kamose	XVII	*/1912?
	-	TPB	Taa I	XVII	*
	-	TPB	Taa II†	XVII	*
	-	R?	Amenophis I†	XVIII	*?
DEIR EL-BAHARI	DBXI.14	R	Montjuhotpe II	XIb	1903
Medinet Habu	MH.1	T	Harsiese	Th.XXIII	1928
	-	T?	Osorkon III	Th.XXIII	*
Biban el-Moluk	KV.1	R	Ramesses VII	XX	‡
(V. of Kings)	KV.2	R	Ramesses IV†	XX	‡
	KV.4	R	Ramesses XI	XX	‡
	KV.6	R	Ramesses IX†	XX	‡
	KV.7	R	Ramesses II†	XIX	‡
	KV.8	R	Merenptah†	XIX	‡
	KV.9	R	Ramesses V†/VI†	XX	‡
	KV.10	R	Amenmesse	XIX	‡
	KV.11	R	Ramesses III†[9]	XX	‡
	KV.14	R	Tawosret/	XIX	
			Sethnakhte	XX	
	KV.15	R	Sethos II†	XIX	
	KV.16	R	Ramesses I†	XIX	1817
	KV.17	R	Sethos II†	XIX	1817
	KV.18	R	Ramesses X	XX	‡
	KV.20	R	Tuthmosis I/		
			Hatshepsut	XVIII	1903
	WV.22	R	Amenophis III†	XVIII	1799
	WV.23	R	Ay	XVIII	1816

6 'Saff el-Bagar'.

7 ''Saff el-Qisasiya'.

8 'Saff e; Dawaba'.

9 Begun for Sethnakhte.

	WV.25	Ru	Amenophis IV/		
			Neferneferuaten?	XVIII	1816
	VK.34	R	Tuthmosis III†	XVIII	1898
	VK.35	R	Amenophis II	XVIII	1898
	VK.38	R	Tuthmosis I[10]	XVIII	1898
	VK.42	R	Tuthmosis II†	XVIII	1900
	VK.43	R	Tuthmosis IV†	XVIII	1903
	VK.47	R	Siptah†	XIX	1905
	VK.55	R	Neferneferuaten[11]	XVIII	1907
	VK.57	R	Horemheb	XVIII	1908
	VK.62	R	Tutankhamun	XVIII	1922
El-Kurru	Ku.15	TPS	Shabaka	XXV	1919
	Ku.16	TPS	Tanutamun	XXV	1919
	Ku.17	TPS	Piye	XXV	1919
	Ku.18	TPS	Shabataka	XXV	1919
Nuri	Nu.1	TPS	Taharqa	XXV	1916

[10] Constructed for reburial by Tuthmosis III.

[11] Reburial.

Abbreviations

AL	*Amarna Letters* (San Francisco).
AR	*Amarna Reports* (London).
ASAE	*Annales du Service des Antiquités de l'Égypte* (Cairo).
A6CIE	*VI Congresso Internazionale di Egittologia: Atti* (Turin, 1992).
ATut	*After Tutankhamun* (ed. C.N. Reeves) (London, 1992).
AUC	American University in Cairo.
BES	*Bulletin of the Egyptological Seminar* (New York).
BIE	*Bulletin de l'Institut égyptien* (Cairo).
BIFAO	*Bulletin de l'Institut Français d'Archéologie Orientale du Caire* (Cairo).
BiOr	*Bibliotheca Orientalis* (Leiden).
BM	British Museum, London.
BMFA	*Bulletin of the Museum of Fine Arts* (Boston).
BMMA	*Bulletin of the Metropolitan Museum of Art* (New York).
BSFE	*Bulletin de la Societé Français d'Egyptologie* (Paris).
CAH	*Cambridge Ancient History* (Cambridge).
CdE	*Chronique d'Egypte* (Brussels).
CCG	*Catalogue Général des Antiquités Egyptiennes du Musée du Caire.*
CM	Egyptian Museum, Cairo.
DE	*Discussions in Egyptology* (Oxford).
EEF/S	Egypt Exploration Fund (later Society), London
EgArch	*Egyptian Archaeology: Bulletin of the Egypt Exploration Society* (London).
GM	*Göttinger Miszellen* (Göttingen).
IFAO	Institut français d'archólogie orientale, Cairo.
JACF	*Journal of the Ancient Chronology Forum* (Orpington)
JARCE	*Journal of the American Research Center in Egypt* (New York, &c).
JE	Journal d'Entree (CM).
JEA	*Journal of Egyptian Archaeology* (London).
JMFA	*Journal of the Museum of Fine Arts, Boston* (Boston).
JNES	*Journal of Near Eastern Studies* (Chicago).
JSSEA	*Journal of the Society for the Study of Egyptian Antiquities* (Toronto).
KMT	*KMT: a Modern Journal of Egyptology* (San Francisco).
LÄ	*Lexikon der Ägyptologie* (Weisbaden).

MDAIK	*Mitteilungen des Deutschen Archäologischen Instituts, Kairo* (Mainz).
MFA	Museum of Fine Arts, Boston.
MMA	Metropolitan Museum of Art, New York.
MMJ	*Metropolitan Museum Journal* (New York).
Muqarnas	*Muqarnas* (Leiden)
NARCE	*Newsletter of the American Research Center in Egypt (New* York).
OMRO	*Oudheidkundige Mededelingen uit het Rijksmuseum van Oudheden te Leiden* (Leiden).
P7ICE	C.J. Eyre (ed.), *Proceedings of the Seventh International Congress of Egyptologists* (Leuven).
RdE	*Revue d'Egyptologie* (Leuven).
RMO	Rijksmuseum van Oudheden, Leiden.
SAK	*Studien zur altägyptschen Kultur* (Hamburg).
SPRS	A.B. Lloyd (ed.), *Studies in Pharaonic Religion and Society in Honour of J. Gwyn Griffiths* (London, EES, 1992).
SR	Special Register (CM).
TAE	B.E. Schafer (ed), *Temples in Ancient Egypt* (London: I.B. Tauris), 1998).
TR	Temporary Register (CM).
UC	Petrie Museum, University College London.
VA	*Varia Aegyptiaca* (San Antonio, TX).
VSK	R.H. Wilkinson (ed.), *Valley of the Sun Kings: New Explorations in the Tombs of the Pharaohs* (Tucson, AZ 1995).
Wb	A. Erman and H. Grapow, *Wörterbuch der ägyptischen Sprache* (Berlin, Leipzig).
ZÄS	*Zeitschrift für Ägyptische Sprache und Altertumskunde* (Leipzig, Berlin).

Bibliography

General

H. Altenmüller, 'Bemerken zu den Königsgraben des Neuen Reiches', *SAK* 10 (1983), 25-62.

D. Arnold, *Building in Egypt: Pharaonic Stone Masonry* (New York: Oxford University Press, 1991).

J.-F. and L. Aubert, *Statuettes égyptiennes: chaouabtis, ouchebtis* (Paris: Librairie d'Amérique et d'Orient, 1974).

J. Baines and J. Málek, *Atlas of Ancient Egypt* (New York: Facts on File, 1980).

G. Belzoni, *Narrative of the Operations and Recent Discoveries within the Pyramids, Temples, Tombs and Excavations in Egypt and Nubia* (London: John Murray, 1820).

J. Cerny, *The Valley of the Kings* (Cairo: IFAO, 1973).

G. Daressy, *Fouilles de la Vallée des Rois 1898-1899* (Cairo: IFAO, 1902). *Cercueils des cachettes royales* (Cairo: IFAO, 1909).

S. D'Auria, P. Lacovara and C.H. Roehrig, *Mummies and Magic: The Funerary Arts of Ancient Egypt* (Boston: Museum of Fine Arts, 1988).

A.M. Dodson, *Egyptian Rock Cut Tombs* (Princes Risborough: Shire Publications, 1991).
The Canopic Equipment of the Kings of Egypt (London: Kegan Paul International, 1992).
The Coffins and Canopic Equipment from the Tomb of Tutankhamun (in preparation).
- 'Valley of the Kings', in Oxford Companion to Archaeology, ed. B. Fagan (New York: Oxford University Press, 1996).

R.O. Faulkner, *The Ancient Egyptian Pyramid Texts* (Oxford: Griffith Institute, 1969).
- *The Ancient Egyptian Book of the Dead* (London: BM Press, 1985).

D.C. Forbes, *Tombs; Treasures; Mummies: Seven Great Discoveries of Egyptian Archaeology* (San Francisco: KMT Communications, 1999).

L. Habachi, *The Obelisks of Egypt* (London: Dent, 1978).

J.E. Harris and K. Weeks, *X-Raying the Pharaohs* (London: Macdonald, 1973).

E. Hornung, *Das Amduat. Die Schrift des verborgenen Raumes*, 3vv (Weisbaden: Otto Harrassowitz, 1963-67).
- *Das Buch der Anbetung des Re im Western (Sonnenlitanei)*, 2vv (Geneva: Editions des Belles Lettres, 1975-76).

- *Das Buch von den Pforten des Jenseits. Nach den version des Neuen Reiches* 2vv (Geneva: Editions des Belles Lettres, 1979-80).
- *The Valley of the Kings: Horizon of Eternity* (New York: Timken Publishers, 1990).
- *The Ancient Egyptian Books of the Afterlife* (Ithaca & London : Cornell University Press, 1999).
S. Ikram and A. Dodson, *The Mummy in Ancient Egypt* (London : Thames & Hudson, 1998).
C. Jacq, *La Vallée des Rois: Images et mystères* (Paris: Perrin, 1993).
E. Lefébure, *Les hypogées royaux de Thebes*, 3vv (Paris: Musée Guimet, 1886-9).
R. Partridge, *Faces of Pharaohs* (London: Rubicon, 1994).
A. Piankoff, *The Litany of Re* (New York: Bollingen, 1964).
B. Porter and R.B. Moss, *Topographical Bibliography of Ancient Egyptian Hieroglyphic Texts, Reliefs and Paintings*: I, *The Theban Necropolis*; II, *Theban Temples*; III, *Memphis*; IV, *Lower and Middle Egypt*; V, *Upper Egypt: Sites*; VI, *Upper Egypt: Chief Temples (excl. Thebes)*; VII, *Nubia, Deserts, and Outside Egypt* (Oxford: Clarendon Press/Griffith Institute, 1960; 1972; 1974-81; 1934; 1937; 1939; 1952).
C.N. Reeves, *Valley of the Kings: the Decline of a Royal Necropolis* (London: Kegan Paul International, 1990).
- and R.H. Wilkinson, *Complete Valley of the Kings* (London: Thames and Hudson, 1996).
J. Romer, *Valley of the Kings* (London: Michael Joseph, 1981).
G.E. Smith, *The Royal Mummies* (Cairo: IFAO, 1912).
R. Stadelmann, 'Totentempel III', LÄ VI (1986), 706-11.
H.M. Stewart, *Egyptian Shabtis* (Princes Risborough: Shire, 1995)
J.H. Taylor, *Egyptian Coffins* (Princes Risborough: Shire, 1989).
E. Thomas, *The Royal Necropoleis of Thebes* (Princeton: Privately Printed, 1966).
K.R. Weeks, (ed.) *Atlas of the Valley of the Kings* (Cairo : AUC Press).
R.H. Wilkinson, 'The Paths of Re: symbolism in the royal tombs of Wadi Biban el Moluk', *KMT* 4:3 (1993), 42-51.
- 'Symbolic Orientation and Alignment in New Kingdom Royal Tombs', *VSK*, 74-81.

Chapter I

D. Arnold, 'Das Labyrinth und seine Vorbilder'. *MDAIK* 35 (1979), 1-9.
- *Der Pyramidbezirk des Königs Amenemhet III in Dahschur I: Die Pyramide* (Mainz: Philipp von Zabern, 1987).
- 'Royal Cult Complexes of the Old and Middle Kingdoms', *TAE*, 86-126.
O. Berlev, 'A Contemporary of King Sewah-en-r', *JEA* 60 (1974), 109-13.

G. Daressy, 'Le cercueil du roi Kamès', *ASAE* 9 (1908), 61-3.

- 'Les cercueils royaux de Gournah', *ASAE* 12 (1912), 64-8.

J. de Morgan, *Fouilles à Dahchour, mars-juin 1894* (Vienna: Adolphe Holzhausen).

A.M. Dodson, 'The Tombs of the Kings of the Thirteenth Dynasty is the Memphite Necropolis', *ZÄS* 114 (1987), 36-45.

- 'On the Internal Chronology of the Seventeenth Dynasty', *GM* 120 (1991), 33-8.

- 'From Dahshur to Dira Abu'l-Naga: the decline and fall of the Royal Pyramid', *KMT* 5:3 (1994), 25-39, 86.

I.E.S. Edwards, *The Pyramids of Egypt* (London: Penguin, 1985).

- 'Sobekemsaf's Heart-Scarab', *Mélanges Gamal eddin Mokhtar*, II Cairo: IFAO, 1985), 239-45.

A. Fakhry, *The Pyramids* (Chicago: University Press, 1969).

S. Harvey, 'Monuments of Ahmose at Abydos', *EgArch* 4 (1994), 3-5.

G. Jequier, *Deux pyramides du Moyen Empire* (Cairo: IFAO, 1938).

P. Lacovara, 'An Ancient Egyptian Royal Pectoral', *JMFA* 2 (1990): 18-29.

C. Lilyquist, 'The Boston/Lafayette jewel and other glass-inlaid ornaments', *VA* 9 (1993), 33-44.

R. Parkinson, R. and S. Quirke, 'The Coffin of Prince Herunefer and the Early History of the Book of the Dead', *SPRS*, 37-51.

W.M.F. Petrie, G.A. Wainwright and E. Mackay, *The Labyrinth, Gerzeh and Mazghuna* (London: BSAE, 1912).

C.N. Reeves, 'A Newly Discovered Royal Diadem of the SIP', *Minerva* 7:2 (March/April 1996), 47-9.

K. Ryholt, *The Political Situation in Egypt during the Second Intermediate Period, c. 1800-1550 B.C.* (Copenhagen : Museum Tusculanum Press, 1997).

N. Swelim and A.M. Dodson, 'On the Pyramid of Ameny-Qemau and its Canopic Equipment', *MDAIK,* 54 (1998), 319-34.

H.E. Winlock, 'The Tombs of the Kings of the Seventeenth Dynasty at Thebes', *JEA* X (1924), 217-77.

- *The Rise and Fall of the Middle Kingdom in Thebes* (New York: Macmillan, 1947).

H. Stadelmann-Sourouzian, 'Rischi-Sarg', *LÄ* 5 (1984), 267-9.

Chapter II

D. Arnold, *The Temple of Mentuhotep at Deir el-Bahri* (New York: MMA, 1979), pl. 42, 44.

E.R. Ayrton, C.T. Currelly and A.E.P. Weigall, *Abydos* III (London: EEF, 1904).

M. Bierbrier, *Tomb Builders of the Pharaohs* (London: British Museum Publications, 1982/Cairo: American University in Cairo Press, 1989).

F.W. von Bissing, *Ein thebanischer Grabfund aus dem Anfang des neuen Reichs* (Berlin: A. Duncker, 1900).

H. Carter, 'Report on the Tomb of Zeser-ka-Ra Amen-hetep I, Discovered by the Earl of Carnarvon in 1914', *JEA* 3 (1916), 147-54.

J. Cerny, *A Community of Workmen at Thebes in the Ramesside Period* (Cairo: IFAO, 1973).

A.M. Dodson, 'The Tombs of the Kings of the Early Eighteenth Dynasty at Thebes', *ZÄS* 115 (1988), 110-23.

- 'Amenhotep I and Deir el-Bahri', *JACF* 3 (1989/90), 42-4.

P.F. Dorman, *The Monuments of Senenmut* (London: Kegan Paul International), 69-70.

M. Eaton-Krauss, 'The Coffins of Queen Ahhotep, consort of Seqeni-en-Re and mother of Ahmose', *CdE* 65/130 (1990), 195-205.

S. Harvey, 'Monuments of Ahmose at Abydos', *EgArch* 4 (1994), 3-5.

C. Lilyquist, *Egyptian Stone Vessels: Khian through Tuthmosis IV* (New York: MMA, 1995).

B. Manley, 'Tomb 39 and The Sacred Land', *JACF* 2 (1988), 41-57.

D. Polz, 'Bericht über die 4. und 5. Grabungskampagne in der Nekropole von Dra' Abu el-Naga/Theben-West', *MDAIK* 51 (1995), 207-25.

- 'Excavations in Dra Abu el-Naga', *EgArch* 7 (1995), 6-8.

- 'The Location of the Tomb of Amenhotep I: A Reconsideration' *VSK*, 8-21.

J. Romer, 'Royal Tombs of the Early Eighteenth Dynasty', *MDAIK* 32 (1976), 191-206.

J. Rose, *Tomb KV 39 : a double Archaeological Enigma* (Bristol : Western Academic & Specialist Press, 2000.

E. Thomas, 'The Tomb of Queen Ahmose(?) Merytamen, Theban Tomb 320', *Serapis* 6 (1980), 171-81.

D. Valbelle, *Les ouvriers de la tombe»: Deir el-Médineh à l'époque Ramesside* (Cairo: IFAO, 1985).

C.C. Van Siclen, 'The Temple of Meniset at Thebes', *Serapis* 6 (1980), 187-207.

R. Ventura, *Living in a City of the Dead* (Freiburg: Universitäts-verlag/Göttingen: Vandenhoeck und Ruprecht, 1986).

H.E. Winlock, 'A Restoration of the Reliefs from the Mortuary Temple of Amenhotep I', *JEA* 4 (1917), 11-15.

- *The Tomb of Queen Meryet-Amun at Thebes* (New York: MMA, 1932).

Z. Wysocki, 'The results of research, architectonic studies and of protective work over the North Portico of the Middle Courtyard in the Hatshepsut Temple at Deir el Bahari', *MDAIK* 40 (1984), 329-49.

Chapter III

B. Adams, *Egyptian Antiquities in the Victoria and Albert Museum* (Warminster: Aris and Phillips, 1977).

P. Bucher, *Les Textes des tombes de Thoutmosis III et d'Aménophis II* (Cairo: IFAO, 1932).

B. Bruyère, *Deir el Médineh, année 1926: Sondage au temple funéraire de Thotmès II (Hat Ankh Shesept)* (Cairo: IFAO, 1952).

Earl of Carnarvon and H. Carter, *Five Years' Explorations at Thebes: a record of work done, 1907-1911* (London: Oxford UP, 1912).

H. Carter, 'Report upon the Tomb of Sen-nefer Found at Biban el-Molouk near that of Thotmes III No. 34', *ASAE* 2 (1901), 196-200.

- 'A Tomb Prepared for Queen Hatshepsuit and Other Recent Discoveries at Thebes', *JEA* 4 (1917), 107-18.

- 'A Tomb Prepared for Queen Hatshepsuit discovered by the Earl of Carnarvon', *ASAE* 16 (1917), 179-82.

T.M. Davis, et al. *The Tomb of Thoutmôsis IV* (Westminster: Archibald Constable, 1904).

- *The Tomb of Hâtshopsîtû* (Westminster: Archibald Constable, 1906).

P. Der Manuelian, P. and C.E. Loeben, 'From Daughter to Father: The Recarved Egyptian Sarcophagus of Queen Hatshepsut and King Thutmose I', *JMFA* 5 (1993), 25-61.

- 'New Light on the Recarved Sarcophagus of Hatshepsut and Thutmose I in the Museum of Fine Arts, Boston', *JEA* 79 (1993), 121-55.

A.M. Dodson, 'The Tombs of the Kings of the Early Eighteenth Dynasty at Thebes', *ZÄS* 115 (1988), 110-23.

P.F. Dorman, *The Monuments of Senenmut* (London: Kegan Paul International, 1988).

D. Dunham, 'A Fragment from the Mummy Wrappings of Tuthmosis III', *JEA* 17 (1931), 209-10.

A. Fakhry, 'The Funerary Temple of Tuthmosis III', *ASAE* 37 (1937), 27-30.

G. Haeny, 'New Kingdom "Mortuary Temples" and "Mansions of Millions of Years"', *TAE*, 86-126.

G. Haeny (ed.), *Untersuchungen im Totentempel Amenophis' III* (Weisbaden: Otto Harrasowitz, 1981).

H.R.H. Hall, 'Three Royal Shabtis in the British Museum', *JEA* 17 (1931), 10-12.

W.C. Hayes, *Royal Sarcophagi of the XVIII Dynasty* (Princeton: University Press, 1935).

- 'The Sarcophagus of Sennemut', *JEA* 36 (1950), 19-23.

E. Hornung, 'Das Grab Thutmosis' II', *RdE* 27 (1975), 125-31.

H. Jaritz, 'What Petrie Missed', *EgArch* 5 (1994), 14-16.

G.B. Johnson, '"No one seeing, no one hearing." KV38 & KV20: the first royal tombs in the Valley of the Kings', *KMT* 3:4 (1992-93), 65-81.

J. Kondo, 'A Preliminary Report on the Re-clearance of the Tomb of Amenophis III', *ATut*, 41-54.

- 'The Re-clearance of Tombs WV 22 and WV A in the Western Valley of the Kings', *VSK*, 25-33.

A. Kozloff, A. and B.M. Bryan, *Egypt's Dazzling Sun: Amenhotep III and his World* (Cleveland, OH: Cleveland Museum of Art/Indiana University Press, 1992).

B. Lesko, 'Royal mortuary suites of the Egyptian New Kingdom', *AJA* 73 (1969), 453-8.

V. Loret, 'Le Tombeau de Thoutmès III à Biban-el-Molouk', *BIE* 3eme ser., 9 (1899), 91-7.

- 'Le Tombeau d'Aménophis II et la cachette royale de Biban-el-Molouk', *BIE* 3eme ser., 9 (1899), 98-112.

C. Lilyquist [See Chapter II.]

E. Naville, *The Temple of Deir el Bahari*, 1+6vv (London: EEF, 1894-1908).

H.H. Nelson, 'The identity of Amon-Re of United-with-Eternity', *JNES* 1 (1942), 127-55.

F. Pawlicki and G.B. Johnson, 'Behind the Third Portico: Polish-Egyptian Restorers Continue Work on the Upper Terrace at Deir el Bahari', *KMT* 5:2 (1994), 40-9.

W.M.F. Petrie, *Six Temples at Thebes 1896* (London, B. Quartitch, 1897).

H. Ricke, *Der Totentempel Thutmoses' III. Baugeschichtliche Untersuchungen* (Cairo: Selbstverlag, 1939).

J. Romer, 'Tuthmosis I and the Bibân el-Molûk: some Chronological Considerations', *JEA* 60 (1974), 119-33.

- 'The Tomb of Tuthmosis III', *MDAIK* 31 (1975), 315-48.

R. Stadelmann, 'hwt-R'w als Kultsätte des Sonnengottes im Neuen Reich', *MDAIK* 25 (1969), 159-78.

C. Vandersleyen, 'Who Was the First King in the Valley of the Kings?', *VSK*, 22-24.

K.R. Weeks, 'A Note on the Tomb of Hatshepsut', *NARCE* 121 (1983), 6-7.

A.E.P. Weigall, 'A Report on the Excavation of the Funeral Temple of Thoutmosis III at Gourneh', *ASAE* 7 (1906), 121-41; 8 (1907), 286.

M. Werbrouck, *Le Temple d'Hatshepsut à Deir el Bahari* (Brussels: Fondation Reine Élisabeth, 1949).

A.C. Western, 'A Wheel Hub from the tomb of Amenophis III', JEA 59 (1973), 91-4.

H.E. Winlock, Notes on the Reburial of Tuthmosis I', *JEA* 15 (1929), 56-68.

- *Excavations at Deir el Bahri 1911-1931* (New York: Macmillan, 1942).

- *The Treasure of Three Egyptian Princesses* (New York: MMA, 1948).

S. Yoshimura and J. Kondo, 'Excavations at the tomb of Amenophis III', *EgArch* 7 (1995), 17-18.

Chapter IV

J.P. Allen, 'Two Altered Inscriptions of the Later Amarna Period', JARCE 25 (1988), 117-28.

H. Beinlich and M. Saleh, *Corpus der Hieroglyphischen Inschriften aus dem Grab des Tutanchamun* (Oxford: Griffith Institute, 1989).

M. Bell, 'An Armchair Excavation of KV 55', *JARCE* 27 (1990), 97-137.

U. Bouriant, G. Legrain and G. Jéquier, *Monuments pour servir à l'étude du culte d'Atounou en Égypte*, I, *Les tombes de Khouitatonou* (Cairo: IFAO).

L.P. Brock, 'Theodore Davis and the Rediscovery of Tomb 55', *VSK*, 34-46.

- 'The Final Clearance of KV 55', in *Ancient Egypt, the Aegean and the Near East: studies in Honor of Martha Rhoads Bell* I, (San Antonio: Van Siclen Books, 1997) 121-36.

H. Carter and A.C. Mace, *The Tomb of Tut.ankh.Amen*, 3vv (London: Cassell, 1923-33).

T.M. Davis, et al. *The Tomb of Iouiya and Touiyou* (Westminster: Archibald Constable, 1907).

- *The Tomb of Queen Tiyi* (Westminster: Archibald Constable, 1910; new edition with introduction by C.N. Reeves, San Francisco: KMT Communications, 1990).

- *The Tombs of Harmhabi and Touatânkhamanou* (Westminster: Archibald Constable, 1912).

A.M. Dodson, 'Death after Death in the Valley of the Kings', *Death and Taxes in the Ancient Near East*, ed. S. Orel (Lewiston: The Edwin Mellen Press, 1992), 53-9.

- 'KV 55 and the End of the Reign of Akhenaten', *A6CIE*, I, 135-9

- 'On the Origin, Contents and Fate of Biban el-Moluk Tomb 55', *GM* 132 (1993), 21-8.

- 'Kings' Valley Tomb 55 and the Fates of the Amarna Kings', *Amarna Letters* 3 (1994), pp. 92-103.

- 'Tutankhamun's Tomb', in *Archaeology of Ancient Egypt: An Encyclopedia*, ed. K. Bard (London : Routledge, 1999).

- 'Tutankhamun's Tomb', in *Encyclopedia of the Archaeology of Ancient Egypt*, ed. B. Fagan (New York, 1997).

- and J.J. Janssen, 'A Theban Tomb and its Tenants', *JEA* 75 (1989), 125-38.

R. Drenkhahn, 'Ein Umbettung Tutanchamuns?' *MDAIK* 39 (1983), 29-37.

M. Eaton-Krauss, *The Sarcophagus in the Tomb of Tutankhamun.* (Oxford: Griffith Institute, 1993).

A. el-Khouli and G.T. Martin, *Excavations in the Royal Necropolis at El-'Amarna 1984* (Cairo: IFAO, 1987).

R. Engelbach, 'Material for a Revision of the History of the Heresy Period of the XVIIIth Dynasty', *ASAE* 40 (1940), 134ff.

E.L. Ertman, 'Evidence of the Alterations to the Canopic Jar Portraits and Coffin Mask from KV 55', *VSK*, 108-19.

R. Germer, 'Die Angebliche Mumie der Teje: Probleme interdisziplinärer arbeiten', *SAK* 11 (1984), 85-90.

J.E. Harris, J.E., E.F. Wente, et. al. 'The Identification of the "Elder Lady" in the Tomb of Amenhotep II as Queen Tiye', *Delaware Medical Journal* 51, no.2 (1979), 39-93.

J.R. Harris, 'Akhenaten and Neferneferuaten in the Tomb of Tutankhamun', *ATut*, 58-75.

R.G. Harrison, 'An Anatomical Eaxamination of the Pharaonic Remains Purported to be Akhenaten', *JEA* 52 (1966), 95-119.

- and A.B. Abdalla,'The Remains of Tutankhamun', *Antiquity* 46 (1972), 8-14.

-, R.C. Connolly, S. Ahmed, A.B. Abdalla and M. El-Ghawaby, 'A mummified foetus from the tomb of Tutankhamun', *Antiquity* 53 (1979), 19-21.

N. Hepper, *Pharaoh's Flowers. Plants of Tutankhamun's Tomb* (London: HMSO, 1990).

U. Hölscher, *The Excavation of Medinet Habu*, II, *The Temples of the Eighteenth Dynasty* (Chicago: University Press, 1939).

E. Hornung, *Das Grab des Haremhab im Tal der Könige* (Bern: Franke Verlag, 1971).

G.B. Johnson, 'Tomb 55 Today', *Amarna Letters* 2 (1993), 70-75.

R. Krauss, 'Kija - ursprüngliche Besitzerin der Kanopen aus KV 55', *MDAIK* 42 (1986), 67-80.

F.F. Leek, *The Human Remains from the Tomb of Tut'ankhamun* (Oxford: Griffith Institute, 1972).

G.T. Martin, *The Royal Tomb at el-'Amarna*, 2vv (London: EES, 1974, 1989).

- 'Queen Mutnodjmet at Memphis and El-'Amarna', *L'Égyptologie en 1979: Axes prioritaires de recherches* (Parsi, 1982), II, 275-8.

- 'Notes on a Canopic Jar from Kings' Valley Tomb 55', *Mélanges Gamal eddin Mokhtar, II* (Cairo, 1985), 111-25.

- 'Shabtis of Private Persons in the Amarna Period', *MDAIK* 42 (1986), 109-29.

- *The Memphite Tomb of Horemheb, Commander-in-Chief of Tut'ankhamun*, 2vv (London: EES, 1989ff).

G. Perepelkin, *The Secret of the Gold Coffin* (Moscow: Nauka, 1978).

A. Piankoff, *Les Chapelles de Tout-Ankh-Amon* (Cairo: IFAO, 1951-2).

- *The Shrines of Tut-Ankh-Amon* (New York: Bollingen, 1955).

- 'Les peintures dans le tombe du rois Ai', *MDAIK* 16 (1958), 247-51.

M.J. Raven, 1994. 'A sarcophagus for Queen Tiye and other fragments from the Royal Tomb at El-Amarna', *OMRO* 74:7-20.

C.N. Reeves, 'A State Chariot from the Tomb of Ay?' *GM* 46 (1981), 11-19.

- 'Tut'ankhamun and his Papyri', *GM* 88 (1985), 39-45.

- *The Complete Tutankhamun* (London: Thames and Hudson, 1990).

O.J. Schaden, 'Clearance of the tomb of King Ay (WV-23)', *JARCE* 21 (1984), 39-64.

- 'Preliminary Report on the Re-clearance of Tomb 25 in the Western Valley of the Kings (WV-25)', *ASAE* 63 (1979), 161-8.

E. Strouhal, 'Queen Mutnodjmet at Memphis: Anthropological and Paleopathological Evidence', *L'Égyptologie en 1979: Axes prioritaires de recherches* (Paris, 1982), II, 317-22.

E. Thomas, 'Was Queen Mutnodjemet the owner of Tomb 33 in the Valley of the Queens?' *JEA* 53 (1967), 161-3.

C. Vandersleyen, 'Royal Figures from Tutankhamun's Tomb: their Historical Usefulness', *ATut*, 76-84.

H.E. Winlock, *Materials Used at the Embalming of King Tut-'ankh-Amun* (New York: MMA, 1941).

Chapter V

C. Aldred, 'Two monuments of the reign of Horemheb', *JEA* 54 (1954), 100-106.

- 'The Parentage of King Siptah', *JEA* 49 (1963), 41-8.

H. Altenmüller, 'Bemerkungen zu den neu gefundenen Daten im Grab der Königin Twosre (KV 14) im Tal der Könige von Theben', ATut, 141-64.

- 'Das Grab des Königin Tausret im Tal des Könige von Thebes', *SAK* 10 (1983), 1-24.

- 'Zweiter Vorbericht in die Arbeiten des Archäologischen Instituts der Universität Hamburg am Grab des Bay (KV 13) im Tal der Könige von Theben', *SAK* 19 (1992), 15-36.

- 'Dritter Vorbericht in die Arbeiten des Archäologischen Instituts der Universität Hamburg am Grab des Bay (KV 13) im Tal der Könige von Theben', *SAK* 21 (1994), 1-18.

E.C. Brock, 'Piecing it All Together: an ongoing study of Late New Kingdom Royal Sarcophagi', *KMT* 2:1 (1991), 42-9.

- 'The Tomb of Merenptah and its Sarcophagi', *ATut*, 122-40.

J. Bonomi and S. Sharpe, *The Alabaster Sarcophagus of Oimenepthah I. King of Egypt* (London: Longman, Green, Longman, Roberts and Green, 1864).

E.A.W. Budge, *An Account of the Sarcophagus of Seti I., King of Egypt, B.C. 1370* (London: Sir John Soane's Museum, 1908).

H. Burton, 'The Late Theodore M. Davis's Excavations at Thebes in

1912-13; 1: the Excavation of the Rear Corridors and Sepulchral Chamber of the Tomb of King Siphtah', *BMMA* 11 (1916), 13-18.

H. Carter, 'Report on the work done in Upper Egypt', *ASAE* 6 (1905), 116-29.

Centre of Documentation, *Le Ramesseum*, 11 vv. (Cairo, 1980).

P.A. Clayton, 'Royal Bronze Shawabti Figures', JEA 58 (1972), 167-75.

Commission des Monuments d'Égypte, *Description de l'Égypte, ou Recueil des observations et des recherches qui ont été faites en Égypte pendent l'expédition de l'armée français: Antiquités* (Planches), 5vv (Paris: Imprimerie impériale, 1809-22).

A.M. Dodson, 'The Tomb of King Amenmesse: Some Observations', *DE* 2 (1985), 7-11.

- 'A Fragment of Canopic Chest in Sir John Soane's Museum', *JEA* 71 (1985), 177-9.
- 'Was the Sarcophagus of Ramesses III begun for Sethos II?', *JEA* 72 (1986), 196-8.
- 'Some Additional Notes on "A Fragment of Canopic Chest in Sir John Soane's Museum," *JEA* 71 (1985), 177-79', DE 4 (1986), 27-8.
- 'The Takhats and some other Royal Ladies of the Ramesside Period', *JEA* 73 (1987), 224-9.
- 'The Canopic Chest of Ramesses II', *RdE* 41 (1990), 31-7.
- 'Amenmesse in Kent, Liverpool and Thebes', *JEA* 81 (1995), 115-28.
- 'The Decoration of the Tomb of Sethos II and its Implications' *JEA* 85 (1999). [See also Chapter IV].

H. Frankfort, A. de Buck and B. Gunn, *The Cenotaph of Seti I at Abydos*, 2vv (London: EES, 1933).

A.H. Gardiner, 'The Tomb of Queen Twosre', *JEA* 40 (1954), 40-44.

L. Habachi, 'Lids of the Outer Sarcophagi of Merytamen and Nefertari', *Festschrift zum 150jahrigen Bestehen des Berliner Ägyptischen Museuems* (Berlin: Akademie-Verlag, 1974), 105-12.

G. Haeny [See Chapter III].

E. Hornung, 'Das Grab einer ägyptischen Königin', *BiOr* 32 (1975), 143-5.

- 'Zum Grab Sethos' I. in seinem ursprünglichen Zustand', *ATut*, 91-8.
- *The Tomb of Pharaoh Seti I/Das Grab Sethos' I.* (Zurich and Munich: Artemis, 1991).
- 'Studies on the Decoration of the Tomb of Seti I', *VSK*, 70-3.
- and E. Staehlin, *Sethos: ein Pharaonengrab* (Basel: Antikenmuseum u. Sammlung Ludwig).

S. Ikram and D. Forbes, 'KV5: Retrospects & Prospects', *KMT* 7:1 (1996), 38-50.

H. Jaritz, 'What Petrie Missed', *EgArch* 5 (1994), 14-16.

-, B. Dominicus and H. Sourouzian, 'Der Totentempel des Merenptah in Qurna: 2. Grabungsbericht (7. und 8. Kampagne), *MDAIK* 51 (1995), 57-83.

C. Leblanc, *Ta set neferou; une necropole de Thebes-Ouest et son histoire*, 5vv (Cairo: Nubar, 1989ff).

- 'The Tomb of Ramesses II and the Remains of his Funerary Treasure', *Eg. Arch.* 10 (1997), 11-13.

C.R. Lepsius, *Denkmaeler aus Aegypten und Aethiopien*, 12vv (Berlin: Nicolaische Buchandlung, 1849-1859).

- *Denkmaeler aus Aegypten und Aethiopien, Text* (Leipzig: J.C. Hinrichs, 1897-1913).

C. Maystre, Le Tombeau de Ramsès II', *BIFAO* 38 (1939), 183-90.

Musée national d'histoire naturelle - Musée de l'homme, *La Momie de Ramsès II: contribution scientifique a l'égyptologie* (Paris, 1985).

M.A. Murray, *The Osirion* (London: Egyptian Research Account).

J. Osing, *Der Tempel Sethos' I. in Gurna* (Mainz: Philipp von Zabern, 1977).

W.M.F. Petrie, *Six Temples at Thebes 1896* (London, B. Quartitch, 1897).

J.E. Quibell, *The Ramesseum* (London, 1898).

C.N. Reeves, 'Excavations in the Valley of the Kings, 1905/6: a Photographic Record', *MDAIK* 40 (1984), 227-35.

J.B. Rutherford, 'KV7, tomb of Rameses II: why save it?', *KMT* 1:3 (1990), 46-51.

O.J. Schaden, 'Some Observations on the Tomb of Amenmesse (KV-10)', in *Essays in Egyptology in honor of Hans Goedicke*, ed. B. Bryan and D. Lorton (San Antonio: Van Siclen Books, 1995).

- and E. Ertman, 'The Tomb of Amenmesse (KV 10) : The First Season', *ASAE* 73 (1998), 116-55.

A. Siliotti and C. Leblanc, *Nefertari e la Valle delle Regine* (Florence: Giunti, 1993).

H. Sourouzian, *Les Monuments du roi Merenptah* (Mainz: Philipp von Zabern, 1989).

E. Uphill, 'Where were the Funerary Temples of the New Kingdom Queens?', *A6CIE*, I, 613-8.

K. Weeks, *The Lost Tomb* (London : Weidenfeld & Nicholson, 1998).

- *KV5 : A Preliminary Report* (Cairo : AUC Press, 2000).

Chapter VI

F. Abitz, *Ramses III. in den Gräbern seiner Söhne* (Freibourg Universitätsverlg/Göttingen: Vandenhoeck und Ruprecht, 1986).

- *Baugeschichte und Dekoration des Grabes Rameses' VI* (Freiburg: Universitätsverlg/Göttingen: Vandenhoeck und Ruprecht, 1989).

- 'The Structure of the Decoration in the Tomb of Ramesses IX', *ATut*, 165-85.

- 'Der Bauablauf und die Dekorationen des Grabes Ramesses' IX', *SAK* 17 (1990), 1-40.

C. Aldred, 'More light on the Ramesside Tomb Robberies', in *Glimpses of Ancient Egypt*, ed. J. Ruffle et al., (Warminster: Aris and Phillips, 1979), 96-9.

E.C. Brock, 'The Clearance of the Tomb of Ramesses VII', *VSK*, 47-63.

J. Capart, A.H. Gardener and B. van de Walle, 'New Light on the Ramesside Tomb Robberies', *JEA* 22 (1936), 169-93.

H. Carter and A.H. Gardiner, 'The Tomb of Ramesses IV and the Turin Plan of a Royal Tomb', *JEA* 4 (1917), 130-58.

L.A. Christophe, 'Ramsès IV et le Musée du Caire', *Cahiers d'histoire égyptienne*, 3e ser., fasc. 1 (November, 1950), 47-67.

M. Ciccarello, *The Graffito of Pinutem I in the Tomb of Ramesses XI* (San Francisco: Privately Printed, 1979).

- and J. Romer, *A Preliminary Report of the Recent Work in the Tombs of Ramesses X and XI in the Valley of the Kings* (San Francisco: Privately Printed, 1979).

P.A. Clayton [see Chapter V].

A.M. Dodson, 'A canopic jar of Ramesses IV and the royal canopic equipment of the Ramesside Period', *GM* 152 (1996), 11-17. [See also Chapter V.]

Epigraphic Survey, *Medinet Habu*, 8vv (Chicago: University Press, 1930-69).

R. Fazzini and J. Manning, 'Work in the Theban Necropolis', *NARCE* 101/102 (1977).

F. Guilmant, *Le Tombeau de Ramsès IX* (Cairo: IFAO, 1907).

G. Haeny [See Chapter III].

F. Hassanein, 'Le probleme historique du Seth-her-khepshef, fils de Ramses III: a propos dela tombe no 43 de la Vallée des Reines', *SAK* Beiheft 4 (1985), 63-6

E. Hornung, *Zwei ramessidischen Königsgräber: Ramses IV. und Ramses VII.* (Mainz: Phillip von Zabern, 1990).

U. Hölscher, *The Excavation of Medinet Habu, III-IV, The Mortuary Temple of Ramses III* (Chicago: University Press, 1941-51).

K. Jansen-Winkeln, 'Der Plünderung der Königsgräber des Neuen Reiches', *ZÄS* 122 (1995), 62-78.

C. Leblanc [see Chapter V.]

W.J. Murnane, *United with Eternity: a Concise Guide to the Monuments of Medinet Habu* (Cairo: American University in Cairo Press, 1980).

O. Neugebauer and R.A. Parker, *Egyptian Astronomical Texts*, II, *The Ramesside Star Clocks* (London: Lund Humphries/Providence, RI: Brown Unversity Press, 1964).

A.J. Peden, *The Reign of Ramesses IV* (Warminster: Aris and Phillips, 1994), 43-8.

T.E. Peet, *The Great Tomb-robberies of the Twentieth Egyptian Dynasty* (Oxford: University Press, 1930).

A. Piankoff, *The Tomb of Ramesses VI* (New York: Bollingen, 1954).

C.H. Roehrig, 'Gates to the Underworld: The Appearance of Wooden Doors in the Royal Tombs in the Valley of the Kings', *VSK*, 82-107.

J.H. Taylor, 'Aspects of the History of the Valley of the Kings in the Third Intermediate Period', *ATut*, 186-206.

R. Ventura, 'The Largest Project for a Royal Tomb in the Valley of the Kings', *JEA* 74 (1988), 137-56.

Chapter VII

S. Adam, 'Recent Discoveries in the Eastern Delta (Dec. 1950-May 1955)', *ASAE* 55 (1958), 301-24.

C.V.A. Adams, 'The manufacture of ancient Egyptian cartonnage cases', *SJH* 1/3 (1966).

A. Badawi, 'Das Grab des Kronprinzen Scheschonk Sohnes Osorkon's II und Hohenpriesters von Memphis', *ASAE* 54 (1956), 153-77.

R. Bianchi, 'Hunting Alexander's Tomb', *Archaeology* 46:4 (July/August 1993), 54-55.

- 'Alexander's Tomb ... Not!', *Archaeology* 48:3 (May/June 1995), 58-60.

P. Brissaud, *Cahiers de Tanis: Mission français des fouilles de Tanis* I (Editions Recherche sur les Civilisations, 1987).

G. Brunton, 'Some Notes on the Burial of Shashanq Heqa-kheper-Re', *ASAE* 39 (1939), 541-7.

J. Capart, 'A propos du cercueil d'argent du roi Chechonq', *CdE* 18 (1943), 191-8.

J. Cerny, 'Studies in the Chronology of the Twenty-first Dynasty', *JEA* 32 (1946), 24-30.

D. Clarke, *Bulletin of the Faculty of Arts, Farouk I University* 5 (1949), 102.

P.A. Clayton [see Chapter V].

M. Ciccarello [see Chapter VI.

H. De Meulenaere and P. Mackay, *Mendes II* (Warminster: Aris and Phillips, 1977).

D. Derry, 'Note on the Remains of Shashanq', *ASAE* 39 (1939), 549-51.

- 'An Examination of the Bones of King Psusennes I', *ASAE* 40 (1940), 969-70.

- 'Report on the Skeleton of King Amenemopet', *ASAE* 41 (1942), 149.

A.M. Dodson, 'Some Notes Concerning the Royal Tombs at Tanis', *CdE* 63/126 (1988), 221-3.

- 'Something Old, Something New, Something Borrowed, Something ... Granite', *KMT* 4:3 (1993), 58-69, 85.

- and J.J. Janssen, 'A Theban Tomb and its Tenants', *JEA* 75 (1989), 125-38.

D. Dunham, 'An Ethiopian Royal Sarcophagus', *BMFA* 43 (1945), 53-7.

- *The Royal Cemeteries of Kush*, 4vv (Boston: Museum of Fine Arts, 1950ff).

C.C. Edgar, 'The Sarcophagus of an Unknown Queen', *ASAE* 8 (1907), 276-81.

J.-Y. Empereur, *Alexandria Rediscovered* (BM Press, 1998).

D.C. Forbes, 'Pinudjem Ist Revealed: Closing in on the Missing Mummy of Cache DB320', *KMT* 6/2 (1995), 86-7.

P.M. Fraser, *Ptolemaic Alexandria*, I (Oxford: University Press, 1972), 15-17.

A.A. Gasm el Seed, 'La Tombe de Tanoutamon à El Kurru (KU. 16)', *RdE* 36 (1985), 67-72.

H. Gauthier, 'Un tombeau de Tell Moqdam', *ASAE* 21 (1921), 21-7.

W.C. Hayes, 'A Canopic Jar of King Nesu-ba-neb-dedet of Tanis', *BMMA* NS 5 (1947), 261-3.

U. Hölscher, *The Excavation of Medinet Habu*, V (Chicago: University Press, 1954).

C.A. Hope, *Gold of the Pharaohs* (Victoria: International Cultural Corporation of Australia, 1988).

S. Ikram and D. Forbes, 'Alexander the Great's Tomb Discovered at Siwa Oasis?', *KMT* 6:1 (1995), 9.

K. Jansen-Winkeln, 'Thronname und Begräbnis Takeloths I', *VA* 3 (1987), 253-8.

J. Leclant, 'Taharqa à Sedeinga', *Studien zu Sprache und Religion Ägyptens. Zu Ehren von Wolfhart Westendorf überreicht von seinem Freunden und Schülern* (Göttingen, 1984).

J. Malek, 'Nekropolen. Late Period', *LÄ* IV (1982), 440-9.

- 'Sais', *LÄ* VI (1985), 355-8.

G. Maspero, *Les momies royales de Déir el-Baharî* (Cairo: IFAO, 1889).

P. Montet, *La necropole royale de Tanis*, 3vv (Paris 1947-61).

A.Y. Mustafa, 'Reparation and Restoration of Antiquities, I. The Golden Mask of Amenemopet', *ASAE* 47 (1947), 77-9.

A. Niwinski, *21st Dynasty Coffins from Thebes: Chronological and Typological Studies* (Mainz: Philipp von Zabern, 1988).

A. Rowe, 'Two royal funerary figurines recently found at Kom El-Shuqafa and the Serapeum', *Societé royale d'Archeologie - Alexandrie Bulletin* 36 (1946), 33-7.

A.H. Rhind, *Thebes: its Tombs and their Tenants* (London: John Murray, 1862).

P.A. and A.J. Spencer, 'Notes on Late Libyan Egypt', *JEA* 72 (1986), 198-201.

R. Stadelmann, 'Das Grab in Tempelhof. Der Typus des Königsgrabes in der Spätzeit', *MDAIK* 27 (1971), 111-23.

H. Stierlin and C. Ziegler, *Tanis: trésors des pharaons* (Fribourg: Seuil, 1987).

Tanis, l'or des pharons (Paris: Association française d'action artistique, 1987).

J.H. Taylor, 'The Valley of the Kings in the Third Intermediate Period', *ATut*, 186-206.

E. Thomas, 'The 'k3y of Inhapy', *JARCE* 16 (1979), 85-92.

G. Vittmann, 'Zwei Königinnen der Spätzeit namen Chedebnitjerbone', *CdE* 49/97 (1974), 43-51.

A. Wace, 'The Sarcophagus of Alexander the Great', *Bulletin of the Faculty of Arts, Farouk I University* 4 (1948), 1-11.

J. Yoyotte, 'Textes et documents de la nécropole royale de Tanis', *Ecole practique des hautes études, section des sciences religieuses: annuaire*, XCV (1986-87), 170-2.

- 'Des lions et des chats: contribution à la prospographie de l'époque libyenne', *RdE* 39 (1988), 155-78.

- 'A propos de Psousennes II', *BSFFT* 1 (1988), 41-9.

Epilogue

M. al-Asad, 'The Mosque of Al-Rifa'i in Cairo', *Muqarnas* 10 (1993), 108-24.

M. Herz, *La mosquée el-Rifa'i au Caire* (n.p., [1912]).

M.V. Seton-Williams and P. Stocks, *Blue Guide: Egypt*^{2}(London: A. &. C. Black, 1988), 300-1, 325-6, 371-3, 388-9.

Index